BIBLE

Oxford University Press Publications
by Gordon Campbell

AS AUTHOR

The Oxford Dictionary of the Renaissance
Renaissance Art and Architecture
John Milton: Life, Work, and Thought (co-author)
Milton and the Manuscript of 'De Doctrina Christiana' (co-author)
Very Interesting People: John Milton

AS EDITOR

The Holy Bible: Quatercentenary Edition
The Grove Encyclopedia of Decorative Arts (2 vols)
The Grove Encyclopedia of Classical Art and Architecture (2 vols)
The Grove Encyclopedia of Northern Renaissance Art (3 vols)
Renaissance Studies (10 vols)
The Review of English Studies (13 vols)
The Complete Works of John Milton (11 vols, in progress)
W. R. Parker, Milton: A Biography (2 vols)
Ben Jonson, The Alchemist and Other Plays

AS CONTRIBUTOR

Grove Art Online
John Bunyan: Conventicle and Parnassus. Tercentenary Essays
The Journal of Theological Studies
The Oxford Chronology of English Literature
The Oxford Companion to English Literature
The Oxford Companion to the Garden
The Oxford Dictionary of National Biography
The Oxford Handbook of Milton

BIBLE

THE STORY OF THE
KING JAMES VERSION
1611–2011

GORDON CAMPBELL

OXFORD
UNIVERSITY PRESS

OXFORD
UNIVERSITY PRESS

Great Clarendon Street, Oxford ox2 6dp

Oxford University Press is a department of the University of Oxford.
It furthers the University's objective of excellence in research, scholarship,
and education by publishing worldwide in

Oxford New York

Auckland Cape Town Dar es Salaam Hong Kong Karachi
Kuala Lumpur Madrid Melbourne Mexico City Nairobi
New Delhi Shanghai Taipei Toronto

With offices in

Argentina Austria Brazil Chile Czech Republic France Greece
Guatemala Hungary Italy Japan Poland Portugal Singapore
South Korea Switzerland Thailand Turkey Ukraine Vietnam

Oxford is a registered trade mark of Oxford University Press
in the UK and in certain other countries

Published in the United States
by Oxford University Press Inc., New York

British Library Cataloguing in Publication Data
Data available

Library of Congress Cataloging in Publication Data
Library of Congress Control Number: 2010935040

Typeset by SPI Publisher Services, Pondicherry, India
Printed in Great Britain
on acid-free paper by
Clays Ltd., St Ives Plc

ISBN 978-0-19-955759-2

2

CONTENTS

PREFACE

The four-hundredth anniversary of the publication of the King James Version of the Bible falls in 2011, and Oxford University Press, which has published King James Bibles since the seventeenth century and has sold uncounted millions of copies over the centuries, has decided to mark the quatercentenary with this account of the fortunes of this translation from 1611 to the present. This project was conceived not as an academic exercise in book history, but rather as an affectionate biography of a book that has had a long life and has, in another sense, given life to Christian readers.

There are more books devoted to the Bible than to any other book in human history, so the addition of another requires some justification beyond the fact that few translations live long enough to have four-hundredth birthdays. The first two centenaries seem to have passed with little note, but, on the occasion of the tercentenary in 1911, Oxford University Press celebrated the anniversary on both sides of the Atlantic. In England the Press commissioned the bibliographer and book historian Alfred Pollard to write a book-length introduction to two editions of the 1611 Bible, one a facsimile of the original, and the other a version of the 1611 Bible set in roman type. In America the Press published *The 1911 Tercentenary Commemoration Bible*, which contained 'a new system of references prepared by C. I. Scofield', who had already published the first edition of his annotated Bible. The text of this edition was corrected and amended by 'a committee of 34 eminent Hebrew and Greek scholars' in the USA and Canada, 'representing all the great evangelical bodies'. The changes that they wrought on this edition are indicative of the issues that will be discussed in this book: Isaiah 9:3, for example, was changed from 'Thou hast multiplied the nation, and not increased the joy' to 'Thou hast multiplied the nation, and increased the joy'.

This book has been prepared in tandem with another project, which is an edition of the 1611 Bible that is as close as possible to the text of 1611; it is entitled *The Holy Bible: Quatercentenary Edition*. In both commissions I have aspired to make the material accessible to modern readers and to take into account the sensibilities of readers of all denominations and none. In the edition of the Bible the typeface is roman (and therefore easier to read than the black-letter type of the original edition), but the initial letters of the first edition have been preserved, because their pictorial images were part of the 1611 Bible. And, just as the roman typeface of the *Quatercentenary Edition* is intended to make the book more accessible, so in this book I have refrained from quoting Hebrew and Greek texts; I have nonetheless felt free to discuss textual issues with reference to these and other languages, because readers of the Bible often have a passionate interest in the subject.

This is not the first account of the history of the KJV, and a reader might reasonably wonder how this book differs from its predecessors, especially as I often draw on their insights. The principal difference is that I have had a large body of recent scholarly material at my disposal, in the form of the *American National*

Biography (*ANB*) published in twenty-four volumes by Oxford University Press in 1999 (under the auspices of the American Council of Learned Societies) and the *Oxford Dictionary of National Biography* (*ODNB*), published in sixty volumes by Oxford University Press in 2004; both are available electronically, and are regularly updated. These extraordinary resources have hugely increased the quality of biographical material available to scholars, and constitute a trustworthy alternative to free material available on the Web. That said, the Web sometimes offers free access to valuable sources. One pertinent example is the early Greek manuscript of the Bible known as the Codex Sinaiticus. I used to admire the British Library segment (which includes the New Testament) in its glass case; now, however, I turn its pages from my desk, thanks to the Codex Sinaiticus Project, which gives me free access to the manuscript in digital form. Such direct access to sources has transformed scholarly enquiry in areas such as biblical studies. I often access these resources from my home in the parish of Knighton, in suburban Leicester. It was from this parish that the fourteenth-century Leicester chronicler Henry Knighton took his name, and it was he (as I explain in Chapter 1) who famously deplored Wyclif, who had foolishly made the Bible available to anyone who could read English—even women! It is oddly satisfying to know that I have written this celebratory chronicle of the KJV in the small parish that more than 600 years ago produced the grumpy chronicler who complained about the first complete translation of the Bible into English; on one level this book is a riposte to my erstwhile neighbour.

I have followed the spelling of names in the *ANB* and *ODNB*, so I refer to George Whitefield (not Whitfield) and John Wyclif (not Wycliffe); in the Further Reading I list individuals who are the subject of *ANB* and *ODNB* entries. In citations from the KJV I have not been consistent, because there are thousands of differences between the text published in 1611 and the text published in the twenty-first century. Sometimes it suits my purpose to quote the original text, but when I do so I usually modernize the letter forms; on other occasions, when textual issues are not at stake, I cite the current Oxford text of the KJV.

ACKNOWLEDGEMENTS

The founding father of textual investigation of the King James Version was F. H. A. Scrivener, whose scholarship, even when I dissent from it, has been an important stimulus to this book. Scrivener's twenty-first-century successor is David Norton, who probably knows the text of the KJV better than anyone now alive; like every other student of the subject, I have drawn deeply on his scholarship, particularly his *Textual History of the King James Bible*.

The circumstances surrounding the commissioning and translating of the KJV have been pieced together over the centuries, but the first scholar to combine a close command of the documentary evidence with a thorough bibliographical understanding of the KJV was Alfred Pollard, who wrote the magisterial bibliographical introduction to the edition of the KJV that Oxford University Press produced on the occasion of the tercentenary in 1911. Of mid-twentieth-century scholars I am particularly indebted to two: A. S. Herbert produced a fine historical catalogue of printed editions of the English Bible, and Ward S. Allen produced an outstanding edition of a document that led to a new understanding of the process by which the first drafts of the KJV were revised by the final committee of reviewers.

Over the centuries the three most important publishers of the KJV have been the king's (or queen's) printer, Cambridge University Press, and Oxford University Press. David McKitterick, the erudite historian of Cambridge University Press, has written illuminatingly about Cambridge editions of the KJV, and his scholarship has made Cambridge the best-understood press in England. His three volumes have no Oxford counterpart, in that Harry Carter's history of Oxford University Press began well with the publication of volume I (to 1780) in 1975, but no successor volume ever appeared; a team led by Simon Eliot has the matter in hand, and a four-volume history of OUP to be published in 2012–13 will include ample material on Oxford's Bible Press. The Cinderella press is the king's printer, which, despite its vast size in comparison to other London printing houses, has been studied much less than the considerably smaller presses that published Shakespeare and Ben Jonson. Indeed, serious study of the king's printer in relation to the KJV was inaugurated as recently as 2005 by John Barnard in a superb article on the financing of the Bible, and has now been hugely advanced by the publication in 2009 of an authoritative account of the king's printers in the Jacobean period by Graham Rees and Maria Wakely.

A scholar, even one with access to the riches of Early English Books Online, needs access to libraries. I am fortunate in that the David Wilson Library at the University of Leicester accommodates the Robjohns Collection, which includes some 500 early printed Bibles; my colleague Evelyn Cornell has been my helpful guide to the collection. In Oxford, the Bodleian Library holds an edition of the 1602 Bishops' Bible that has been annotated by the translators, and access to its readings has greatly assisted my endeavours. Elsewhere in Oxford, Julian Reid and Joanna Snelling of Corpus Christi College kindly made the notes of John Bois available to me and supplied me with a photograph that enabled me to enlarge a particularly intractable passage. The Cambridge University Library holds an edition of the 1769 Oxford folio with annotations by Gilbert Buchanan that record the thousands of changes to the text between 1611 and 1769; in Cambridge, as on previous occasions, I have been grateful for the support of John Wells. In the British Library I was able to consult early Bibles and several manuscripts relating to the preparation of the KJV. The Lambeth Palace Library kindly gave me access to the manuscript of a draft translation by the Second Westminster Company. Finally, my work on the Revised Version has been illuminated by a draft translation in the library of Wesley College in Bristol; the librarian, Michael Brealey, was immensely helpful, and his generosity even extended to taking the photograph of the draft reproduced in this book.

At Oxford University Press, my commissioning editor was Tom Perridge, who entrusted me with the commission and then supported the process of writing and publishing with a conscientiousness that is remarkable even by the high standards of the Press; indeed, he read a draft version of the book, an exemplary editorial practice that is now all too rare. The assistant commissioning editor was Lizzie Robottom, whose command of production issues and unfailing efficiency eased my way through a complex phase of the project. Production was ably managed by Tessa Eaton. My copy-editor, Hilary Walford, was a model of tact as she purged my text of inconsistencies; my highly-skilled proof-reader was Nicola Sangster. Across the Atlantic, I benefited from the wise advice of Don Kraus, who is responsible for Bible publishing at OUP New York. I had the benefit of two marketing teams, one in Oxford led by

Phil Henderson (whose colleague Kirsty McHugh arranged publicity) and the other in New York led by Brian Hughes; the helpfulness of both extended to offering shrewd advice on the content of the volume. Picture research was undertaken by Emmanuelle Peri, and my very efficient indexer was Gillian Northcott, with whom I have worked happily on previous books.

I have enjoyed huge support from within the academic community. Three colleagues with a variety of confessional and secular perspectives kindly read the entire book in draft: Stella Fletcher (Secretary of the Ecclesiastical History Society), Timothy Larsen (Wheaton College), and David Crystal (Bangor), whose most recent book, *Begat. The King James Bible and the English Language* (2010), enabled me to restrict myself to a broad-brush treatment of material on which he has vast expertise. Others read smaller portions or helped with individual queries, including Jonathan Beck (Arizona), Stuart Campbell (SOAS), Julie Coleman (Leicester), Anne Marie D'Arcy (Leicester), Ian Gadd (Bath Spa), Peter Lindenbaum (Indiana), Diarmaid MacCulloch (Oxford), Thomas Keymer (Toronto), William Poole (Oxford), Sam Richardson (HarperCollins), Joel Silver (Indiana), Elaine Treharne (Florida State), and Henry Woudhuysen (UCL). All can say with the Preacher that 'of making many books there is no end; and much study is a weariness of the flesh', but, despite their busy schedules, all assisted me with gladsome heart.

Closer to home, my wife, Mary, cheerfully endured many breakfast monologues about textual issues, and in Canada my brother-in-law, the Revd Dr Gordon Freeland, read part of the manuscript and cheered me on from a safe distance.

Leicester   G.C.
2010

INTRODUCTION

On 20 January 2009 Barack Obama took the presidential oath of office on a copy of the King James Version of the Bible published by Oxford University Press in 1853; it was the same Bible that had been used by Abraham Lincoln in 1861. Similarly, a series of twentieth-century presidents (Warren Harding, Dwight Eisenhower, Jimmy Carter, and George Bush Senior) chose to take their oath on the copy of the KJV published in London in 1767; it was the same Bible that had been used by George Washington in 1789. These two Bibles (which will be discussed in Chapter 10) are, like Paul Revere's Sons of Liberty Punch Bowl, artefacts that represent turning points in American history. They have become part of American history, just as the KJV is part of America's religious culture. This version of the Bible is similarly honoured in the United Kingdom. In 1953 (the coronation year), for example, Queen Elizabeth commanded that a copy of the KJV be given to every child born in Britain that year.

The King James Version of the Bible, which is known in the United Kingdom as the Authorized Version, is the most celebrated book in the English-speaking world. In other religious traditions it is the version of the sacred book in the original language that is honoured. In the Islamic world, for example, many Muslims memorize the entire Qur'an, but often have only the vaguest idea what the words mean, unless their first language happens to be Arabic. Protestant Christianity, however, places a high value on a translation, and it is passages from this translation rather than the original that Protestants have committed to memory. Why should this be so?

The answer lies in an emphasis on understanding the meaning of the words rather than committing the original words to heart. In the century before 1611, at the time of the Reformation, Protestants had championed the idea of the priesthood of all believers. This led to a resistance to 'implicit faith', which is faith subordinated to the doctrine of the Church, in favour of 'explicit faith', in which faith derives from the individual believer's understanding of the Bible under the guidance of the Spirit. The resurgence of this doctrine in the late sixteenth century, together with the ability of print to make books available to an increasingly literate public, led to translations of the Bible into all of Europe's vernacular languages. In the case of English, it was the KJV that eventually triumphed.

This book is the story of that triumph. There have been many translations in the 400 years since the KJV was first published, but it is highly valued even by those who use another translation. The reasons for the universal respect for this version vary enormously. Some admire its resonant prose, which sometimes has the rhythms of poetry: when Adam says to God that 'she gave me of the tree, and I did eat' (Genesis 3:12), his words are cast in iambic pentameter, the five-beat metre of Shakespeare's plays. Others travel beyond admiration to reverence, especially if they believe that, as the translators asked in their prayers, God guided the translation. By any account, this is a history of the most important book in the English language.

That history includes the printing history. This may sound dry, but is both important and, at times, comical in the difficulties that arise in the printing of such a large book. These problems can be illustrated by some of the more memorable errors. In the first edition of the KJV designed for private study (1612), as opposed to reading aloud in church, Psalm 119:161 read 'Printers have persecuted me without cause'; 'printers' was a misprint for 'princes'. The 1631 edition now known as the Wicked Bible made adultery compulsory by omitting 'not' in Exodus 20:14, which read 'Thou shalt commit adultery'. The printers were heavily fined, but in 1641 the same press printed an edition in which they omitted 'no' in Revelation 21:1, which read 'And there was more sea'. The problem with negatives cropped up again in 1653, when another printer omitted the second negative in 1 Corinthians 6:9, which read 'Know ye not that the unrighteous shall inherit the kingdom of God?' From negatives we move uneasily to murderers. A Bible of 1795 rendered Mark 7:27 as 'Let the children first be killed', when Jesus had in fact asked that they be filled (that is, fed). Similarly, in a Bible of 1801 the murmurers of Jude 16 became murderers, and so the Bible became known as the Murderers' Bible. Murder can arise from wife-hating, and in 1810 a Bible printed Luke 14:26 as 'if any...hate not...his own wife also', when what Jesus had said was 'life'.

Misprints are an easy target, but printing history extends far beyond the occasional memorable error, because the text of the KJV was not fixed in 1611. There was no master text from which all subsequent editions descended, and later editors, printers, and publishers were not always certain which text was the first edition. The absence of an agreed master text gave licence to a long tradition of corrections, and there was not always a clear line drawn between corrections of printers' errors and corrections of translators' errors. The stabilization of the text finally came in 1769, when Benjamin Blayney's Oxford folio was published. The KJV that one can buy now is essentially this late-eighteenth-century text, not the text of 1611.

In addition to this printing history, the KJV also has a political, ecclesiastical, and cultural history, for in the course of its long life it has been championed by various confessional groups, as well as by those whose interest is in its literary style and influence. The monarch whose name it bears was an active participant in debates about the structure of organized Christianity in the post-Reformation period. He firmly rejected the presbyterianism practised by many of his Scottish subjects, opting instead for the episcopally led Church of England and expressing that preference with admirable succinctness: 'No bishop, no king'. This was a sharp rebuke to England's hotter Protestants, the puritans who rejected bishops as a relic of popery. Some puritans also initially mistrusted the KJV, though it duly came to be central to the lives and witness of their evangelical heirs throughout the English-speaking world.

When the KJV was published in 1611, all English Protestants were members of the national church. In the late seventeenth century, groups such as Baptists, Congregationalists, and Quakers asserted their independence from the established Church, thereby initiating the dissenting tradition. Over the following centuries, dissenters were identified as nonconformists and came to identify themselves as free churches. In the eighteenth century, the Methodist movement initiated by John and Charles Wesley provided a model for other popular revivalist movements in the nineteenth and twentieth centuries. Some evangelicals remained within the Church of England, finding outlets for their energies among the newly urbanized populations of industrial towns and cities or in missionary work throughout Britain's expanding empire. No less zealous and, indeed, no less devoted to biblical scholarship were the high churchmen of the Oxford Movement in the mid-nineteenth century, some of whom converted to the Church of Rome while others remained ritually minded Anglicans. Thus the Church of England attained its reputation for breadth and inclusivity, with the KJV of the Bible as one of the bonds holding together the increasing diversity of religious practice not just within the Church of England but also throughout what emerged as the worldwide Anglican communion. In the late twentieth and early twenty-first century this cohesion has weakened as the inclusive character of the Church of England has been assaulted from one side by secularizing influences and from the other by internal tensions between Anglo-Catholics and evangelicals.

There is a parallel tradition in the United States, where the impact of the KJV extends well beyond the Episcopal Church, which is one province of the Anglican communion, for many of the non-episcopal Protestant denominations have been and continue to be thoroughly Bible centred, and the KJV has a large following among evangelicals. In this context, my use of the term 'evangelical' requires some clarification. In the United Kingdom the term is used beyond the Anglican communion in nonconformist churches, including English Presbyterians (in Scotland Presbyterianism is the established Church), Congregationalists (many now in the United Reform Church), Methodists, and Baptists. In America the term may cover an even wider range of opinion, as there are more denominations and an increasing number of independent, non-denominational churches, some of which are very large indeed. In post-war America, it is also helpful to distinguish fundamentalism from the New Evangelical movement, but each of those movements accommodates varying opinions on many issues. The term 'evangelical' thus covers a wide range of Christian opinion, but there is, in the analysis of the historian David Bebbington, a cluster of four common emphases: conversionism (the necessity of a conversion experience), activism (encouraging conversion experiences in others), biblicism (the inerrancy of the Bible and its standing as the sole source of doctrine), and crucicentrism (a stress on the redemptive sacrifice of Christ on the cross). These features emerge in the eighteenth century, and in the preceding centuries the contours of debate were different. Church government, for example, was a prominent issue, and the rift between episcopalians and presbyterians ran deep; on the other hand, there was no notion of a conversion experience, except from other religions. Debates within Christianity have never stood still, so the religious contexts of the KJV are remarkably protean.

This is a complex history, and I have been able to survey it in the compass of these pages only by concentrating on the two countries in which the greatest number of King James Bibles have been printed: England and the United States. No one with my name or background would claim that the contiguous countries of Scotland and Canada are unimportant, but the histories of the KJV in those countries are intertwined with those of their neighbours, and I have chosen to concentrate on the two principal centres rather than yield to atavistic urges to write at length on other countries. That said, I cannot help but note one possible misprint that seems to have persisted through all editions of the KJV. Genesis 24:63 invariably reads 'and he lifted up his eyes, and saw, and behold, the camels were coming'; this is, I am confident, an allusion to my clan march, and should read 'the Campbells were coming'.

1

THE BIBLE IN ENGLISH

Pre-Reformation Translations

The language of England before the Norman Conquest of 1066 is variously known as Old English or Anglo-Saxon. To the untrained eye it does not look very much like English, so the opening line of the Lord's Prayer ('Our father which art in heaven' in the King James Version (KJV)) as translated into the Mercian dialect of Old English (which was spoken in the English Midlands) is *Fæder ure þu þe in heofunum earð*. This looks impossible to read because of the archaic letters, but once it is understood that *æ* is the vowel sound in 'hat', *þ* is the 'th' sound in 'thin', and *ð* is the 'th' sound in 'with', the words become recognizable.

There was no complete translation of the Bible into Old English, but parts of the Bible were translated for specific purposes. Sermons delivered in parish churches, for example, quoted passages of Scripture, but, as the only available Bibles were in Latin, preachers had to translate these passages into Old English. In the early eighth century the Venerable Bede translated (in the final days of his life) the Gospel of John into Old English. It is a happy coincidence that the man who first tried to translate the Bible into English was the same person who tried to create the

7

idea of the English people, but his translation has been lost; had it survived, it would have been honoured as the first translation of a book of the Bible into English and as the earliest substantial piece of English prose. The earliest surviving English translation is attributed to King Alfred (the Great), who ruled Wessex in the late ninth century; he translated (or commissioned translations of) Psalms 1–50 and the four Gospels into the West Saxon dialect, and translated Exodus 20–3 in the introductory section of his Laws.

After the Norman Conquest the English language changed, because French words of Latin origin began to enter the language. This new form of English is known as Middle English, and it is the language of poets such as Chaucer. In the late thirteenth century there were metrical translations into Middle English of individual books of the Bible (notably Genesis, Exodus, and the Psalms) and in the early fourteenth century the Yorkshire hermit Richard Rolle undertook a prose translation of the Psalms in a northern dialect of Middle English. His sentences read oddly, because they follow the word order of the ancient Latin translation of the Bible known as the Vulgate. Compare, for example, the opening of Psalm 23 in the Latin of the Vulgate with Rolle's translation:

> *Dominus regit me et nihil mihi deerit: in loco pascuae ibi me collocavit.*
> Lord govern me and nothing shall me want: in stead of pasture there he me set.

The question of the extent to which translations should follow the word order of the original texts was destined to perplex translators for generations to come.

The most famous translations of the fourteenth century are those associated with John Wyclif, the theologian and religious reformer who has been praised since the sixteenth century as the 'morning star of the Reformation'. Wyclif is a seminal figure in the period leading to the Reformation, but the idea that he was the first translator of the entire Bible into English is a myth; indeed, he seems to have encouraged a number of translations by his followers, but there is no evidence that he undertook any translating himself. It is possible that Wyclif had some sort of role in the early stages of this vast enterprise, but no evidence has survived; by the end of the century, however, the English Bible was firmly associated with his name. Its purpose was wholly consistent with Wyclif's objectives, which were widely deplored. As the chronicler Henry Knighton complained in the early 1390s, Wyclif 'translated from Latin into the language not of angels but of Angles (Englishmen), so that he made the Bible common and open to the laity, and to women who were able to read, which used to be reserved for literate and intelligent clergy'. Knighton was clearly appalled at the prospect of women being able to read the Bible in their own language.

The translation was certainly inspired by Wyclif, so, even if he was not directly involved in the translation, it is rightly known as the 'Wycliffite Bible'. This Bible circulated in manuscript, and indeed the New Testament was not printed until 1731 (in only 160 copies); the complete Wycliffite Bible was first printed by Oxford University Press in 1850. Although more than 100 manuscripts survive, there is little evidence that the Wycliffite translations were consulted in the sixteenth or seventeenth centuries. Wyclif did, however, enjoy a posthumous reputation as the herald of the Reformation. John Milton's attitude was typical. When God speaks, Milton explained, he speaks first to his Englishmen. The Reformation was said to have been started by Luther, but Milton thought that unlikely, because he was not English. In fact, Milton opined, the Reformation was started by Wyclif, and, had the bishops not persecuted him, Milton added, 'the glory of reforming all our neighbours had bin compleatly ours'. Wyclif thereby became the first English Protestant.

Tyndale

William Tyndale is rightly known as 'the father of the English Bible'. The Dutch scholar Erasmus produced an edition of the Greek New Testament, which he published in 1516 together with his translation into Latin, which was the international language of Europe. Tyndale, who was an excellent linguist (he knew Greek, Latin, Hebrew, German, Spanish, and French), decided to translate Erasmus's Greek text into English. He resolved, in the teeth of bitter opposition, to 'defy the Pope and all his laws' and proclaimed ringingly that, 'if God spare my life ere many years, I will cause a boy that driveth the plough, shall know more of the Scripture than thou dost'. On being refused permission to print his New Testament in English, Tyndale left for Germany, where his Lutheran sympathies made him welcome in Reformation circles. In 1525 he began to print the New Testament in the Catholic city of Cologne, but, when the printing house was raided by the authorities, Tyndale fled; all that remains of the historic Cologne printing is a single copy of the first twenty-two chapters of Matthew's Gospel, now in the British Library. The Cologne fragment has a prologue by Tyndale, parts of which are translations of Luther; it also has marginal notes, many of which derive from Luther. It also has some illustrations. The beginning of John's Gospel, for example, has on its facing page a woodcut of John (who was traditionally portrayed with an eagle), and a text undivided into verses, with a commentary on the right side of the page. This edition of Tyndale's Bible is the first printing of a gospel in English, and its translation proved to be enormously influential. Some of the phrases that we associate with the KJV first appear in this fragment, such as 'Ask and it shall be given you; seek and ye shall find; knock and it shall be opened unto you'.

Tyndale sought refuge in Worms, where there was a strong Lutheran presence, and in 1526 published his New Testament. Unlike the Cologne fragment, it had no prologue, no notes, and no attribution to Tyndale. It was a pocket-sized book, and was quickly smuggled into England, where it was sold cheaply. By October the book had been banned as a 'pestiferous and most pernicious poison dispersed throughout all our dioceses of London in great numbers'. At a public burning of confiscated copies of Tyndale's New Testaments at St Paul's Cathedral on 27 October 1526, the Bishop of London, Cuthbert Tunstal, claimed to have found 2,000 errors in the translation. Tunstal had excellent Greek, and so could not have meant errors in Tyndale's understanding of Greek; the most charitable way to interpret his comments would be to assume that there were more than 2,000 deviations from the literal sense of the Latin Vulgate Bible, which was the official Bible of the Church. The banning order did not work, and soon an Antwerp printer was publishing large numbers of copies of Tyndale's Bible, albeit in an unreliable text. Bishop Tunstall visited Antwerp and arranged for an English merchant to buy the entire printer's stock of Tyndale's Bibles, which he

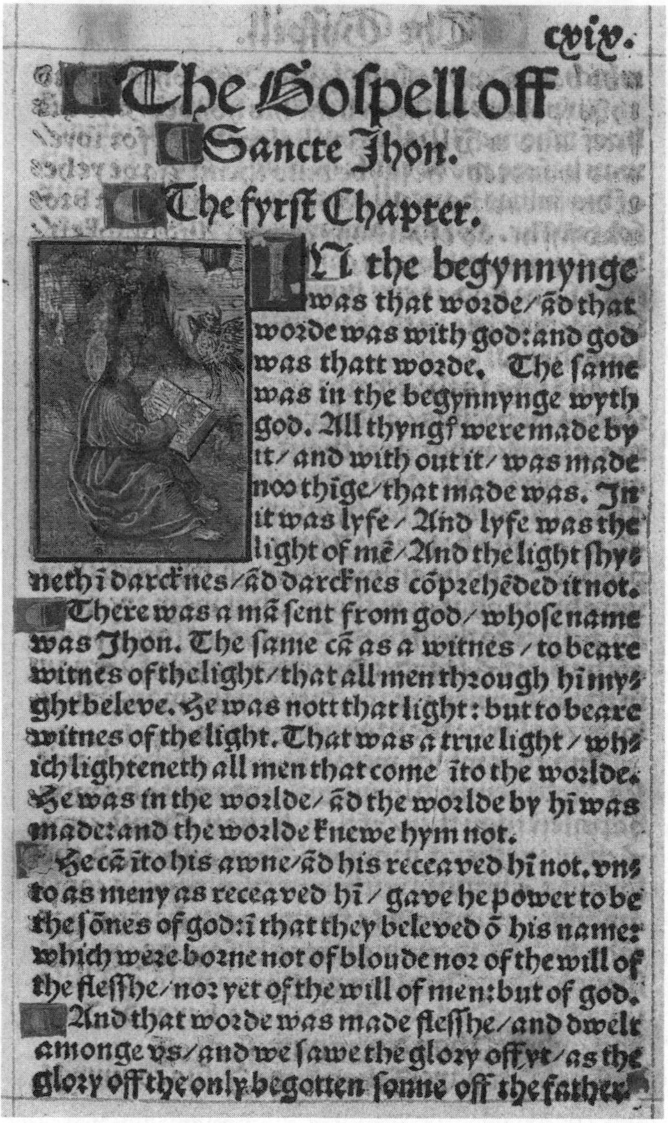

☞ The Gospell off
☞ Sancte Jhon.
☞ The fyrst Chapter.

IN the begynnynge was that worde/ād that worde was with god: and god was thatt worde. The same was in the begynnynge wyth god. All thyngf were made by it/ and with out it/ was made noo thige/ that made was. In it was lyfe/ And lyfe was the light of mē/ And the light shyneth i darcknes/ ād darcknes cōprehēded it not.

There was a mā sent from god/ whose name was Jhon. The same cā as a witnes/ to beare witnes of the light/ that all men through hī myght beleve. He was nott that light: but to beare witnes of the light. That was a true light/ whi̅ch lighteneth all men that come ito the worlde. He was in the worlde/ ād the worlde by hī was made: and the worlde knewe hym not.

He cā ito his awne/ ād his receaved hī not. vnto as meny as receaved hī/ gave he power to be the sōnes of god: i that they beleved ō his name: which were borne not of bloude nor of the will of the flesshe/ nor yet of the will of men: but of god.

And that worde was made flesshe/ and dwelt amonge vs/ and we sawe the glory off yt/ as the glory off the only begotten sonne off the father

FIGURE I. The opening of John's Gospel in Tyndale's translation, printed in Cologne in 1525.

12

promptly burnt. The first edition seems to have consisted of about 3,000 copies, but now only two complete copies survive, in London (British Library) and Stuttgart (Württembergische Landesbibliothek).

Eventually Tyndale would also be burnt, but the language of his New Testament lives on, preserved by the KJV, which adopted phrases such as 'fight the good fight' and 'the powers that be'; both phrases (and many others) are now embedded in English, but their origins in Tyndale's New Testament have been forgotten. On a broader front, Tyndale set the linguistic style for New Testament translations for centuries to come, in that the studied simplicity of his language, which was designed to make the New Testament accessible to ploughboys, has become established as the dominant idiom of subsequent translations.

Somehow Tyndale learned Hebrew, and embarked on a translation of the Old Testament. It was never completed, and the only parts that were published in his lifetime were the Pentateuch and the Book of Jonah. Many phrases from these published translations survived into the KJV, such as 'Let there be light, and there was light'. This translation also brought into the English language the term 'Jehovah' (Exodus 6:3), which requires some explanation. The four consonants that make up the name of God in Hebrew (known technically as the Tetragrammaton, a Greek term meaning 'four letters') are usually transliterated as JHVH or YHWH. Because the name of God was deemed by Jews to be too sacred for utterance, they substituted the word 'adonai' (the Hebrew word for 'Lord'). When vowel points were added to Hebrew consonants, the vowels of 'adonai' were inserted into the consonants 'JHVH' to produce the compound word 'Jehovah', which was first used in Latin in 1516, and first appeared in English in Tyndale's Pentateuch of 1530; the form of the word used by modern scholars is Yahweh.

The popularity of Tyndale's New Testament continued to antagonize the English clerical establishment. In 1529 Sir Thomas More condemned Tyndale as a Lutheran (which he was) and declared his New Testament to be heretical. He also touched on an issue that was destined to be revived by the KJV translators, which was the use of ecclesiastical terms. The instructions given to the KJV translators included 'the old ecclesiastical words to be kept, viz. the word "church" not to be translated "congregation" etc.'. One of the pillars of More's denunciation of Tyndale as a heretic was that he had used 'congregation' instead of 'church', 'senior' instead of 'priest', 'love' (the noun) instead of 'charity', and 'repent' instead of 'do penance'.

Tyndale replied to More's attack, page by page, and in his reply explained his lexical decisions. On 'congregation' and 'church', for example, Tyndale said:

> In as much as the clergy...had appropriat[ed] unto themselves the term [Church] that of right is common unto all the whole congregation of them that believe in Christ...therefore in the translation of the New Testament where I found this word *Ecclesia*, I interpreted it by this word *congregation*.

More issued a counter-reply that ran to more than 2,000 packed pages, many of which attack Tyndale in the vitriolic language typical of the period ('discharging a filthy foam of blasphemies out of his brutish beastly mouth'). Tyndale did not reply, and the tasks to which he turned instead include a revision of his New Testament, which was published in 1534. It is this revised version that had the greatest impact on subsequent translations.

Indeed, it has been estimated that 83 per cent of the KJV published in 1611 derives from Tyndale, either directly or indirectly through other Bibles.

In the event, both More and Tyndale, both of whom had offended King Henry VIII, were destined to be executed. More succumbed to the executioner's axe in July 1535. The following year Tyndale was tried for heresy (as a Lutheran) in what is now Belgium. According to the Protestant martyrologist John Foxe, Tyndale was tied to a stake, and, as a chain encircled his neck, cried 'Lord, open the king of England's eyes'. He was then strangled with the chain and his body was burnt.

Coverdale

Tyndale's most important successor was Miles Coverdale, a former Augustinian friar who eventually became the Protestant bishop of Exeter. It was Coverdale who in October 1535, living in exile in Antwerp, published the first edition of the entire Bible in English. As he explains in his dedication to King Henry VIII, Coverdale had 'with a clear conscience purely and faithfully translated this out of five sundry interpreters'. The most important of the 'interpreters' was Tyndale, whose New Testament is printed in revised form. Tyndale had not, however, published a complete Old Testament, so Coverdale had to assemble an Old Testament from other sources. On the title page he (or the printer) explains that the book has been 'faithfully and truly translated out of Dutch and Latin into English'. By 'Dutch' Coverdale meant German (German *deutsch*), and he was acknowledging a debt to Luther's Bible and to its Swiss-German derivative, the Zwinglian 'Zürich Bible'. His Latin sources were the Vulgate and a Latin translation (from Hebrew and Greek) of the Bible by the Dominican friar Sante Pagnini, which had been published in Lyons in 1528. It was the Bible of Pagnini that transmitted the division of Old Testament chapters into numbered verses from its origins in a Hebrew Bible of 1440 to a long line of English Bibles, beginning with Coverdale.

Coverdale's Old Testament is his own translation of these German and Latin Bibles. On a point of principle he followed Tyndale in his rejection of ecclesiastical terms, using 'congregation' instead of 'church' and 'love' (the noun) instead of 'charity'. Beyond principle, Coverdale had an excellent ear, and many of his fine phrases have resonated down the centuries, transmitted by the KJV. His magnificent rendering of Psalm 25:6, for example ('call to remembrance, O Lord, thy tender mercies and thy loving kindnesses, which have been ever of old'), brought the word 'lovingkindness' and the phrase 'tender mercies' into English and into the mainstream of biblical translation. His translations are in prose, but often have the quality of verse. His translation of Isaiah 55:6 ('Seek ye the Lord while he may be found, call upon him while he is nigh'), for example, passed into the KJV with two tiny changes (the addition of a second 'ye' after 'call', and the substitution of 'near' for 'nigh'), and in that form became a hymn, one that captures the parallel structures of the Hebrew original, and sounds natural in English; this is no small accomplishment. Similarly, in Matthew 25:21 and 23, the translators of the KJV bypassed Tyndale ('go into thy master's joy') in favour of the translation that originated with Coverdale's 'enter thou into the joy of thy lord'.

Coverdale's most enduring translation was his psalter. His version of Psalm 137:1 ('By the waters of Babylon we sat down and wept when we remembered Sion'), for example, was reworked by later translators, so the KJV has 'By the rivers of Babylon, there we sat down, yea, we wept, when we remembered Zion'. However, it was Coverdale's translation of the Psalms, as revised for the Great Bible of 1539, that became the psalter of the Book of Common Prayer, and so served as the liturgical text for the Church of England for centuries to come. The eventual challenge to Coverdale's psalms related to his sources. He knew very little Hebrew, and so translated the Latin text of the Vulgate, which embodies many readings from the Greek version of the Old Testament that are not found in the Hebrew text; this ancient Greek version (third century BC) is known as the Septuagint (which means '70', hence the abbreviated form LXX), which was said to have been translated in Egypt by 72 elders in 72 days. The authors of the Revised Psalter of 1964 attempted to preserve the beauty of Coverdale's language while rooting their version in the Hebrew text rather than the Vulgate or the Septuagint. The final exclusion of Coverdale came in 1980, when the Alternative Service Book incorporated a psalter based on a fresh translation of the Hebrew into modern English.

The Coverdale Bible is a handsome volume, but its finest feature is the title page rather than the text. The illustration is the work of Hans Holbein the Younger, who was the greatest northern Renaissance artist to have worked in England. At the bottom of the magnificent woodcut King Henry VIII sits enthroned, distributing the Bible to his bishops while the laity kneel in attendance. The fact that Henry sits directly beneath the Tetragrammaton makes a Protestant point, in that there is no papal figure between them. The theme of the scenes in Holbein's design is the propagation of the gospel. The most resolutely Protestant of the scenes shows Jesus sending the apostles away to preach the gospel; each apostle has been issued with a large key, which reflects the Protestant rejection of the primacy of Peter.

The Matthew Bible

In 1537, the publisher John Rogers (*c.*1500–55), who was eventually to be burnt alive for his Protestant faith, produced the first authorized English Bible. The Pentateuch and the New Testament were Tyndale's, and Rogers also used Tyndale's unpublished translations of the Old Testament books from Joshua to 2 Chronicles. The rest of the Old Testament and the Apocrypha were taken from Coverdale's versions. Tyndale was a heretic, so he could not be named, but the ornamental initials 'WT' appear at the end of Malachi, immediately before the Apocrypha; similarly, Rogers is acknowledged only through initials. The name 'Thomas Matthew', which Rogers chose as a pseudonym, has long been a puzzle. The key to the puzzle is a polemical 'table of principal matters' translated from the first French Protestant Bible, which had been published two years earlier. This table, which was said to be the work of one Matthieu Gramelin, was a militantly Protestant attack on the mass, religious images, free will, the priesthood, confession, holy days, purgatory, and every other doctrine that separated the widening gulf between Catholics and Protestants. The name Matthieu Gramelin is a pseudonym for the ex-Dominican French Calvinist Matthieu Malingre: 'Gramelin' is an anagram of 'Malingre', and sometimes Malingre's first name is given as 'Thomas', which may have been his Dominican name, revived for need to hide his identity. As Malingre was known as

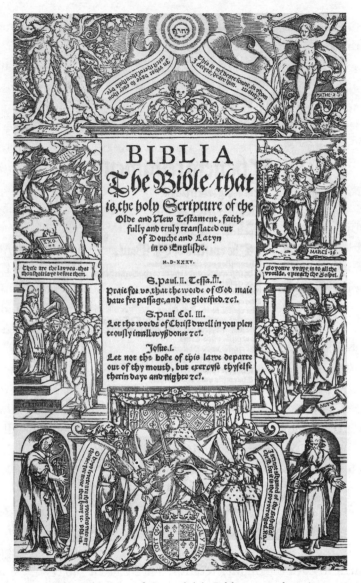

FIGURE 2. The title-page of Coverdale's Bible, printed in Antwerp in 1535.

both Thomas and Matthieu, Rogers chose to use the name 'Thomas Matthew'.

The Matthew Bible, like the Coverdale Bible, was dedicated to King Henry VIII, but there was a difference: whereas the title page of Coverdale's Bible was adorned with a picture of King Henry VIII distributing Bibles, the title page of the Matthew Bible went a step further, declaring it to have been printed by 'the King's most gracious licence'. The timing was propitious, as a debate was already underway about the desirability of authorizing an English translation of the Bible. As recently as 1530, Archbishop Warham had declared on behalf of the church that translation of the Bible into English could do no good but could cause much harm, and English translations of the Bible continued to be burnt. Four years later Thomas Cranmer, by now archbishop of Canterbury, tried to force the bishops to work on a translation of the New Testament, and they either ignored the request or undertook the work grudgingly.

The importation of 1,500 copies of the Matthew Bible in 1537 signalled a shift in ecclesiastical opinion. Cranmer wrote to Thomas Cromwell, sending by the same messenger a copy of the Matthew Bible; his comment on the translation was wholly positive: 'as for the translation, so far as I have read thereof I like it better than any other translation heretofore made.' He was, as it were, speaking to the converted. Cromwell had the previous year embarked on a campaign to place an English Bible in every parish church, but there were more than 8,000 parishes and only 1,500 Bibles. In any case, the Matthew Bibles were too small to have the dignity requisite for a church Bible, so it was decided to commission a new version that was suitable for churches.

FIGURE 3. The title-page of the Matthew Bible, printed in Antwerp in 1537.

The Great Bible

The task was entrusted to Miles Coverdale, who, instead of revising his own Bible, undertook a version of the Matthew Bible. As the finest presses were in Paris rather than London, it was decided to use the Paris printing house of François Regnault, who had supplied English service books since 1519. Coverdale moved to Paris to prepare the edition for the press. Printing began in May 1538, and, in expectation of rapid publication, Thomas Cromwell ordered that 'a Bible of the largest volume in English' be distributed to every parish in England by Christmas 1538. He spoke too soon, because the enterprise began to unravel. There was opposition from the English ambassador in France (Stephen Gardiner, bishop of Winchester) and from the Sorbonne, and by mid-December most of the bound copies had been seized by the Inquisition, and unbound pages had been sold to a haberdasher for use in the making of hats. The English publishers rescued their staff, the type, the unused paper, and some printed sheets of the Old Testament (Genesis to Job) and the New Testament (Matthew to 1 Peter), and returned to London, where printing resumed. By April 1539 the print run of 3,000 copies was ready, but they were kept in storage because Cromwell was negotiating for the release of the 2,500 copies confiscated by the Inquisition. In November the Bible was published.

The term 'Great Bible' reflects its size (337 mm × 235 mm, roughly 15 inches × 9 inches), but the edition is also remarkable for its editorial scrupulousness. The Old Testament was revised in the light of the publication in 1535 of a new edition of the Hebrew Bible (with a literal Latin translation) by the German Hebraist

Sebastian Münster, and the New Testament with reference to the Latin version by Erasmus. The sole exception to this process was the Psalms, which remained in Coverdale's own version. The title page demonstrates that the argument about priests and laity had moved on. Whereas on the Coverdale Bible a small Henry VIII distributed Bibles to the clergy, in the Great Bible a large Henry VIII distributes Bibles to clergy and laity alike. In 1526, smuggled copies of Tyndale's New Testament had made it available in English to anyone who could secure a copy; thirteen years later, the English king was portrayed distributing English Bibles to his subjects. The Reformation had been accompanied by a revolution, one in which a book that had been imprisoned in Latin had become accessible in the everyday language of the English people.

The printers of the Great Bible were Edward Whitchurch and Richard Grafton, and often only one of their names appears on the title page. The name that stuck, however, was Whitchurch's, so, in the instructions to the translators of the KJV, the Great Bible is described as Whitchurch's Bible.

The Geneva Bible

The accession of the resolutely Catholic Queen Mary to the throne in 1553 put an end to the printing of English Bibles and to their use in churches. Protestants fled from the fiery persecution that she inaugurated with the judicial murder of John Rogers, the publisher of the Matthew Bible. One of the Marian exiles was William Whittingham (later dean of Durham), who became a senior of the English church in Geneva. On the accession of Queen Elizabeth, most of the congregation returned to England,

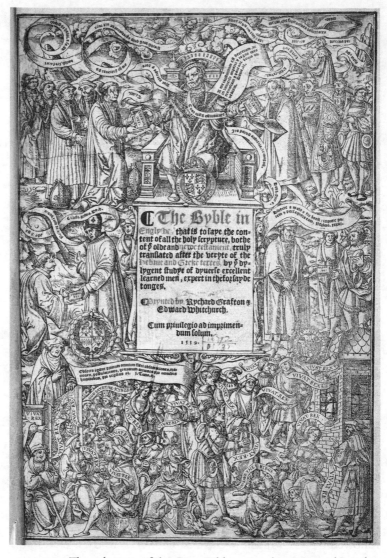

FIGURE 4. The title-page of the Great Bible, printed in Paris and London in 1539.

and Calvin suggested that Whittingham became pastor of the Geneva church; as the pastoral responsibilities eased with the diminution of the congregation, he was able to devote himself to scholarship. He was the powerhouse of the Geneva Bible, translating the New Testament himself (published 1557) and helping to coordinate the translation of the Psalms (1559) and the Old Testament (published with the Apocrypha and the New Testament in 1560); the complete Bible was dedicated to Queen Elizabeth. The Old Testament is largely based on the Great Bible; many of the changes reflect scholarly study of the Hebrew original and of translations into Greek and Latin. The New Testament also uses the Great Bible, but Tyndale's phrasing is sometimes adopted, and attention is paid to the Latin translation by Theodore Beza, Calvin's successor in Geneva.

Whittingham's collaborators were Anthony Gilby (a Leicestershire clergyman), Thomas Wood (first identified in 1960 as an army officer), Christopher Goodman (later Lady Margaret Professor of Divinity at Oxford), William Cole (later dean of Lincoln), Miles Coverdale, and the Scottish reformer John Knox. Four members of the group (Knox, Whittingham, Goodman, and Cole) had been members of the English church in Frankfurt, but had been expelled from the church and the city over a dispute about the reintroduction of the Book of Common Prayer. In Geneva, Goodman and Knox had become ministers of a new English church, and Gilby and Wood became elders. The allocation of responsibilities and the procedures followed by the translators are not known. Knox and Coverdale seem to have played minor roles in the process, but their presence was symbolically important. The tradition that the English clergyman Thomas Sampson, who had been in Frankfurt with the other anti-ceremonialists, was one of the translators seems to be mistaken, as he was not in Geneva at the right time, but other members of the congregation may have been involved.

The Geneva Bible was intended for private study. Most editions were printed in roman type and published in small octavo editions that were easy to hold. It was the first English Bible to adopt verse numbers. The translation was not eccentric, despite the fact that the rendering of Genesis 3:7 (in which Adam and Eve are said to have 'made themselves breeches') has led to the nickname 'Breeches Bible'. Indeed, the fact that several of the translators would later become embroiled in the vestiarian controversy, which arose from puritan scruples about the continued use of traditional Catholic canonical vestments within the English Church (the surplice, and later the cope, were deemed to violate the principle of the priesthood of all believers) meant that terms relating to clothing were chosen with particular care; their Adam and Eve could not be dressed in anything that might recall the dress of bishops.

Private study was assisted by a system of chapter headings, maps, 'tables' of theological material and marginal notes, many of which are helpfully explanatory, but a few of which were deemed to be anti-monarchical. The presence of notes that reflected a particular theological position offended those who maintained opposing positions; the decision to ban notes in the KJV was a direct reaction to the notes in the Geneva version. Bibles were thereafter reprinted without notes for centuries, until the Scofield Bibles reintroduced a similar system in the early twentieth century.

The Geneva Bible remained in print until 1640, but did not remain stable throughout the eighty years that it was in print. The Apocrypha was often omitted, and the text and notes of Revelation existed in two versions, one with notes deriving from John Bale and Heinrich Bullinger, and the other (available from 1599) with notes by Franciscus Junius. In England, many editions had notes by the learned polyglot Laurence Tomson, translated from continental sources.

The Geneva Bible became enormously popular, and was published in more than seventy editions between 1560 and 1640. In England, where about half a million copies were sold, it was printed (sometimes by the king's printer) from 1576 to 1640, and it became the Bible of the puritan faction in England and in the puritan disapora on the Continent and in America. Its readership, however, extended well beyond the puritan party, because it was cheap and easily available. Despite its anti-episcopacy, its readers included ceremonialists such as Lancelot Andrewes, Richard Hooker, John Whitgift, and William Laud; such readers continued to read it, or at least to consult it, long after the KJV had been published. The friendship of Whittingham and John Knox meant that it was the first English Bible to be published in Scotland (1579; New Testament title page dated 1576), where it was printed by the king's printer for Scotland, was dedicated to King James VI, and displayed the royal coat of arms on its cover. The Bible was in English, but the dedication by the General Assembly was in Scots: 'this holy boke of God callit the Bible, newly imprentit, was brocht before us be the prenter thereof... and desyrit to be dedicate to zour Hienes with a convenient preface in our common Scottis language' ('this holy book of God, called the Bible, newly printed, was brought before us by the printer thereof... and desired to be dedicated to your Highness with a convenient preface in our common Scots language').

This royal endorsement did not mean that King James was to remain an admirer of the Geneva Bible. Indeed, he turned against its annotations, some of which he deemed to be subversive of royal authority. In the first chapter of Exodus the Pharaoh orders the Jewish midwives to kill all male children born to Jewish mothers. The midwives disobey this royal command, explaining to the credulous Pharaoh that the physiology of Jewish mothers differs from that of Egyptian mothers: in the words of the Geneva translation, 'And the midwives answered Pharaoh, Because the Hebrew women are not as the women of Egypt: for they are lively, and are delivered ere the midwife come at them'. The marginal note in the Geneva Bible reads 'their disobedience herein was lawful, but their dissembling evil'. To a modern reader this seems an extraordinary view, rather like asking someone hiding Jews during the Second World War to be honest when a Nazi at the door enquires about whether there are any Jews inside. King James, however, took the opposite view. Not only would the dissembling of the midwives be evil, but so would their failure to yield to royal authority. The commands of kings must always be obeyed. It was this view that determined that the KJV would be published without marginal notes.

The Bishops' Bible

The anti-episcopal notes to the Geneva Bible displeased the Bishops, and in 1568 a revised version of the Great Bible was published; a second edition with more revisions was published four years later. Coverdale's lively prefatory material was replaced by a solemn preface by Archbishop Thomas Cranmer. The large number of bishops on the revision committee led to it becoming the trespace of the seruants of thy fathers God. And Ioseph wept, when they spake vnto him.

18 Also his brethren came vnto him, and fel downe before his face, & said, Beholde, we be thy seruantes.

19 To whome Ioseph said, Feare not : for am not I vnder God?

20 When ye thoght euil against me, God disposed it to good, that he might bring to passe, as it is this day, and saue muche people aliue.

21 Feare not now therefore, I wil nourish you, and your children : and he comforted, and spake kindely vnto them,

22 ¶ So Ioseph dwelt in Egypt, he, and his fathers house : and Ioseph liued an hundreth and ten yeres.

23 And Ioseph sawe Ephraims children, euen vnto the third generation : also the sonnes of Machir the sonne of Manasseh were broght vp on Iosephs knees.

24 And Ioseph said vnto his brethren, I am ready to dye, & God wil surely viset you, and bring you out of this land vnto the land, which he sware vnto Abraham, vnto Izhák, and vnto Iaakób.

25 And Ioseph toke an othe of the childré of Israél, saying, God wil surely viset you, and ye shal cary my bones hence.

26 So Ioseph dyed, when he was an hundreth and ten yere olde : and they enbaumed him, & put him in a chest in Egypt.

THE SECONDE BOKE
OF MOSES, CALLED
EXODVS.

THE ARGVMENT.

AFTER that Iaakob by Gods commandement Gen. 46, 3. had broght his famille into Egypt, where they remained for the space of foure hundreth yeres, and of seuenty persones grewe to an infinite nombre, so that the King and the countrey grudged and endeuored bothe by tyrannie and cruel slauery to suppresse them : the Lord according to his promes Gen. 15, 14. had compassion of his Church & deliuered them, but plagued their enemies in moste strange and sondry sortes. And the more that the tyrannie of the wicked enraged against his Church, the more did his heauy iudgements increase against them, til Pharaoh & his armie were drowned in the same Sea, which gaue an entrie and passage to the children of God. But as the ingratitude of man is great, so did they immediatly forget Gods wonderful benefites, and albeit he had giuen them the Passeouer to be a signe & memorial of the same, yet they fel to distrust, and tempted God with sondry murmurings and grudgings against him and his ministers, sometime moued with ambition, sometime for lacke of drinke or meate to content their lustes, sometime by idolatrie, or suche like. VVherefore God visited them with sharpe roddes and plagues that by his corrections they might seke to him for remedy against his scourges & earnestly repentihim for their rebellions and wickednes. And because God loueth them to the end whome he hathe once begonne to loue, he punished them not according to their desertes, but dealt with them in great mercies, and euer with newe benefites labored to ouercome their malice : for he first gouerned them and gaue them his worde & Law, bothe concerning the maner of seruing him, & also the forme of iudgements and ciuil policie. to the intent that they shulde not serue God after their owne inuentions, but according to that ordre, which his heauenlie wisdome had appointed.

¶ CHAP. I.

2 The children of Iaakob came into Egypt. 8 The newe Pharaoh oppresseth them. 12 The prouidence of God towards them. 15 The Kings commandement to the midwiues. 22 The sonnes of the Ebrewes are commanded to be cast into the riuer.

NOw these are the names of the children of Israél, which came into Egypt (euerie man and his houtholde came [thither] with Iaakób) Reubén, Simeón, Leui, and Iudáh,

3 Issachár, Zebulún and Beniamin,

4 Dan, and Nephtalí, Gad, and Ashér.

5 So all the soules that came out of the loynes of Iaakób, were seuentie soules : Ioseph was in Egypt already.

6 Now Ioseph dyed and all his brethren, and that whole generation.

7 ¶ And the children of Israél broght forthe the frute, and encreased in abundance, and were multiplied, and were exceeding mightie, so that the land was ful of them.

8 Then there rose vpa newe King in Egypt, who knewe not Ioseph.

9 And he said vnto his people, Beholde, the people of the children of Israél [are] greater and mightier then we.

10 Come, let vs worke wiselie with them, lest they multiplie, & it come to passe, that if there be warre, they ioyne them selues also vnto our enemies, & fight against vs, and get them out of the land.

11 Therefore did they set taskemasters ouer them, to kepe them vnder with burdens, and they buylt the cities Pithóm & Ramasés for the treasures of Pharaóh.

12 But the more they vexed them, the more they

known as the Bishops' Bible. In 1570 the Convocation of Canterbury (the southern provincial assembly of the clergy of the Church of England) instructed that copies be placed in all cathedrals, and thereafter it was widely purchased by parish churches. There is no surviving parallel instruction from the Convocation of York (the northern provincial assembly), but churches in the north bought it as well. There were twenty editions, of which the last was published in 1602.

The Bishops' Bible is more notable for its dignity and its aspirations to majesty than for its clarity. The plain English of Tyndale and Coverdale, elevated slightly to reflect the standing of the Bible as a holy book, has been edged aside in favour of Latinate rotundity. Its scholarship is, alas, as lax as its prose is inflated. It was clearly the work of senior churchmen who had more pressing duties on their minds. Because it was authorized, it became the Bible that was read in churches; at home, however, readers preferred the good demotic English of the Geneva Bible.

Douai–Reims

The popularity of the Geneva Bible distressed Roman Catholics as well as Anglican bishops, and, although the Catholic Church did not yet acknowledge the right of the laity to read the Bible in the vernacular, there was clearly a practical need for an antidote to Geneva. The translation was begun at the English College in Douai (then spelt Douay), but the College moved to Reims (then spelt Rheims) in 1578, and the work was completed there; the driving force behind it was the Oxford Hebraist Gregory Martin. The New Testament was published in 1582 (with notes by Martin's colleague Richard Bristow), and the Old Testament followed in

1609 (as far as Job) and 1610. In both Testaments the translation was from the Vulgate, the standing of which had been affirmed by the Council of Trent, though, in the case of the New Testament, it is clear that the Greek was consulted. Much of the translation can be fluent and elegant, but sometimes dogma or literalism intrude, so, in the Lord's Prayer (Matthew 6:11), our daily bread becomes 'supersubstantial bread', and, in Philippians 2:7 (2:8 in KJV), Jesus is said to have 'exinanited Himself'; neither phrase trips off the tongue, because readability has been sacrificed on the altar of theological precision. The scholarly probity of the Douai–Reims Bible meant that it had to be taken seriously by later translators, as indeed was its New Testament by the translators of the KJV; had the Old Testament been published sooner, it might have had a comparable influence.

2

THE COMMISSIONING OF
THE KING JAMES VERSION

The Hampton Court Conference

In the second half of the sixteenth century Queen Elizabeth presided over a church that was increasingly divided. The enthusiastic Roman Catholicism of her half-sister, Mary Tudor, had driven many Protestants abroad in the mid-1550s, and on the Continent they had experienced forms of Protestantism that were deemed 'purer' than English Protestantism, which still retained many ceremonial vestiges of its Catholic origins. When the exiles returned, on the accession of Queen Elizabeth, they became known as 'puritans'. In 1559 Elizabeth established a Protestant church, but there was a growing minority of puritans who felt uncomfortable with church government by bishops, the ceremonialism of the 1552 Prayer Book, and the Queen's attempts to keep ceremonial conservatives on side by advocating traditional vestments, reintroducing a crucifix in her chapel, and, at a later stage, limiting puritan preaching.

The firm government of Elizabeth kept the puritan party in check, but her death in 1603 and the accession of James VI of

FIGURE 6. James I. Engraving by Crispijn van de Passe, 1613.

FIGURE 7. Richard Bancroft by unknown artist, c.1600.

Scotland to the throne of England (as James I) afforded an opportunity to the puritans to present their views to the new monarch. A petition said to have contained more than 1,000 signatures (and so known as the millenary petition) was drawn up and presented to the King; it centred on issues such as 'popish' ceremonies and vestments, married clergy, the requirement that clergy be educated, and the grounding of doctrine in Scripture rather than authority of the clergy and the tradition of the Church. James loved theological debate, and decided to convene a conference for which the agenda would be the millenary petition.

In January 1604 King James assembled a group of bishops and moderate puritans at Hampton Court Palace for a three-day conference; the leader of the bishops was Richard Bancroft (bishop of London), and the leader of the puritans was John Rainolds (president of Corpus Christi College, Oxford). The debates proved inconclusive, but one item not on the agenda was to prove of historic importance. On the second day of the conference (16 January), according to William Barlow's grumpily anti-puritan *Sum and Substance of the Conference* (1604), John Rainolds proposed 'that there might be a new translation of the Bible, because those that were allowed in the reigns of Henry VIII and Edward VI were corrupt, and not answerable to the truth of the original'. This account is puzzling, because it was the Great Bible that was in use in the reigns of Henry and Edward, and from which Rainolds drew his three examples of erroneous translations. The Bishops' Bible in use in 1604 was a product of Queen Elizabeth's reign, but, in Barlow's account, it is not mentioned. Clearly something has been lost in the retelling, but, whatever was said, the King was convinced.

The bishops, who were content with the Church's use of the Bishops' Bible of 1568, were unhappy about the idea, but it appealed to King James, because it offered the prospect of an authoritative alternative to the Geneva Bible, which contained notes that were critical of the authority of monarchs; it had the added advantage of conceding something to the puritan side, which would otherwise have emerged from the conference with every proposal rejected. Beyond these practical considerations, a Bible emerging from a conference convened by the King and that would be dedicated to him was in effect an endorsement of the idea of a monarchical national church of which King James was the head. That is why the dedication to the King describes him as the 'principal mover and author' of the translation; indeed, the phrase sets up a parallel with God, the 'first mover' and the 'author of all things', so eliding obedience to God with obedience to the king, and ratifying the claim of James to be king by divine right.

Instructions and Procedures

Bishop Bancroft's objection to a new Bible had been overruled, but he was wily enough to ensure that, if the project was to proceed, he should have a controlling hand in the selection of translators and in the formulation of the terms of reference that would guide their work. There were fifteen 'rules to be observed in the translation of the Bible'.

1. The ordinary Bible read in the church, commonly called the Bishops' Bible, to be followed, and as little altered as the truth of the original will permit.

This rule specified the version of the Bible was to be a revision of the Bishops' Bible (for which the 1602 edition was used) rather than a fresh translation from the ancient languages. As the revisers say in the preface to the King James Version (KJV), 'The Translators to the Reader', their purpose 'was not to make a new translation... but to make a good one better'.

2. The names of the prophets, and the holy writers, with the other names of the text, to be retained, as nigh as may be, according as they are vulgarly used.

The term 'vulgarly' does not have its modern sense of 'coarsely', but specifies a preference for the English form of names over the Hebrew and Greek forms. This, as will be seen below, is the rule that was most often transgressed.

    3. The old ecclesiastical words to be kept, viz. the word
'church' not to be translated 'congregation' etc.

The implementation of this rule was to be a persistent source of
puritan objections to the KJV, as puritans, appropriating Tyndale's
argument, preferred 'congregation' to 'church', 'wash' to 'baptize',
'elder' or 'senior' to 'bishop', and 'minister' to 'priest'.

    4. When a word hath divers significations, that to be kept
which hath been most commonly used by most of the
ancient fathers, being agreeable to the propriety of the
place, and the analogy of the faith.

'Divers significations' means 'more than one meaning', and
'propriety of the place' means 'the context in which the word is
used'. The assertion of the authority of the church fathers ('ancient
fathers') and the need to conform to the doctrine of the church
('the analogy of the faith') were anti-puritan rules, because puritans
tended to believe that the church fathers had no authority and that
doctrine should spring from the Bible, not the other way round.

    5. The division of the chapters to be altered, either not at all,
or as little as may be, if necessity so require.

By this time the division of chapters into verses had become
embedded, because verse references were an aid to memory.
Hebrew and Greek manuscripts had been divided in various ways
since late antiquity, but the system adopted by the KJV revisers
had been introduced by the French publisher Robert Estienne,
who divided chapters into verses in a series of Bibles (in Greek
and Latin) published in Geneva. These divisions had first appeared
in an English version in the Geneva Bible of 1560, and had since
become established.

6. No marginal notes at all to be affixed, but only for the explanation of the Hebrew or Greek words which cannot, without some circumlocution, so briefly and fitly be expressed in the text.

The interdiction against expository marginal notes may have originated in King James's dislike of anti-monarchical notes in the Geneva Bible, but also reflected unease about the prospect that marginal notes might reflect a particular theological perspective.

7. Such quotations of places to be marginally set down as shall serve for the fit reference of one scripture to another.

'Places' are verses; this rule gave the authority for the revisers to produce a system of cross-references.

8. Every particular man of each company to take the same chapter or chapters, and having translated or amended them severally by himself, where he thinketh good, all to meet together, confer what they have done, and agree for their parts what shall stand.
9. As any one company hath dispatched any one book in this manner, they shall send it to the rest, to be considered of seriously and judiciously, for His Majesty is very careful in this point.
10. If any company, upon the review of the book so sent, doubt or differ upon any place, to send them word thereof; note the place and withal send their reasons, to which if they consent not, the difference to be compounded at the general meeting, which is to be of the chief persons of each company, at the end of the work.

11. When any place of special obscurity is doubted of, letters to be directed, by authority, to send to any learned man in the land for his judgement of such a place.

The phrase 'by authority' probably means 'by authority of the synod of bishops' rather than 'by the king's authority', but in either case would have the force of law, which meant that those in receipt of enquires were commanded (rather than asked) to give an opinion.

12. Letters to be sent from every bishop to the rest of his clergy, admonishing them of this translation in hand, and to move and charge as many as being skilful in the tongues; and having taken pains in that kind, to send his particular observations to the company, either at Westminster, Cambridge or Oxford.
13. The directors in each company to be the deans of Westminster and Chester for that place, and the King's professors in Hebrew or Greek in each university.

'King's professors', more commonly known as regius professors, are nominated by the Crown; they had originated as acts of royal beneficence at the time of the Reformation, when Henry VIII had funded the original regius professorships, but by the early seventeenth century had become an important mechanism by which the Crown exercised authority in the universities. The dean of Westminster was the dauntingly learned Lancelot Andrewes, and the dean of Chester was William Barlow, the official historian of the Hampton Court Conference. The regius professors of Hebrew (Edward Lively at Cambridge, John Harding at Oxford) and Greek (Andrew Downes at Cambridge, John Perrinne at Oxford), all of whom are discussed in the next chapter, did not all go on to play an important role in the translation (indeed, Lively died before it began), but they were not appointed simply for their personal qualities; they had all been appointed to their chairs by the monarch, and so were expected to keep the king's wishes in mind as they directed the translators.

14. These translations to be used when they agree better with the text than the Bishops' Bible: Tyndale's, Matthew's, Coverdale's, Whitchurch's, Geneva.

Whitchurch's Bible was the common name for the Great Bible, so called from one of its printers, Edward Whitchurch.

15. Besides the said directors before mentioned, three or four of the most ancient and grave divines, in either of the universities, not employed in translating, to be assigned to the Vice-Chancellor, upon conference with the rest of the heads, to be overseers of the translations as well Hebrew as Greek, for the better observation of the 4th rule above specified.

This rule was a late addition formulated at the suggestion of the vice-chancellor of Cambridge. The vice-chancellor was always drawn from the heads of colleges (masters, wardens, principals, etc.), hence the reference to 'the rest of the heads'.

These rules were quite unprecedented in their rigour. Whereas previous translations had been the work of a small number of individuals or a group of slapdash bishops, the KJV was a carefully meditated enterprise in which panels of translators worked collaboratively. Nothing comparable had been attempted since antiquity, when the elders of Israel gathered in Alexandria to translate the Hebrew Bible into Greek, and created a Greek text (the Septuagint) with consistent principles and a remarkably even style. The KJV translators were determined to improve upon that precedent, because (as the translator Miles Smith explained in the preface to the KJV), the Septuagint translators were said to have finished the task in seventy-two days, but the KJV translators had sufficient time for revision: 'neither were we barred or hindered from going over it again, having once done it.'

To what extent were these guidelines followed? Anyone who has worked with untried procedures set out in advance of a project will be aware that the practicalities of implementation mean that some procedures will not be followed. It is difficult to judge exactly how the translators worked, but there are several documents that afford glimpses into their practices. The most important of these from the perspective of guiding principles was a report by one of the translators to the Synod of Dort.

In 1618, seven years after the KJV had been published, the assembly now known as the Synod of Dort was convened in Dordrecht by the Dutch Reformed Church to deal with the dispute between Calvinists and Arminians; just as the Hampton Court Conference had commissioned a new version of the Bible, so the Synod of Dort approved a new translation of the Bible into Dutch. The five English delegates to the Synod included the resolute Calvinist Samuel Ward, a member of the Cambridge company that translated the Apocrypha. Ward submitted an account, written in the international language of Latin, which set out the procedures that governed the work of the KJV. He also listed eight rules that had guided the process of translation. Although the first two simply summarize elements in the original fifteen rules, the other six are, in effect, supplementary rules; because they were formulated retrospectively (and in Ward's Latin are sometimes phrased in the past tense), they have the inestimable advantage of reflecting what actually happened rather than what was supposed to happen.

1. The translators were not being asked to create a new version of the Bible, but rather to revise the established version, removing any blemishes or inaccuracies.
2. Parallel pages would be recorded in the margins, but there would be no marginal commentary.
3. Where a Hebrew or Greek word admits two meanings of a suitable kind, the one was to be expressed in the text, the other in the margin. The same to be done where variant readings were found in different (but reputable) versions of the Hebrew and Greek texts.

The use of the margin for alternative readings was controversial, because, as Miles Smith explains in the preface to the KJV, such a 'show of uncertainty' could shake belief 'in the authority of the Scriptures for deciding of controversies'. He therefore mounts a carefully argued defence of the practice, noting that nothing essential to salvation is ambiguous, but that there are instances, such as 'rare names of certain birds, beasts and precious stones', when it is better to be honest about uncertainty than to 'dogmatize upon this or that peremptorily'.

4. The more difficult Hebraisms and Graecisms were consigned to the margin.
5. In the translation of Tobit and Judith, when any great discrepancy is found between the Greek text and the old vulgate Latin, they followed the Greek text by preference.

The 'old vulgate Latin' refers to Jerome's translation from the Aramaic text of the apocryphal books of Tobit and Judith; that text was based on the Greek rather than the lost Hebrew originals. The Greek text followed by preference is the Septuagint.

    6. Words that it was anywhere necessary to insert into the text to complete the meaning were to be distinguished by another type, small roman.

    7. New arguments were to be prefixed to every book, and new headings to every chapter.

An 'argument' is a summary of contents, but in the event 'arguments' were never prefixed to the books of the Bible. Headings were, however, furnished for each chapter.

    8. A very perfect genealogy and map of the Holy Land was to be joined to the work.

Procedures in Practice

Perhaps the most impractical of the rules was number 4, which implied that all members of the company would translate or amend all the books that had been assigned to the company. There is some evidence that in practice the work was divided up. The contemporary biographer of John Bois, a member of the Cambridge company responsible for the Apocrypha, says that 'part of the Apocrypha was allotted to him... [and] when he had finished his own part, at the earnest request of him to whom it was assigned, he undertook a second'. Similarly, one manuscript list (now in the British Library) of the ten members of the Westminster company responsible for the books from Genesis to 2 Kings divides the company into two groups, one responsible for the Pentateuch and the other for the remaining books in their section.

The rule that seems to have been broken most often is number 2, on the spelling of proper names. Isaiah, the English name of the prophet, derives from the abbreviated form of his Hebrew name used in the title of his book (a fuller Hebrew form is used in the text). It must, however, have been the precedent of the Bishops' Bible that caused the revisers to call him 'Esai' in the 1611 text of 2 Kings 19:2; from 1629 onwards the name was spelt Isaiah. On the twenty-one occasions in which he appears in the New Testament, however, the name is spelt Esaias, its Greek form. Similarly, Jeremiah is so spelt in the Old Testament, but in Matthew's Gospel he appears as Ieremie on three occasions (2:17; 16:14; 27:9) in the 1611 text, and in modern texts of the KJV as Jeremy; we may be relieved that he is not 'vulgarly' called Jerry.

Rules formulated in advance of a project are inevitably adjusted to accord with the practicalities of the job. In the case of the KJV, there is evidence both of short cuts and of going the extra mile.

The Canon and the Inclusion of the Apocrypha

For twenty-first-century readers, the most surprising feature of the early editions of the KJV is the inclusion of the Apocrypha. The Protestant canon now consists of the 39 books of the Old Testament and 27 books of the New Testament. The Old Testament is identical with the Jewish and Roman Catholic canon, though some of the 24 books of the Hebrew canon have been subdivided; the order of the books is also different, in that the Prophets are placed at the end by Christian editors, so that the last two verses of Malachi (the final book) concerning Elijah form a transition to the New Testament and a foreshadowing of the link between Elijah and John the Baptist (for example, Matthew 11:14). As for the New Testament, Luther had doubts about the canonicity of Hebrews, James, Jude, and Revelation, and disliked James for its insistence that 'faith without works is dead', but his decision to include these books in his Bible meant that the Protestant New Testament canon became identical with the Roman Catholic canon. Differences arose, however, over the body of writings known to Roman Catholics as deuterocanonical and to Protestants as apocryphal. The term 'deuterocanonical' implies that these writings belong to a second layer of the canon, distinguished by the fact that they survive only in Greek, whereas the term 'apocryphal' is pejorative, and implies that these writings are of doubtful authorship, in contrast to canonical writings of which God is the author. The standing of these books, which entered the early church through the Hellenistic Jews of Alexandria, had long been a matter for contention. Unease first surfaced in the fourth century, when Greek theologians began to give a privileged place to books that were canonical in Hebrew; in the West, it was Jerome who, under the influence of Greek churchmen and as a result of his own Hebrew studies, first introduced the term 'Apocrypha' to denote 'books of the church', as distinct from 'books of the canon'. In the event, most churchmen accepted these books as canonical, though a muted debate continued through the centuries, especially in the East. Throughout the centuries preceding the Reformation, the disputed books were inserted at appropriate places in the Old Testament, so giving them the same status as canonical books, but Protestant reservations led to their being gathered together and published as a separate section of the Bible, labelled Apocrypha. The Catholic

Church responded at the Council of Trent (1546) by declaring these books to be deuterocanonical.

Protestants were divided about the Apocrypha. Lutherans argued that the Apocrypha were valuable (but uninspired) supplements to the inspired Scriptures, and encouraged their study; Luther's Bible included the Apocrypha (except for 1 and 2 Esdras) as an appendix. The Geneva Bible also included the Apocrypha, noting that they were useful 'for knowledge of history and instruction of godly manners'. The Church of England insisted (and still insists) that the Apocrypha be included in any Bible intended for use in public worship (though not in Bibles intended for private study), and includes passages from the Apocrypha in its lectionary and liturgy, but insists in Article 6 of the Thirty-Nine Articles that 'the other Books' (the term 'Apocrypha' is not used) 'the Church doth read for example of life and instruction of manners; but yet doth it not apply them to establish any doctrine'. Puritans such as the Hebraist Hugh Broughton, who is notably absent from the list of translators, inveighed against the inclusion of the Apocrypha, arguing that 'all who make the Apocrypha part of the Holy Bible make God the author of lying fables and vain speech'. John Rainolds, who was one of the translators, had given a series of 250 lectures in which he argued that the Apocrypha were uncanonical; after that many lectures, any listener who was still awake would surely be convinced.

The consequence of these views was that the Apocrypha were included in early editions of the KJV, and that any puritan dissent was suppressed. Under the puritan ascendancy of the 1640s, however, the Westminster Confession asserted that the Apocrypha were not 'to be otherwise approved or made use of than other human writings'. After the Restoration of the monarchy in 1660, Bibles used for reading in churches contained the Apocrypha, as did some Bibles produced for private study, but in the nineteenth century the decision of the British and Foreign Bible Society to exclude the Apocrypha from their Bibles dealt a mortal blow to their inclusion, and thereafter the Apocrypha disappeared from Bibles on sale to the general public.

3

⸘⸙⸘

TRANSLATORS AND
TRANSLATING

The Companies

The principles for choosing the members of the companies, as the committees were called, made the process relatively straight-forward, and, within five months of the Hampton Court Confer-ence, Bishop Bancroft had chosen his teams, assisted in small measure by Thomas Bilson, bishop of Winchester, whose infirmities (sciatica, arthritis, vertigo, tinnitus, and 'many obstructions and extreme windiness') precluded more active involvement. The process of translation and revision was to be undertaken by six companies, two in each of Westminster, Oxford, and Cambridge. The reason for the choice of Westminster (as opposed to London, from which it was then separate) was that Westminster Abbey was a royal peculiar, and so exempt from any jurisdiction other than that of the monarch.

The surviving lists of translators are not entirely consistent, but we know a good deal about most of them, and a majority were of sufficient standing in their profession to have been included in the *Oxford Dictionary of National Biography*. I list all the known translators in Appendix 1 (pp. 278–295) together with short biographical sketches.

Vera Effigies Reverendi in Cristo
Patris Dni. IOH. OVERALL
Epiſcopi Norwicenſis.

FIGURE 8. Lancelot Andrewes, by Simon de Passe, 1618.

FIGURE 9. John Overall by Wenceslaus Hollar, 1657.

The First Westminster Company was charged with the translation of the Old Testament from Genesis to 2 Kings. There were ten men in the company, but four manuscripts now in the British Library supply four slightly different lists. The company met in the Jerusalem Chamber of Westminster Abbey, and was chaired by Lancelot Andrewes, who was then dean of Westminster. He was by some measure the most powerful figure among all the translators, partly because he exercised very considerable powers of patronage, but also because he was one of the most learned men in England, and he offered intellectual as well as spiritual leadership. Six of the men that Andrewes recruited are well known. John Overall, the dean of St Paul's Cathedral, had participated in the Hampton Court Conference, and was, like

Andrewes, a convinced high churchman, comfortable with epis-copacy and ceremonialism. William Bedwell, England's leading Arabist, had fallen under the spell of Andrewes at Cambridge. Richard Thomson, who was half Dutch and known as 'Dutch Thomson', was also a member of the Andrewes circle at Cambridge; he had a drink problem, but was able to lend his outstanding philological expertise to the project. Adrian Saravia, a canon of Westminster, was an outstanding apologist for episcopacy; like Thomson and Andrewes, he enjoyed a European reputation for scholarship. The other members of the company were all broadly sympathetic to Andrewes's theology and ecclesiology, but also had serious credentials as Hebraists. The rigorous study of the Old Testament requires a range of other languages (Aramaic, Syriac, Samaritan, Ethiopic, Arabic), but members of the company had an ample competence in such languages. It comes as no surprise to realize that Andrewes had assembled one of the two most learned of the six companies, and that almost all of its members were drawn from Cambridge. Whether they all pulled together on the project is harder to judge. As early as November 1604 Andrewes complained to the secretary of the College of Anti-quaries that 'most of our company are negligent'.

The central section of the Old Testament, from 1 Chronicles to the Song of Solomon, was the responsibility of the First Cambridge Company. The company was supposed to be directed by the regius professor of Hebrew at Cambridge, Edward Lively, but, although he was nominated for the post, he died before the company had had its first meeting; his loss meant that the company did not have anyone with particular expertise in rabbinical Hebrew. His successor, Robert Spalding, was a member of the company, so he may have become the new director; alternatively, Lancelot

Andrewes may have taken advantage of the vacancy to advance the claims of his brother Roger, who was as bad tempered as Lancelot was serene. Patronage played a part in some of the other appointments. Francis Dillingham was a theologian rather than a distinguished Hebraist, but he was well connected in both the royal court and the Church. Similarly, Andrew Byng may have been appointed because he was the godson of Archbishop Whitgift, though he also had excellent Hebrew. John Richardson was one of the earliest English Arminian theologians (an unpopular position at Cambridge), and had scholarly strength in biblical Hebrew. The final two members of the company both had puritan leanings. Laurence Chaderton had been one of the four puritan delegates at the Hampton Court Conference, and was a good Hebraist; his age contributed to his standing: he was 75 when the King James Version (KJV) was published, and lived to be 103. Thomas Harrison had, despite his puritan sympathies, been a friend of Lancelot Andrewes at school and university. He was the heavyweight intellectual on the committee, with daunting expertise in both Greek and Hebrew; he was also the only translator in any company whose prodigious learning rivalled that of Andrewes. It seems possible that the Orientalist William Eyre (a product of Emmanuel College and later chaplain to Archbishop George Abbot) was appointed as overseer of this company. In a letter of December 1608 to James Ussher (whose chronology would eventually be incorporated into the KJV), he seems to write as a member of the company, but he was not a translator. The purpose of the letter is to ask for the return of the copy of the draft translation that had been sent to William Daniel, who had translated the New Testament into Irish; it seems possible that Daniel was one of the learned men whose judgement was sought in

FIGURE 10. John Rainolds by unknown artist.

compliance with rule 11, but it is equally possible that Daniel wanted to see a specimen draft translation as part of his current work on the translation of the Book of Common Prayer into Irish or a future project on the translation of the Old Testament.

The First Oxford Company was responsible for the final third of the Old Testament, from Isaiah to Malachi. Its nominal director was John Harding, regius professor of Hebrew at Oxford, but the presence in the company of John Rainolds, the leader of the puritan delegation to the Hampton Court Conference who had successfully argued the case for a new Bible, meant that leadership may have passed to him; it is striking that the company met in Rainolds's rooms at Corpus Christi College (of which he was president) rather than Harding's at Magdalen, but that may be related to Rainolds's impaired mobility. As a seventeenth-century account explains, the translators 'had recourse once a week to Dr Rainolds his lodgings in Corpus Christi College, and there 'tis said perfected the work, notwithstanding the said Doctor, who had the chief hand in it, was all the while sorely afflicted with the gout'. Another possible reason for the move to Corpus was the college library, whose holdings in Latin, Greek, and Hebrew books rightly enjoyed a European reputation. This was the only company whose collective linguistic expertise rivalled Andrewes's First Westminster Company. Thomas Holland (a moderate puritan) had a command of rabbinical as well as biblical Hebrew. Richard Brett's languages included Latin, Greek, Hebrew, Aramaic, Arabic, and Ethiopic. Richard Kilbye had an incomparable command of Hebrew sources. The company also included Miles Smith, one of the few translators with no university affiliation, but a scholar with an extraordinary knowledge of the Jewish exegetes, and a knowledge of ancient languages that gave rise to the folk belief that Hebrew, Aramaic, Syriac, and Arabic were as familiar to him as English. His quality must have been noticed, because he also sat on the revision committee for the whole Bible, and it was he who composed the learned and elegant preface, 'The Translators to the Reader', that was included among the preliminaries of the KJV. Finally, the company included William Thorne in a capacity that is not entirely clear, but probably that of overseer. At the time of the Hampton Court Conference, Thorne had been regius professor of Hebrew, but, before work on the translation had begun, he had been succeeded by Harding, who therefore became director of the company. Thorne's Hebrew was good enough for him to correspond in the language, and he composed at least one poem in Hebrew, so he was not merely an ornament to the company.

The Second Cambridge Company was responsible for the Apocrypha, which was the most sensitive task in the project, because there was opposition to its inclusion from other translators, notably John Rainolds. According to Archbishop Bancroft's rules, the director of the company should have been Andrew Downes, regius professor of Greek at Cambridge and regarded by contemporaries as 'the ablest Grecian of Christendom'. For whatever reason, the directorship was assumed by John Duport, a senior academic who was also a moderate puritan, and so a politically astute choice. Samuel Ward was a second puritan member, and in his case it must have been advocacy of episcopacy that made him acceptable; it was Ward who was later to give an account of the translation process to the Synod of Dort. William Branthwaite had court connections that may have secured his place on the company, but he also had excellent Greek. John Bois, whose tutor had been Andrew Downes, was a former child prodigy who had grown into an adult haunted by imagined illnesses; like Miles Smith, he had no current university connection, but was recruited from his rural parish because of his extraordinary command of Greek. He went on to serve on the Revisers' Committee. His recently discovered notebooks, to which I shall return, offer substantial insights into the work of the companies.

The Second Oxford Company was responsible for the bulk of the New Testament: the Gospels, Acts, and Book of Revelation. The notional director of the company was presumably John Perrinne, the regius professor of Greek, but the company met in the lodgings of Sir Henry Savile, the warden of Merton College; Savile is now known as an astronomer, but he was also an eminent student of patristic Greek. The only other member of the company with serious holdings in Greek was John Harmar, who was a former regius professor of Greek. Other members of the company were no doubt competent in Greek (in which competence is more easily achieved than in Hebrew), but seem to have been appointed for reasons other than eminence in scholarship. Thomas Ravis and Giles Thomson, for example, had attended the Hampton Court Conference; Ravis took notes (which were later used for the official account), and Thomson seems to have remained silent. George Abbot, the future archbishop of Canterbury, was a rising star who combined Calvinist zeal with advocacy of episcopacy. Three members of the company were royal chaplains, and therefore deemed to be safe pairs of hands, which was certainly required for the company responsible for the Book of Revelation.

The Second Westminster Company was responsible for the New Testament epistles, which was a relatively small task. Its director was William Barlow, the dean of Chester. Other members of the company seem to have been included for reasons other than their scholarly standing in Greek, though all were no doubt competent. The group included John Spenser, a royal chaplain best known as the editor of Richard Hooker's *Laws of Ecclesiastical Polity*, and Roger Fenton, a friend of Lancelot Andrewes with a particular interest in the spiritual life of the Christian. Fenton's sermons and publications were praised for 'the natural majesty of the style, like a master bee without a sting'; in 1609 the beekeeper Charles Butler showed in *The Feminine Monarchy* that master bees were female, but the metaphor nonetheless works, and we might reasonably assume that Fenton's abilities as a writer contributed to the high quality of the prose in the KJV epistles. Another member with powerful connections was Arthur Lake, a fellow of Winchester College whose older brother was Sir Thomas Lake, secretary of state to James I; it seems possible that he was appointed through royal patronage. In addition to the company members, George Ryves, the warden of New College, Oxford, was appointed as an overseer for this section, in compliance with the fifteenth of Bancroft's rules. The same document that names Ryves as an overseer also mentions the involvement of Nicholas Love, the headmaster of Winchester College, but his role is not specified.

The learning embodied in the men of these six companies is daunting. It is sometimes assumed that people in the twenty-first century know more than the benighted people of the seventeenth century, but in many ways the opposite is true. The population from which scholars can now be drawn is much larger than that of the seventeenth century, but it would be difficult now to bring together a group of more than fifty scholars with the range of languages and knowledge of other disciplines that characterized the KJV translators. We may live in a world with more knowledge, but it is populated by people with less knowledge. To give but one example, the preface to the KJV ('The Translators to the Reader') affirms 'that the Syrian translation of the New Testament is in most learned men's libraries...and the Psalter in Arabic is with many.' As one who has struggled with both Syriac ('Syrian') and Arabic, I can attest how difficult they are for modern Anglophone readers; I am also confident that books in these languages are no longer 'in most learned men's libraries'.

Work-in-Progress Documents

The procedures described in the previous chapter seem to have been treated as guidelines rather than rules. This was a case not of cutting corners, but rather of recognizing that the task, unprecedented since antiquity, was in some respects impracticable. Means had been found, chiefly through the provision of sinecures, to relieve the translators of many of their daily responsibilities, so they had far more time to devote to the task than did their predecessors on the Bishops' Bible; on the other hand, they were vastly more scrupulous than those predecessors, and the procedures as set out in the rules demanded huge tracts of time. In particular, the requirement that every man in a company translate all the books assigned to that company seems to have been too onerous, because there are signs of the subdivision of labour. The First Westminster Company, for example, seems to have established separate working parties for the Pentateuch and the historical books, and the Second Westminster Company seems to have separated the Pauline epistles from the canonical epistles. There is evidence in the case of the Second Cambridge Company that individuals were given separate assignments: John Bois's biographer, Andrew Walker, asserted that

> sure I am, that part of the Apocrypha was allotted to him (for he hath showed me the very copy he translated by) but, to my grief, I know not which part.... When he had finished his own part, at the earnest request of him to whom it was assigned, he undertook a second... but I forbear to name... the person.

If Walker's recollection is correct, then the practice he describes may imply a lower level of scholarly probity in the translators of the Apocrypha than in the companies responsible for the canonical parts of the Bible. Indeed, the practice of assigning individual books to individual translators was the one used for the Bishops' Bible, and it accounts in significant part for its scholarly failings.

The king's printer, Robert Barker, supplied forty copies of the 1602 edition of the Bishops' Bible for the use of the translators;

the sheets were unbound, and so could be subdivided for the companies, members of which annotated the sheets. A small number of these sheets survive, and are bound into a Bible now in the Bodleian Library in Oxford. The annotations in this Bible offer insights both into the process by which one company went about its work and into the proceedings of the revision committee. This Bible is not a simple document. The sheets were annotated before the book was bound, so annotations disappear into the binding. And, whether or not the sheets were all from one of the forty copies, it is clear that the two marked sections were annotated during different phases of the editorial process. The Old Testament annotations, to which I shall return below, seem to reflect the stage at which translations were being revised. The New Testament annotations, however, reflect an earlier stage of the process.

The New Testament annotations record the work of the Second Oxford Company, which was responsible for the Gospels, Acts, and Revelation. The surviving annotations are all in the gospels, and are written in three distinct hands: one annotated Matthew and John 17, another Mark and Luke 1 18, and a third Luke 19–24 and John 18–21. The unannotated first part of John's Gospel is a puzzle, and the work of all three scribes is well advanced, but none of the sections is finished. The annotations would, therefore, seem to catch a series of moments in time. Careful analysis of the comments shows that the draft translation was twice reviewed in a systematic way; probably both reviews were undertaken by the company, but it is possible that one was the work of another company, in compliance with rules 9 and 10, which required review by other companies. In any case, many (but not all) of the revisions in the margins of these pages survived the process of scrutiny, and were duly incorporated into the KJV.

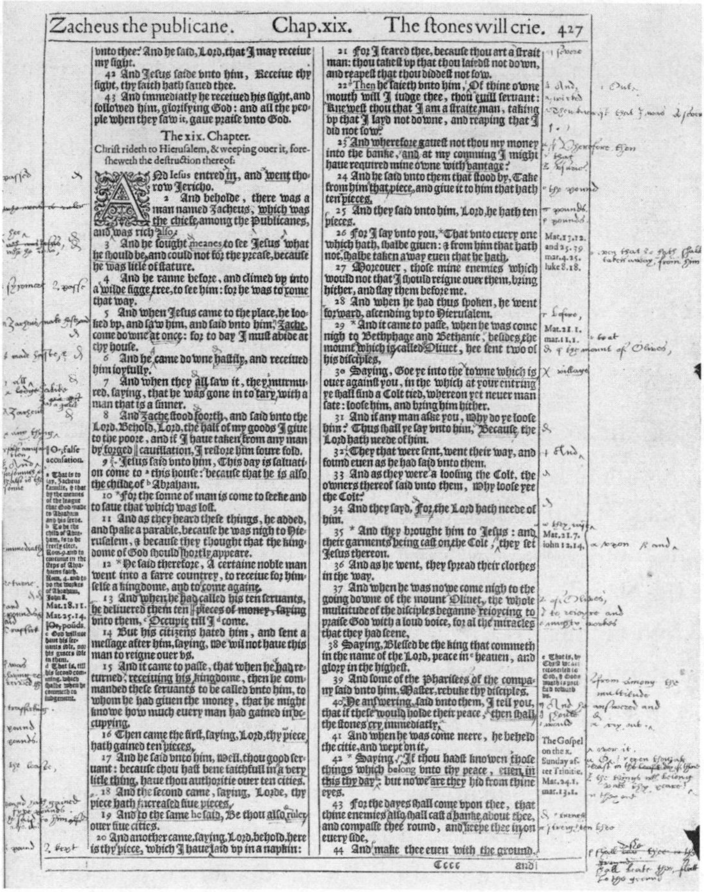
Zacheus the publicane. Chap.xix. The stones will crie. 427

The xix. Chapter.

Christ rideth to Hierusalem, & weeping ouer it, foreshewethe the destruction thereof.

FIGURE 11. Luke 19: folio from the annotated Bishops' Bible, 1602, The Bodleian Library.

The Old Testament annotations bear mute witness to the revision process. The annotations are in the hands of the same three scribes, and so these pages would seem to have been in the possession of the same company; that said, the annotations occur in

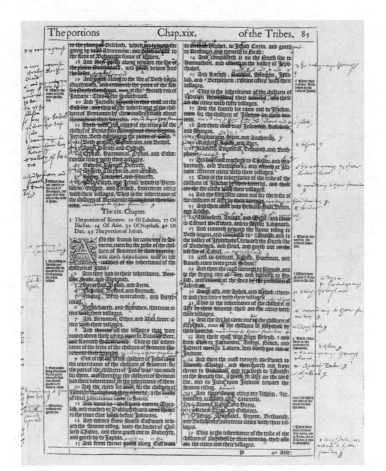

FIGURE 12. Joshua 19: folio from the annotated Bishops' Bible, 1602, The Bodleian Library.

extended patches throughout the Old Testament, from Genesis to Malachi, and so cover material that was the responsibility of all three companies responsible for the Old Testament. It is possible that the First Oxford Company saw the work of the other two Old Testament companies, and, alternatively, possible that it is annotation produced by the Committee of Revision, which met in 1610 in the Stationers' Hall in London—in which case the three scribes would have had to travel to London. The annotations represent a stage of revision more advanced than the last of the New Testament revisions, though they are not quite final; beyond the choice of words, there are also unfinished matters such as italics and chapter headings. Whatever the manuscript is, it is not the final copy that was sent to the printer. Indeed, it is not even clear, as is sometimes assumed, that printer's copy took the form of an annotated Bishops' Bible, though that remains a possibility.

The Lambeth Palace Library in London contains a working document from the Second Westminster Company, which was responsible for the epistles. The text is a draft translation of the epistles, laid out on the page in the style of a printed book, with ruled lines separating two columns of text. Indeed, it resembles the layout of the Bishops' Bible, from which it was evidently transcribed in modified form. The formality of the document may imply that it was intended to be sent to an overseer or another company (or more than one company) for comment, or that it was kept as a master copy on which comments from other readers could be recorded. In either case, what is striking is that the process is unfinished, as is also the case with the annotated Bishops' Bible. The unfinished state of these documents may reflect haste occasioned by the command of the King to bring the project to completion; a process that was thorough but slow had to be hastened in the final stages. So it was, as will become apparent in the next chapter, with the printing of the first edition of the KJV.

The Revision Process

When the six companies had finished their work, a 'general meeting' (as it is called in rule 10) was convened daily over a period of nine months in 1610 in the Stationers' Hall in London. The Hall was then Abergavenny House, adjacent to the City wall on Ave Maria Lane. The setting was doubly appropriate: first, the Hall was the nerve centre of the London book trade, and so the presence of the revision committee marked the transition of the KJV from a translation to a book; second, the Hall was opposite the residence of the bishop of London, and the nine-month process of revision fitted wholly within the sixteen-month tenure of George Abbot as bishop of London, who, like his predecessor Thomas Ravis, had served on the Second Oxford Company. The Stationers' Company contributed to the project by paying each of the revisers 30 shillings a week, which was a generous rate.

There is conflicting evidence of the size of this revision committee, which probably consisted of twelve members (two from each company), but may have had only six members (two from each of Westminster, Oxford, and Cambridge), or some other number dictated by practicalities. The committee included Bois and Andrew Downes, who represented either their company (if there were twelve) or Cambridge (if there were six); the notes of John Bois have recently revealed the name of a third member, John Harmar, a former regius professor of Greek at Oxford. Bois's notes also refer to 'Hutch.', which cannot refer to Ralph Hutchinson, who had been appointed to the Second Westminster Company but had died in 1606, before work had begun. It therefore seems likely that the reference is to Lancelot Andrewes's colleague William Hutchinson, a prebendary of St Paul's (and archdeacon of

St Albans) who had not been one of the translators, but who had been brought in at a late stage for the revision committee. No other names are known. Downes was evidently a reluctant participant, for it was said that he 'would not go till he was either fetcht or threatened with a Pursuivant'—that is, a royal messenger with power to execute warrants; that said, the evidence of Bois's notes is that Downes participated energetically when he was present.

The evidence for the procedures followed in the general meeting has long consisted of remarks by the lawyer John Selden and by Andrew Walker, the biographer of John Bois. Selden recorded:

> That part of the Bible was given to him who was most excellent in such a tongue (as the Apocrypha to Andrew Downes), and then they met together; and one read the translation, the rest holding in their hands some Bible of the learned tongues or French, Spanish, Italian etc.; if they found any fault they spoke, if not he read on.

It would be hard to imagine a more rigorous procedure. Rule 14 had specified five English versions that could be used in the preparation of the new Bible, but the practice of using Bibles in other languages introduced a new level of scholarly rigour. The three vernacular Bibles mentioned were Protestant translations into French (the Olivétan Bible), Italian (the Diodati Bible), and Spanish (the Reina-Valera Bible), all of which are still in use. The 'etc.' includes Luther's Bible in German and two new Latin versions (one Catholic, one Protestant). The rule seems to imply that the Douai–Reims New Testament should not be used, but in fact it was taken into account; the translators cast their nets as widely as possible. Selden's account is collaborated by Miles Smith in the preface to the KJV, where he explains that the translators did not hesitate to consult the 'Chaldee [i.e. Aramaic], Hebrew,

Syrian, Greek or Latin...nor the Spanish, French, Italian or Dutch [i.e. German]'.

The consultation of a variety of translations was in part a way of clarifying meaning, but it also exposed issues of textual authority. 2 Timothy 3:16 is a good example. In the Wyclif version it is rendered: 'All scripture is given by inspiration of God, and profitable to doctrine, to reprove, to correction, to instruction which is in righteousness.' Tyndale, on the other hand, writes: 'For all scripture gave by inspiration of god is profitable to teach to improve to amend and to instruct in righteousness.' There is a significant difference, in that Wyclif's version asserts that all Scripture is inspired, whereas Tyndale's is open to the interpretation that only some Scripture is inspired. The difference is apparent in many other translations. Coverdale is identical to Tyndale, and similar versions can be found in Spanish and German Bibles; the Wyclif reading, however, is echoed in the Geneva Bible, the Bishops' Bible, and in the Italian and French versions. The difference relates to the choice of Greek text, which in some traditions (and in Erasmus's edition) includes the word 'and' and in others does not. If 'and' is part of the text, the sentence breaks into two parts, the first part of which must mean that all Scripture is inspired; if 'and' is not included, the structure of the sentence shifts, and it need not mean that all Scripture is inspired. The rigorous process whereby the revisers consulted alternative translations forced them to confront difficult issues of textual authority, some of which had important theological implications. Was that word 'and' inspired or not?

Andrew Walker's brief account of the revision process in his life of John Bois ends with a teasing sentence: 'he [Bois] and he only took notes of their proceedings, which he diligently kept to his dying day.' Students of the KJV long bemoaned the loss of these notes. It is pleasing to note that the two greatest scholars of the KJV in the late twentieth century, Ward Allen and David Norton, each found a copy of Bois's notes: Allen in Corpus Christi College, Oxford (reported 1969) and Norton in the British Library (reported 1996). The notes are incomplete, in that they cover only the epistles and Revelation, which raises the question of whether more notes survive. They puzzle in another respect, in that the discussions of more than 500 details in the New Testament are more often focused on the meaning of the original Greek than on the suitability of the draft translations. That said, they are hugely rewarding to study, in part because of Ward Allen's brilliant editing. The annotated Bishops' Bible, on the other hand, still awaits an editor with the requisite linguistic abilities and the diplomatic skills necessary to persuade the Bodleian Library to unbind it and so render visible annotations hidden in the binding.

The work of revision did not end with the general meeting, for the translators' work was in turn reviewed by Thomas Bilson (who had been too ill to serve as a translator) and Miles Smith. It was Smith who wrote the majestic preface on behalf of the translators; the dedication to King James is anonymous, but may be the work of Bilson. Finally, the completed revision was sent to Archbishop Bancroft, who made fourteen alterations; it is not now known what they were, but one might speculate that the changes were designed to buttress episcopacy.

4

THE TRANSLATION

Revising the Bishops' Bible

The aspiration of the translators, in the words of Miles Smith's 'The Translators to the Reader', was not 'to make a new translation, nor yet to make of a bad one a good one...but to make a good one better'. By 'better' Smith meant 'truer to the original', but 'original' is a problematical concept with respect to the Bible. The difficulty centres on the biblical languages of Hebrew, Aramaic (in which a few passages, such as Jeremiah 10:11 and Daniel 2:4b–7:28, are written), and Greek, in that the texts in those languages are not altogether stable (manuscripts offer tiny variations in readings), and, in the case of Hebrew, the meaning is not always straightforward, because the ancient texts consist entirely of consonants. In order to endow the words with meaning and with grammatical features such as tense, recourse must be made to the way the words are spoken. The Hebrew consonants MLK, for example, can be vocalized as 'MeLeK' (which means 'king') or as 'MoLeK' (the wicked god of the Ammonites). The pronunciation of Hebrew was preserved over many centuries (during which Hebrew ceased to be a living language), and was finally recorded in the Middle Ages by means of vowel signs and accent markings (both integrated into the consonants) and marginal notes; these additions, which are collectively known as the Massorah ('tradition'), were compiled between the sixth and tenth centuries AD by the Jewish grammarians known as Massoretes, and the text that derives from their labours is known as the Massoretic text.

The principal alternative version of the Old Testament on which the translators could draw is the Septuagint, the Greek version prepared by Alexandrian Jews in the third century BC. These scholars also worked with a consonantal Hebrew text, and their translation is in effect a rival to the Massoretic text. For the most part the two versions agree, but there are differences in the canon of the Old Testament, in the order of the books, and, most importantly for the translators, in the meanings of particular words.

The doctrine of the verbal inspiration of the Bible, which in the nineteenth century became a shibboleth for many conservative evangelicals and now has millions of adherents in the evangelical tradition, takes the Hebrew (and Aramaic) text of the Old Testament to be the original, and, although there is some debate about whether the Massoretic vowels and accents were inspired by God, the Hebrew text is deemed to be authoritative. The translators of the King James Version (KJV) took a different view. As Miles Smith explained in the 'The Translators to the Reader', a translation of the Bible 'containeth the word of God, nay is the word of God: as the King's speech which he uttered in Parliament, being translated into French, Dutch, Italian and Latin, is still the King's speech'. The same thinking led the translators to assume that there was an authoritative text, and that various versions, including the Massoretic text and the Septuagint, enabled scholars to come ever closer to the original text. They also took into account other texts, including the Syriac Bible (the Peshitta, translated in the first and second centuries AD), the Targums (Aramaic paraphrases), early Latin texts (including the Vulgate and quotations in the church fathers), and the Samaritan text of the Pentateuch. These languages were part of the scholarly equipment of many of the translators. The more learned among them could also venture into the 'daughter translations' of the Septuagint (into Coptic, Ethiopic, and Arabic) and the Peshitta (into Persian and Arabic). In the New Testament, the most important secondary language was Syriac. These languages may now seem to be the domain of specialists, but such was not the case in the seventeenth century. Edward Phillips, the nephew of poet John Milton, recorded how as a child he was taught by his uncle:

> Nor did the time thus studiously employed in conquering the Greek and Latin tongues hinder the attaining of the chief oriental languages, *viz* the Hebrew, Chaldee [Aramaic] and Syriac, so far as to go through the Pentateuch...in Hebrew, to make a good entrance into the Targum, or Chaldee Paraphrase, and to understand several chapters of St Matthew in the Syriac Testament.

These languages, together with French and Italian, were learned by Milton's nephews, and were widely known in scholarly circles. Versions of the Bible in these languages (and others) were all taken into account by the translators as they revised the Bishops' Bible. There was, for example, an edition of the Hebrew Bible (1534–5) published with a Latin translation by Sebastian Münster. In a verse subsequently made famous by its incorporation into Handel's *Messiah*, the translators rendered the Hebrew as 'he was wounded for our transgressions, he was bruised for our iniquities: the

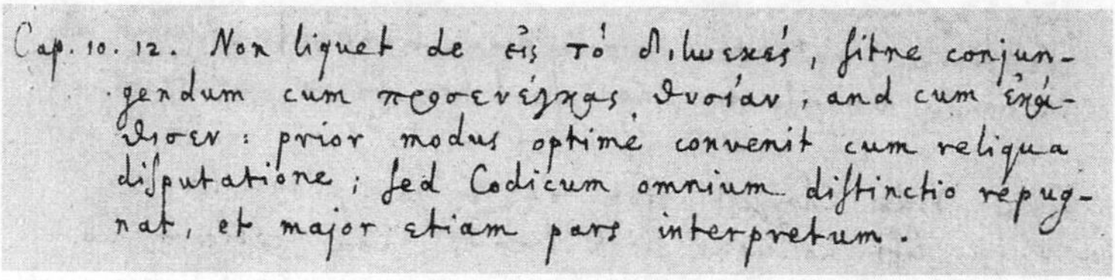
Cap. 10. 12. Non liquet de εἰς τὸ διηνεκές, ſitne conjungendum cum προσενέγκας θυσίαν, and cum ἐκάθισεν: prior modus optime convenit cum reliqua diſputatione; ſed Codicum omnium diſtinctio repugnat, et major etiam pars interpretum.

FIGURE 13. John Bois' Notes (on Hebrews 10:12).

chastisement of our peace was upon him, and with his stripes we are healed' (Isaiah 53:5). Some of the phrasing derives from the Bishops' Bible (for example, 'with his stripes we are healed'), but 'the chastisement of our peace' does not (the Bishops' Bible has 'for the pain of our punishment'); it is rather a direct translation of Münster's elegant Latin rendering of the Hebrew (*castigatio pacis nostrae*).

The notes of John Bois (described in Chapter 3) record translation issues that arose in the sequence from Romans to Revelation, and they afford important insights into the way the translators made their decisions. In Hebrews 10:12, for example, there is a grammatical ambiguity about the phrase meaning 'for ever'. The Bishops' Bible (and earlier translations) presented it as modifying 'sat down': 'But this man, after he hath offered one sacrifice for sinnes, is sit downe for ever on the ryght hande of God' ('sit' is an archaic form of 'sat'). As Bois's notes recorded, it is not clear whether 'for ever' should modify 'sat down' or 'had offered a sacrifice'. His note goes on to observe (in Latin) that the former view ('sat down for ever') fits better with the remaining argument, but that the latter ('had offered a sacrifice for ever') is consistent with the punctuation of every known manuscript and most translations. In the event, the argument from the manuscript tradition prevailed against the argument from context, and the translators chose to render the line as 'But this man after he had offered one sacrifice for sinnes for ever, sate downe on the right hand of God'. On other occasions the translators borrowed a good idea from a surprising source: Douai–Reims. In Colossians 2:18, for example, the Bishops' Bible printed 'Let no man begile you of victorie, in the humblenesse and worshippyng of Angels'. The translators scrutinized the Greek text and realized that 'humbleness' missed the point that the humility was wilful. Bois notes 'Rheims, *willing in humility*, and in the margin, that is, *wilful, or self-willed in voluntary religion*'. This was the solution that they adopted, so the KJV reads 'Let no man beguile you of your reward, in a voluntary humility, and worshipping of Angels'.

If translators must resist literalism, they must also resist its opposite, which is an ironing-out of complexities in order to create a smooth flow of words. There is a good example in 2 Corinthians 8:4, which the Bishops' Bible printed 'that we woulde receave this grace and societie of the ministerie to the saintes'. The difficulty, as Bois noted, is that the Greek word for 'receive' signifies two things: 'recovering' and 'taking upon oneself'. The KJV therefore printed 'that we would receive the gift, and take upon us the fellowship of the ministring to the Saints'. It is one of the moments in the translation when I am tempted to applaud.

One of the most surprising passages in Bois's record of the process of revision concerns a moment of silence: there is no comment on 1 John 5:7 ('For there are three that bear record in heaven, the Father, the Word and the Holy Ghost: and these three are one'), the verse known to biblical scholars as the Johannine Comma (a comma is a short clause). The canonicity of the verse was a matter of much scholarly contention, and it was not included in early editions of Erasmus's Greek New Testament, or in Luther's translation into German. It was, however, included in the third edition of Erasmus's New Testament, which underlay the text used by the KJV translators. The translators must have known that the verse was contentious, and so it remains (several modern translations omit it or relegate it to a footnote), but it passed the scrutiny of the Revisers' Committee, apparently without comment.

Textual and Critical Apparatus

In 1637 the theologian William Chillingworth famously proclaimed that 'the Bible, I say, the Bible only, is the religion of Protestants'. This resonant phrase, which was intended to displace the authority of the traditional teachings of the Church in favour of a theology based squarely on the Bible, raises the question of what constitutes 'the Bible only'. The ideal was a Bible free of bias, and accordingly the sixth rule in Bancroft's instructions to the translators specified that 'no marginal notes at all [were] to be affixed, but only for the explanation of the Hebrew or Greek words which cannot, without some circumlocution, so briefly and fitly be expressed in the text'.

In practice, however, there were opportunities for expressions of the translators' understanding of the text, beyond the obvious medium of the translation itself. The margins did not contain theological notes, but nonetheless accommodated three sorts of commentary. First, in accordance with rule 7 ('such quotations of places to be marginally set down as shall serve for the fit reference of one scripture to another'), the translators devised a system of some 9,000 cross-references linking passages in different parts of the Bible; the number of cross-references has expanded over the centuries, and there are more than 60,000 in modern editions of the KJV. In compiling the cross-references the translators took a short cut, borrowing more than half from printed editions of the Latin Vulgate Bible; this practice had one disadvantage, which is that the Psalms are numbered differently in the Vulgate, so most of the cross-references to the Psalms were wrong; they were to be corrected in the Cambridge editions of 1629 and 1638. Some of the original cross-references express the view of the translators that many passages in the Old Testament are prophetic. Second, in keeping with rule 4 of the report to the Synod of Dort ('The more difficult Hebraisms and Graecisms were consigned to the margin'), the margins are used to record literal translations in cases where an interpretative translation has been necessitated by the requirement that the text make sense in English; such notes are restricted to the three original languages of the Bible: 'Heb[rew]', 'Cald[ee]' (the old name for Aramaic), and 'Gr[eek]'. Third, in keeping with rule 3 of the report to the Synod of Dort ('Where a Hebrew or Greek word admits two meanings of a suitable kind, the one was to be expressed in the text, the other in the margin. The same to be done where variant readings were found in different (but reputable) versions of the Hebrew and Greek texts'), the margins recorded alternative readings and translations in notes that begin with 'or'; some of these readings reflect minority opinions among the translators.

In addition to using the margins to convey their understanding of the text, the translators were able to formulate book titles that reflected their view of authorship ('The First Booke of Moses, called Genesis', 'The Epistle of Paul the Apostle to the Hebrewes', 'The Revelation of S. John the Divine'), and their sense that the writers of the gospels and the Book of Revelation should be designated as 'saints', but that the writers of the epistles need not be so styled: they are simply named as Paul the Apostle, James, John, and Jude. The translators also devised running heads and chapter summaries. The clearest example of these devices being turned to interpretative use is the Song of Solomon. In the Jewish traditions embodied in the Aramaic Targums, the Song is interpreted as an allegory of God's love for Israel. In the Christian tradition originating with Origen in the third century, however, the Song is interpreted as a celebration of Christ's love for his Church. The translators agreed, and so the running heads at the top of the pages include 'Christ and his Church' and 'The beautie of the Church'. Similarly, the chapter summaries embody this reading: chapter 5, for example, is summarized 'Christ awaketh the Church with his calling'; 'The Church having a taste of Christes love, is sicke of love'; 'a description of Christ by his graces'. The text never mentions God, much less Christ, so these summaries embody the traditional understanding of the Church, not the 'Bible only', but such was the consensus about their meaning within the Church that there was no recorded unease about their formulation. Puritans had reservations about the use of the word 'saint', but they were at one with other Christians in their understanding of the Song of Solomon.

The Song of Solomon is the extreme example of interpretative apparatus, but there are many minor instances of prophetic readings being embodied in the apparatus. The chapter summary at the beginning of Isaiah 53, for example, proposes a Messianic reading: 'the Prophet complaining of incredulitie, excuseth the scandal of the crosse.' There is no cross mentioned in the text, so references to the New Testament citations of this passage (John 12:38, Romans 10:16) are inserted in the margins. Similarly, the summary at the beginning of Ecclesiastes 5 begins 'Vanities in divine service', though there is no mention of a service in the visit to the temple described in the text.

The Language

If asked to characterize the language of the KJV, many readers of the Bible would point to its archaic elements, notably the use of 'ye' and 'thee' and 'thou' and '-eth' endings, and some would point to its sonority. Some would assume, if pressed, that the language was rooted in the spoken language of 1611. In several respects, however, the language was archaic when the KJV was published, and that points to the background of the translators as well as the history of the translation. Just as the use of archaic formal words such as 'chastise' and archaic informal terms such as 'crack on' by Boris Johnson (the mayor of London) point to his educational background (Eton and Oxford), so the language of the translators reflects their conservatism and slightly out-of-touch language. They were content to leave in place the language of earlier generations that was embodied in previous translations.

In the early sixteenth century, the second-person nominative form of the personal pronoun was 'thou' for the singular and 'ye' for the plural; the accusative forms were 'thee' for the singular and 'you' for the plural. The distinction between 'ye' and 'you' was fading by the mid-sixteenth century, and thereafter 'you' was used for both forms—except in plays written in a formal idiom (notably those of Shakespeare) and in the KJV. Matthew 5:11, for example, reads 'Blessed are ye, when men shall revile you'; the distinction between nominative 'ye' and accusative 'you' would have struck ordinary readers in 1611 as archaic.

The use of 'thou' and 'thee' is an even more striking example of archaic language. By 1611 the distinction between 'you' and 'thou' had ceased to be one of number and had become a marker of the social relationship between the speaker and the listener, and also of the emotional relationship between speaker and listener—as when Lear switches from 'you' to 'thou' in addressing Cordelia in the opening scene of *King Lear*. 'You' was the polite, deferential form, used by children to their parents, by employees to their employers, by citizens to aristocrats, and by aristocrats to each other; those who had been addressed as 'you' normally responded with 'thou', that being the form of address used by parents to children, by employers to employees, by aristocrats to citizens, and by citizens to each other. A breach of the rules was deemed to be provocative, so when in Shakespeare's *Twelfth Night* (*c*.1600) Sir Toby Belch counsels Sir Andrew Aguecheek on how to be insulting to Cesario/Viola, he says 'if thou "thou'st" him some thrice, it shall not be amiss'. And when Sir Walter Raleigh was being insulted at his trial in 1603, his wickedness was attributed to 'thy instigation, thou viper; for I "thou" thee, thou traitor'. In this context, it seems odd that in the KJV God should always be addressed as 'thou', as a God who is both our Father and our King should be addressed respectfully as 'you'; that said, all supernatural beings were so addressed (for example, Jupiter in Shakespeare's *Cymbeline*). There are two possible reasons for this anomaly. First, the usage may reflect the conventions of the previous century, when 'thou' was the only available form of address in the singular; second, it may reflect the distinction in Hebrew, Greek, and Latin between singular and plural in second-person pronouns.

As God is singular, he was addressed in Latin, for example, in the singular form, which was 'tu'; English translators preserved this distinction by addressing God as 'thou'. Uncertainty about the reason for the choice is paralleled by uncertainty about how readers understood the usage, because thereafter 'thou' moved in two different directions: on the one hand, it slowly acquired the solemn respectful sense that it has now, but, on the other, it could also imply intimacy, treating Jesus as a friend. The latter sense gradually disappeared, though it was retained for centuries in Quaker circles.

One word that is notable by its absence in the KJV is the neuter possessive pronoun 'its'. Until about 1600, there was no distinct ive neuter form, so 'his', which was both masculine and neuter, was always used; by 1620, however, 'its' was in almost universal use, except by a few linguistic reactionaries. The KJV occasionally uses the archaic alternatives of 'of it' ('groweth of it own accord' (Leviticus 25:5), 'great was the fall of it' (Matthew 7:27)) or 'thereof' ('in all the coasts thereof' (Matthew 2:16)), but for the most part it uses 'his' ('if the salt have lost his savour, wherewith shall it be salted' (Matthew 5:13)).

The principal relative pronouns are 'who' (in its various forms), 'which' (including 'the which'), and 'that'. In twenty-first-century prescriptive usage, the distinction between 'that' and 'which' is that the former is used in defining clauses ('an arrow is a piece of wood that has been adapted as a weapon') and the latter in non-defining clauses ('the arrows, which were still in the quiver, were broken'); the distinction between 'who' and 'which' is that the former is used if the antecedent is a person, and the latter if the antecedent is a thing ('the class, which consisted of twelve students, included six women, who sat at the front'); the distinction between 'who' and 'that' is that the former is used for particular persons ('my students, who have been studying Greek') and the latter for generic persons ('students that study Greek will learn'). These distinctions were gradually developed in grammatical treatises, from the end of the seventeenth century, but many native speakers of English neither know nor observe them.

A similar distinction between educated and popular usage existed in the early seventeenth century, but the conventions were slightly different. The KJV shows a consistent preference for older forms such as 'the which', so John's Gospel refers to 'the same hour, in the which Jesus said' (John 4:53) and 'the hour is coming, in the which all that are in the graves' (John 5:28). On the who/which distinction, 'who' is widely preferred by the writers of the period (Shakespeare, Donne, Ben Jonson) for reference to particular persons, but the KJV adheres to an older convention, so the Lord's Prayer opens 'our father which art in heaven' (Matthew 6:9 and Luke 11:2, the latter with an initial capital on 'Father'). The distinction between 'that' and 'who' (or 'whom') was much the same as it is now. In Shakespeare's *Henry VI Part III*, for example, there is a distinction between the generic stage direction ('Enter a Son that hath killed his Father') and the particular persons of the speech that follows ('it is my father's face, | Whom in this conflict I unawares have killed'). Similarly, the KJV reads 'blessed are they that mourn' (Matthew 5:4), but 'take thy only son Isaac, whom thou lovest' (Genesis 22:2).

In the early sixteenth century the '-eth' ending in third-person verbs in the present tense was in universal use, but in the course of the century it disappeared for plural forms, and in the singular was displaced by the '-es' ending. By the 1590s '-es' was the norm in educated speech, but in the written form of the language there was a distinction between formal '-eth' and informal '-es'. In the boisterous city comedies of the period, the '-eth' ending is rare, but in the plays of Shakespeare, whose language was more formal than that of his fellow playwrights, '-eth' often appears instead of '-es', especially in words such as 'doth', 'hath', and 'saith'. The KJV text of the Testaments, however, is more formal still, and always uses '-eth' for singular verbs; the formal ending may reflect the importance of the subject matter, the conservative inclinations of the translators, and the precedent of earlier translations. This formality had a lasting legacy in that 'doth', 'hath', and 'saith' persisted into the nineteenth century (and beyond in ecclesiastical circles). The Cambridge Company responsible for the Apocrypha, however, used the modern form on five occasions; modern texts of the KJV Apocrypha archaize four of these, but Ecclesiasticus 22:2 survives in its original modernized form, 'every man that takes it up'.

The language choices made by the translators of the KJV would have seemed to many listeners and readers slightly formal and slightly archaic, and this may have been thought to be entirely appropriate to the dignity and standing of a sacred text. For twenty-first-century listeners and readers, the language of the KJV is distinctly formal and archaic, though there is no consensus about the appropriateness of these effects.

Modern English grammar of the formal type that attempts to regulate written English makes distinctions that are at odds with the more fluid grammar of the KJV. The distinctions between 'will' and 'shall' (in grammatical terminology, two of the modal auxiliaries) are typical examples. 'Shall' (and the older form 'shalt') could express futurity, as it does now in educated usage, but it could also signal obligation or necessity ('thou shalt love thy neighbour as thyself'); on the other hand, 'will' (and the older form 'wilt') not only expressed intention or willingness ('Caleb said unto her, what wilt thou' (Judges 1:14)), but could also retain that meaning when a modern reader might expect simple futurity: 'wilt thou be angry with us for ever?' (Psalm 85:5) is a question not simply about the future, but about God's intention.

Similarly, grammar that is now regarded as incorrect was wholly acceptable in 1611. We no long use double comparatives, so it would be unacceptable to describe someone as the 'most oldest' person in the room, but, just as in Shakespeare's *Julius Caesar* the dying Caesar says 'this was the most unkindest cut of all', so the apostle Paul can refer to 'the most straitest sect of our religion' (Acts 26:5).

Finally, a word about the marking of direct speech. Since the eighteenth century written English has marked direct speech with single inverted commas in the UK or double inverted commas ('quotation marks') in the USA. In the KJV, however, the beginning of direct speech is marked with a comma and a capital letter ('And saying, The time is fulfilled' (Mark 1:15)). The end of direct speech is unmarked, which can give rise to confusion. The phrase 'saith the Lord', for example, sometimes indicates direct speech of which it is not a part, but sometimes appears to be used as part of that direct speech, in which the Lord is indicating himself. Isaiah 66 opens:

> Thus saith the LORD, The Heaven *is* my throne, and the earth *is* my footstool: where *is* the house that ye build unto me? and where is the place of my rest? For all those *things* hath mine hand made, and all those *things* have been, saith the LORD: but to this *man* will I look.

The capital letter on the fifth word ('The') indicates the onset of direct speech, but it is not clear whether the second 'saith the LORD' is part of the direct speech or a narrative intervention in direct speech, so it is not clear where the Lord stops speaking.

Style

The passage on style in Miles Smith's 'The Translators to the Reader' is phrased in terms of an aspiration to avoid confessional bias and to be accessible to uneducated listeners and readers. The translators explicitly rejected a striving after effect ('niceness in words was always counted the next step to trifling') in favour of a vocabulary that was clear. Their translation was not an act of exhibitionism, but one of communication, and it was designed to take a middle way:

> We have on one side avoided the scrupulosity of the Puritans, who leave the old ecclesiastical words, and betake them to others, as when they put 'washing' for 'baptism', and 'congregation' instead of 'church': as also on the other side we have shunned the obscurity of the Papists, in their 'azymes', 'tunic', 'rational', 'holocausts', 'praepuce', 'pasche' and a number of such like whereof their late translation is full, and that of purpose to darken the sense, that since they must needs translate the Bible, yet by the language thereof it may be kept from being understood. But we desire that the Scripture may speak like itself, as in the language of Canaan, that it may be understood even of the very vulgar.

The closing phrase recalls Tyndale's aspiration to speak to the 'boy that driveth the plough', and it explains the choice of vocabulary used by the translators. The Douai–Reims Bible had favoured a Latinate vocabulary, not for the defamatory reason suggested by Smith ('that it may be kept from being understood'), but rather because its translators aspired to be faithful to the Vulgate. In Leviticus 8:7, for example, the priestly garment is said in Douai–Rheims to be a 'tunic' because the Latin is *tunica*, whereas the KJV follows the Bishops' Bible in calling it a 'robe'; the word 'tunic' was too classical to be in common use, whereas 'robe' was understood by everyone.

Similarly, the KJV translators also had a distinct preference for monosyllables: the Bishops' Bible reads 'God is my shepherd, therefore I can lack nothing' (Psalm 23:1), but in the KJV two of the three polysyllables are eliminated: 'The LORD is my shepherd, I shall not want.'

The balance between the public reading and private study of the Bible has shifted over the centuries with the rise in literacy. In the seventeenth century the Bible was more often heard than read, and it is clear that the translators had the practice of reading aloud (in homes as well as churches) in mind. Part of the evidence for this is punctuation, which tends to be rhetorical rather than grammatical, but the clearest manifestation of the emphasis on the need to provide a text that can be read aloud is the rhythms of the KJV. The text is prose, but it often has the pulse of poetry. Adam, blaming Eve for the fall, says 'she gave me of the tree, and I did eat' (Genesis 3:12), a perfect iambic pentameter line (and one that Milton incorporated intact into *Paradise Lost*); in the next verse, God says to Eve 'what is this that thou hast done?' (Genesis 3:13), a perfect iambic tetrameter line. The seventeen words that I have quoted are all monosyllables cast in prose, but their regular rhythm makes them easy to read aloud.

The style of the KJV is conventionally described in terms of majestic cadences, but such terms seem inappropriate, except in the case of Smith's epistle, which has passages of soaring eloquence. The translation, however, aspires to literal accuracy rather than majesty, and on occasion leaves the job of translation half-done. Here is a verse in which the Hebrew is translated word for word, but the translation is stylishly incomprehensible: 'Then the Angel of the Lord went forth, and smote in the camp of the Assyrians a hundred and fourscore and five thousand: and when they arose early in the morning, behold, they were all dead corpses' (Isaiah 37:36). The notion that the Assyrians got up in the morning before noticing that they were dead is exceedingly unhelpful. The Revised Standard Version, for example, deals with the problem by translating the second half of the sentence 'and when men arose early in the morning, behold, these were all dead bodies'. The meaning could be captured by translating the second phrase as 'at dawn it became clear that they were all dead', but the KJV translators preferred literal fidelity to interpretative translating.

That aspiration to translate literally led to some idioms that now seem formal, because the translators decided that certain words, especially in the Hebrew of the Old Testament, should be translated in the same way whenever they occurred; the effect is an incantatory quality that can be mistaken for majesty. The clearest example is the past and future tenses of the copula 'to be', which are often translated 'and it came to pass' and 'and it shall come to pass'. These phrases are instantly recognizable as biblical partly because of the frequency of their occurrence (for example, 'and it came to pass' occurs more than 450 times), but also because they did not become part of the stock of the English language;

indeed, the phrases are used only in books that mimic the language of the KJV, such as the Book of Mormon (where the phrase occurs more than 1,000 times), or in phrases that evoke the biblical idiom. When used in close proximity, as in Genesis 38:27–9 (where all three verses begin 'and it came to pass') and Isaiah 7:21–3 (where all three verses begin 'and it shall come to pass'), such phrases give the impression of prose that verges on the ritualistic.

Theology

As languages never correspond word for word, translators have to make choices. In the case of the KJV, some of these choices were laid down in the guidelines, such as 'church' rather than 'congregation', which is the example given in the rule. The decision to retain 'bishop' (instead of 'elder' or 'senior') reflects a decision to favour episcopacy rather than presbyterianism as a model of church government; as disagreement about the form of government was a gaping fault line between the church hierarchy and the puritan minority, this decision was critically important: the KJV was not intended to be a puritan Bible.

Other decisions are not covered by the guidelines, but nonetheless have theological implications. The question of whether 'spirit' should be capitalized, for example, rests with the translators. 1 Peter 3:18 as translated in the Bishops' Bible asserts that 'Christe…was kylled as parteynyng to the fleshe, but was quickened in the spirite'. This translation was problematical, because it seemed to endorse the radical heresy that denied the hypostatic union (the union of the divine and human natures in Christ) and instead asserted the separateness of the human nature of Christ embodied in his flesh and the divine nature of Christ as expressed in his spirit. The translators took evasive action by changing the final preposition from 'in' to 'by' and by capitalizing 'Spirit', deftly transforming the sentence from its endorsement of a heresy into an affirmation of the resurrection: in the KJV Christ is described as 'being put to death in the flesh, but quickened by the Spirit'. This solution is neat, and is certainly countenanced by the Greek, but it may have seemed to some of the translators to have closed down other interpretations: Bois's note records an alternative reading that did not make it into the margin: Christ 'was indeed put to death according to the flesh, but quickened according to the Spirit'. The repetition of 'according to' preserves the parallel structure of the phrases in Greek and shuts out the heretical doctrine, but allows for the possibility that the phrase is intended to limit the extent to which the flesh and spirit of Christ were transformed by death, and not necessarily to affirm the resurrection. This softer alternative was clearly rejected in favour of an unambiguous affirmation of the resurrection.

The tendency to emphasize prophetic interpretations of the Bible is embedded in seventeenth-century theology and lives on in twenty-first-century evangelical exegesis. Hebrews 11, for example, records that by faith Abraham was willing to sacrifice Isaac, 'his only begotten son', and that 'God was able to raise him up, even from the dead'. The parallel with the sacrifice and resurrection of Jesus is made in the final phrase of verse 19, which in the Bishops' Bible is rendered 'he receaved hym in a similitude'. The difficulty was that this translation (which is true to the Greek) implies that this was nothing more than a comparison. The translators therefore turned to Chrysostom (a fourth-century bishop of Constantinople), who had explained that the Greek also had the sense of 'prefiguring'. The translators happily adopted this insight, and so the KJV prints 'Accounting that God was able to raise him up, even from the dead: from whence also he received him in a figure'.

The principal theological debate of the early seventeenth century concerned predestination. A distinction was sometimes drawn between foreknowledge and predestination: if God foreknew the future, he need not have caused everything in the future to happen, but if he predestined the future, then he was the cause of everything that happened. In the language of biblical translation, an act such as the appearance of Christ or the choice of a believer for salvation could be 'foreknown' (the Arminian view) or 'foreordained' (the Calvinist view). 1 Peter 1:20, referring to the coming of Christ, is rendered in the Bishops' Bible 'which was ordeyned beforehande, euen before the worlde was made, but was declared in the last tymes for your sakes'; the KJV reads 'who verily was foreordained before the foundation of the world, but was manifest in these last times for you'. 'Ordained beforehand' and 'foreordained' convey the same Calvinist interpretation, but the congruence obscures a debate among the translators and revisers. One consideration is the influence of Douai–Reims on the translators; that translation reads 'Foreknowen in deede before the constitution of the world, but manifested in the last times for you'. The second half of the sentence in the KJV ('but was manifest in these last times for you') clearly comes from Douai–Reims, the only other translation to use 'manifested' and 'for you'. That translation proposed 'foreknown', which favours the Arminian view. The translators were mostly Calvinists, but a few were Arminians, and the appropriate word to use became a matter for debate. Bois's notes record an etymological analysis by Theodore

Beza (Calvin's successor), who argued that the root of the relevant Latin word meant 'to ordain', not 'to know'. The committee also noted a passage in Ausonius (a fourth-century Latin poet) that supported Beza's contention. After due deliberation, it was decided that the Calvinist reading was the correct one, so 'foreordained' was chosen. Posterity has not been unanimous in its approval: the Revised Version and the New American Standard Version, for example, print 'foreknown', which is consistent with the Arminian theory of salvation of Anglo-Catholic members of the Church of England and the Episcopalian Church in America.

5

———— ⊸⊷⊶ ————

THE FIRST EDITION

Printing

The first edition of the King James Version (KJV) of the Bible was printed in 1611 by Robert Barker, the king's printer, who held the right to print all Bibles published in England in English translation (works in other languages published in England and royal books published in Scotland were separate rights). Barker was the son of the queen's printer, Christopher Barker, who had printed large numbers of Bibles as well as official publications such as statutes and proclamations during the reign of Queen Elizabeth. In 1599 Robert succeeded his father as queen's printer, and was subsequently confirmed as king's printer by King James, who succeeded Elizabeth in 1603. He was, therefore, the inevitable choice for the printing of the KJV; later in the century the university presses of Cambridge and Oxford were to exercise their right to print Bibles, but in 1611 Barker was the sole authorized printer. The printing house of the king's printer was Northumberland House, a large medieval palace in Aldersgate (on the site of what is now Northumberland Alley) recently vacated by the earls of Northumberland for a new palace on the Strand; the old palace was refurbished as a workshop, and there the first edition of the KJV was printed.

Printing the KJV was an expensive undertaking, not least because Barker seems to have had to pay the enormous sum of £4,000 for the rights to the translation. He financed the project by selling or mortgaging shares in the office of king's printer to two rival printers: Bonham Norton and John Bill. The names of Barker, two Nortons (Bonham and his cousin John), Bill, and their descendants were to appear on Bibles for generations. Because the KJV was classified as a revision rather than a fresh translation, it does not appear in the register of new books known as the Stationers' Register. In the absence of a dated entry in the register, we are left without any knowledge of when in 1611 the KJV began to be sold. The popular notion that it was published on 2 May is often repeated, but is a myth: there was no such thing as a publication date in the seventeenth century, and there is no evidence to link the KJV to May or any other month.

There were two folio editions of the KJV published in 1611, and they are known as the 'He' Bible and the 'She' Bible. The names arise from a well-known crux at Ruth 3:15: one 1611 Bible reads 'he went into the city', 'he' referring to Boaz; the other reads 'she went into the city', referring to Ruth. The difficulty is that the Hebrew text has 'he', but the sense of the passage demands that Ruth rather than Boaz go into the city. Setting aside the question of which version is correct, it is now clear that the earlier of the two Bibles is the 'He' Bible, and that the translators seem deliberately to have changed the pronoun from 'she' in the Bishops' Bible.

A folio is a large book (see p. 112), and the first edition of the KJV was large even by the usual standard of folios; its thick pages measure approximately 11 inches by 16 inches. It was a heavy volume designed to sit on a lectern in a church; as the title page explains, it was 'appointed to be read in churches'. At the beginning of most surviving copies there is a thick section of preliminaries (74 pages), consisting of

- a title page
- a dedicatory epistle to King James
- a preface from the translators to the reader
- a calendar
- an almanac
- a table for the calculation of Easter
- a table and calendar setting out the order of psalms and lessons to be said at morning and evening prayers throughout the year
- a list of the books of the Testaments and the Apocrypha
- the royal coat of arms and the Latin phrase indicating that the book was printed 'by authority of the king'
- genealogies
- a table of place names in Canaan
- a map of Canaan

The title page is discussed below (pp. 98–102) and the other preliminaries in Appendix 2 (pp. 304–310).

The preliminaries are followed by 1,464 unnumbered double-columned pages of text. The two columns of text on each page consist of fifty-nine lines of type enclosed within ruled margins. The right-hand pages (of which an example is shown) have the chapter numbers in the centre of the header (except in the Psalms), and on either side is a summary of the subject of the page; the left-hand pages have the title of the book in the centre, together with a summary of the subject. There is a catchword at the bottom of the right-hand column indicating what the first word will be brought him into my mothers houſe, and into the chamber of her that conceiued me.

5 *J charge you, O ye daughters of Jeruſalem, by the Roes and by the hindes of the field,that ye ſtirre not vp, nor awake my loue,till he pleaſe.

6 ¶ *who is this that commeth out of the wildernes like pillars of ſmoke, perfumed with myrrhe and frankincenſe , with all powders of the merchant ?

7 Behold his bed , which is Solomons : threeſcore valiant men are about it,of the valiant of Iſrael :

8 They all hold ſwords , being expert in warre : euery man hath his ſword vpon his thigh , becauſe of feare in the night.

9 King Solomon made himſelfe a charet of the wood of Lebanon.

10 He made the pillars thereof of ſiluer, the bottome thereof of gold, the couering of it , the inuot thereof being paued with loue, for the daughters of Jeruſalem.

11 Goe foorth, O yee daughters of Zion,and behold king Solomon with the crowne wherewith his mother crowned him in the day of his eſpouſals, and in the day of the gladneſſe of his heart.

CHAP. IIII.

1 Chriſt ſetteth forth the graces of the Church. 8 He ſheweth his loue to her. 16 The Church prayeth to be made fit for his preſence.

*Ehold,thou art faire, my loue, behold thou art faire, thou haſt doues eyes within thy lockes : thy haire is as a *flocke of goats,that appeare from mount Gilead.

2 Thy teeth are like a flocke of ſheepe that are euen ſhorne , which came vp from the waſhing : whereof euery one beare twinnes , and none is barren among them.

3 Thy lips are like a thred of ſcarlet ,and thy ſpeach is comely : thy temples are like a piece of a pomegranate within thy lockes.

4 Thy necke is like the tower of Dauid builded for an armorie , whereon there hang a thouſand bucklers, all ſhields of mightie men.

5 *Thy two breaſts , are like two yong Roes , that are twinnes, which feed among the lillies.

6 *Untill the day breake , and the ſhadowes flee away, J will get mee to the mountaines of myrrhe , and to the hill of frankincenſe.

7 *Thou art all faire, my loue, there is no ſpot in thee.

8 ¶ Come with me from Lebanon (my ſpouſe,) with me from Lebanon : looke from the top of Amana, from the top of Shenir *and Hermon,from the Lions dennes,from the mountaines of the Leopards.

9 Thou haſt rauiſhed my heart, my ſpouſe, my ſiſter; thou haſt rauiſhed my heart ,with one of thine eyes,with one chaine of thy necke.

10 How faire is thy loue, my ſiſter, *my ſpouſe ! how much better is thy loue then wine ! and the ſmell of thine oyntments then all ſpices !

11 Thy lips,O my ſpouſe! drop as the hony combe : hony and milke are vnder thy tongue , and the ſmell of thy garments is like the ſmell of Lebanon.

12 A garden † incloſed is my ſiſter, my ſpouſe : a ſpring ſhut vp,a fountaine ſealed.

13 Thy plants are an orchard of pomegranates , with pleaſant fruits, Camphire,with Spikenard,

14 Spikenard and Saffron, Calamus and Cynamom , with all trees of Frankincenſe,Mirrhe and Aloes,with all the chiefe ſpices.

15 A fountaine of gardens, a well of liuing waters, and ſtreames from Lebanon.

16 ¶ Awake, O Northwinde, and come thou South, blow vpon my garden , that the ſpices thereof may flow out : let my beloued come into his garden,and eate his pleaſant fruits.

CHAP. V.

1 Chriſt awaketh the Church with his calling. 2 The Church hauing a taſte of Chriſtes loue , is ſicke of loue. 9 A deſcription of Chriſt by his graces.

Am come into my garden, my ſiſter, my ſpouſe, J haue gathered my Myrrhe with my ſpice, J haue eaten my hony combe with my hony , J haue drunke my wine with my milke : eate , O friends, drinke, yea drinke abundantly,O beloued !

2 ¶ J ſleepe , but my heart waketh :

Chap.2.7. and 8.4.

Chap.8.5

||Or, a bed.*

Chap.1. 15.and 5. 12

Chap.6 5.6. ||Or, that eate of, &c.

Chap.7.3.

Chap.2. 17. †Hebr. breathe.

Epheſ.5. 27

Deut.3.9.

||Or, taken away my heart*

Chap.1.2.

†Hebr barred.

||Or,Cypres.

||Or, and be drunken with loues.*

FIGURE 14. A sample page from the 1611 text of the King James Version: Song of Solomon chapter IV and the beginning of chapter V.

on the next page (its purpose is to ensure that the pages, which are unnumbered, are sorted in order); in this case the catchword is a syllable ('keth'), because the word 'waketh' is divided between two pages. Each chapter begins with a summary of its contents with references to particular verses; in this case, almost uniquely, the summaries are highly interpretative readings of the Song of Solomon. After the summary, each chapter opens with an initial capital, normally of five lines and normally with a floral design; the second letter of the first word is also a capital. Each verse begins on its own line, and after verse one its number appears at the beginning of the line. Some verses (for example, Song of Solomon 4:8 and 4:16) are preceded by a paraph (of which the modern form is ¶) to indicate a new paragraph; oddly, there is only one paraph in the Psalms (Psalm 92:8) and none at all after Acts 20, so it would seem that the book went to press before the marking-up was completed. The other marks, all of which refer to marginal annotations, are an asterisk (*) to indicate a biblical cross-reference, a dagger (†) to indicate a literal translation, and parallel vertical lines (‖) to indicate an alternative translation into English.

The typeface of the text is black letter (an imitation of Gothic script), and roman type is used for headers, chapter summaries, and words that have been supplied by the translators to make the text more intelligible, and so do not translate anything in the original Greek and Hebrew. In the 1611 Bible the small roman type of the supplied words makes them appear relatively insignificant, which was the intended effect, but in modern Bibles the supplied words are placed in italics, which wrongly makes them look particularly significant. In the Old Testament the name of God (the four Hebrew letters known as the Tetragrammaton (see

p. 13)) is translated as 'Lord'. In Genesis the word is printed as LORD, in large capitals, and thereafter as LORD, with only the initial letter in a full-sized capital and the rest of the word in small capitals; clearly a policy decision was taken after printing had started. Black-letter type is not particularly easy to read, in part because m, n, and u look similar; there is also a problem (shared with roman type) with f and s, because the latter had two forms: at the end of a word it was always 's', but elsewhere it was often 'ſ', a letterform that now survives only as a mathematical symbol but was then in universal use; this form leads to occasional confusion, so the 'He Bible' reads 'he shall flay the burnt offering' (Leviticus 1:6) but the 'She Bible' reads 'he shall slay the burnt offering'. Another difficulty arising from archaic letter formation is the occasional representation of the 'th' sound by the letter 'y', which in such instances derives from the Old English thorn (þ); in the KJV this most commonly occurs when the printer wishes to contract 'the' (e.g. Job 1:9, Romans 15:29) or 'that' (2 Corinthians 13:7), and so prints ỹ and ẏ. This is the convention that leads to pseudo-archaisms such as 'Ye Olde Cheshire Cheese' and 'Ye Olde Trip to Jerusalem' (ancient pubs in London and Nottingham), in which 'Ye' simply means 'The'.

For twenty-first-century readers there are other conventions that seem odd. Consider, for example, the illustration of 1 Corinthians 7:32. The long 's' in 'carefulnesse' is not the only oddity. The hyphen signalling a break in the word 'careth', for example, is represented by a slanted version of the sign now used in mathematics to denote 'equals'. The word 'belõgeth' is another puzzle: the wavy line that survives in romance languages such as Spanish (where it indicates a nasal consonant) was used in seventeenth-century Europe as an abbreviation: when 'm' or 'n' followed a

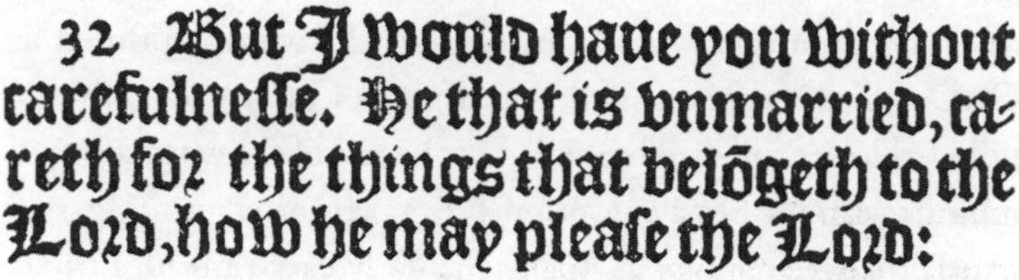

32 But J would haue you without carefulneſſe. He that is vnmarried, careth for the things that belōgeth to the Lord, how he may pleaſe the Lord:

FIGURE 15. I Corinthians 7:32, 1611, King James Version.

vowel, the letter was often omitted, and instead a tilde was placed over the preceding vowel: the reader would therefore expand the abbreviation as 'belongeth'. The conventions about lower-case 'u' and 'v' have also changed, because 'v' was always used at the beginning of a word, even if a vowel was intended (hence 'vnmarried'), and 'u' was always used in the middle of a word, even if a consonant was intended (hence 'haue'). There is a similar difficulty with 'i' and 'j', which now represent a vowel sound and a very different consonant sound. In the early seventeenth century they were regarded as variant forms of the same letter. The 'j' was rare, and in the KJV occurs only as the final letter in lower-case roman numerals used in the running heads at the top of the right-hand pages, where chapters 1–8 are numbered as j, ij, iij, iv, v, vj, vij, and viij; capital 'J', on the other hand, never appears in the KJV, so the 'iust' God of the 'Iudges' is 'Iehovah'.

Artwork

One of the features that has disappeared in modern editions of the KJV is the artwork, which consists of thirty-six pages of genealogies, a map of Canaan, two decorated title pages (an engraving for the whole volume and a woodcut for the New Testament), and, at the beginning of each chapter, a decorative initial, some of which have a pictorial element.

The genealogy begins with God's creation of Adam and Eve and ends with the birth of Christ; it includes in the first ten pages pictorial representations of Adam and Eve (in naked innocence), Noah's ark (beached on Ararat), the Tower of Babel (in its unfallen state), the cities of the plain (under fiery rain), and Jacob in Egypt (on his deathbed); for unknown reasons, the remaining twenty-four pages of the genealogy contain no pictorial art. At the end of the genealogy, the fact that Joseph was not the natural father of Jesus is handled by making him the father 'by law', whereas Mary is the mother 'by nature'.

The title page that reflects the injunction to follow the Bishops' Bible is the one to the New Testament, which is a slightly modified version of the overall title page of the last edition of the Bishops' Bible (1602). Indeed, all that has been changed is the boxed text at the centre: whereas the Bishops' Bible version said 'The Holy Bible containing the Old Testament and the New. Authorised and appointed to be read in churches', the KJV says (in modernized spelling):

> The New Testament of our Lord and Saviour Jesus Christ. Newly translated out of the original Greek: and with the former translations diligently compared and revised, by his Majesty's special commandment.

The woodcut is the work of two craftsmen (possibly a designer and an engraver) who have left their initials at the bottom of the title compartment. 'R.L.', on the left, may be the painter and goldsmith Rowland Lockey, who is known to have been a print collector, but not known to have been a woodcut designer. 'C.S.',

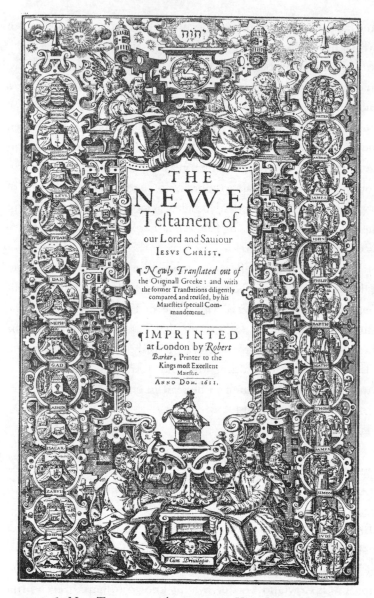

THE
NEWE
Teſtament of
our Lord and Sauiour
IESVS CHRIST.

¶ Newly Tranſlated out of
the Originall Greeke : and with
the former Tranſlations diligently
compared and reuiſed, by his
Maieſties ſpeciall Com-
mandement.

¶ IMPRINTED
at London by Robert
Barker, Printer to the
Kings moſt Excellent
Maieſtie.
ANNO DOM. 1611.

Cum Priuilegio.

FIGURE 16. New Testament title-page, 1611, King James Version.

94

on the right, is certainly the woodcutter Christopher Switzer; the tiny coat of arms beneath the initials is a reversed image of the arms of Zurich, his home before he moved to England; it was Switzer who cut the design for Speed's map of Canaan in the preliminaries of the KJV.

At the top of the woodcut there are images of the Trinity. At the centre of the top are the four Hebrew letters of the name of God (then transliterated as 'Jehovah' and now as 'Yahweh'). Below these letters is a medallion portraying a lamb bearing a cross, the ancient image of Jesus as the sacrificial lamb of God; the diamond wedding ring around the base of the medallion represents the marriage of Christ and the Church. Below the ring is a dove, representing the Holy Ghost. Protestant dislike of images meant that God the Father and God the Son could not be portrayed as humans, as was sometimes the case in Catholic publications. What is remarkable, however, is that this was the first representation of the trinity on the title page of an English Bible. In the 1602 Bishops' Bible, the depiction of the trinity constitutes a defiant affirmation of the centrality of trinitarianism in the face of unitarian movements on the Continent and among English radicals; in the 1611 KJV the symbolism was even more pointed, because in 1604 a Latin version of the unitarian Racovian Catechism had been dedicated to an enraged King James without his permission. Indeed, in the year that the KJV was published, two English anti-trinitarians were burnt.

To the left of the trinity sits Matthew with his traditional attribute, the angel; to the right, sitting on the other end of the bench, is Mark, accompanied by his lion. At the bottom left of the design Luke sits with his ox, and opposite him is John with his eagle. Luke and John look up to a second image of the lamb, this time trussed on an unadorned altar. The lamb's legs are straight because the passover lamb could not have broken bones (Numbers 9:12), and, in the New Testament, the bones of Jesus remained unbroken (John 19:33); this link was peculiar to Protestantism, and in the Church of England is affirmed in the liturgy for Easter Day, when the priest says (in the 1662 version) 'he is the very paschal lamb, which was offered for us'. In the upper corners, the sun with a face and the new moon, which are in the reverse order from what would be expected in Catholic iconography, represent the new and old dispensations, and allude to the day when the Lord made the sun and moon stand still (Joshua 10:12) and the the ends of the earth to which the apostles will travel to 'teach all nations' (Matthew 28:19).

The sides of the design are dominated by two columns of ovals. On the left the ovals contain the tents and armorial shields of the twelve tribes of Israel: from top to bottom, Ruben (water), Simeon (sword), Levi (book), Judah (lion), Dan (serpent), Nepht[ali] (hind), Gad (lion), Asher (cup), Isacar (ass), Zebul[on] (ship), Joseph (bullock), and Benja[min] (wolf). The idea of emblematic representation may be implied in the Bible (Numbers 2:2), but the iconography was elaborated in rabbinical commentaries that could be read only in Hebrew, so the designer must have had some learned advice. On the right are the twelve apostles, each with a traditional attribute (usually the instrument of his martyrdom): from top to bottom, Peter (keys), Andre[w] (diagonal cross), James the Greater (pilgrim's hat and walking stick), John (chalice), Philip (book and staff), Barth[olomew] (book and knife), Math[ew] (builder's square), Thomas (book and staff), James the Lesser (fuller's club), Simon (book and saw),

Jude (sword), and Matthias (halberd). These attributes were not altogether stable: the builder's square, for example, was traditionally (and in the main title page of the KJV) associated with Thomas, who was said to have built a palace in India; here it is given to Matthew, who in a much later tradition was said to have constructed a church in Ethiopia.

The more important of the two title pages in the 1611 Bible is a fine engraving at the beginning of the volume. It is signed 'C. Boel fecit in Richmont, 1611', which means 'C. Boel made this in Richmond, 1611'. Cornelis Boel was a Flemish draughtsman and engraver who had previously worked in Antwerp and subsequently worked in Spain. The reference to Richmond may imply that he was living in Richmond Palace, which since 1610 had been the residence of Prince Henry, the crown prince (whose portrait Boel engraved).

The design is organized around a wall with two niches and a central recess. At the top of the wall is a cornice with the tents and heraldic shields of the twelve tribes; the designs are adapted from those in the Bishops' Bible, but have been stripped of their landscape backgrounds. In the niche on the left stands Moses with his tablets and rod; in the right niche, Aaron stands in his priestly robes. The juxtaposition of Moses and Aaron is not unprecedented, but it is very unusual (it exists only in two Bibles printed in Louvain), in part because Aaron so rarely appears on title pages. The purpose of his inclusion is to emphasize the role of the priest in the English Church; whereas puritans insisted on the priesthood of all believers, the Church saw the priest as mediator of the teaching of the Church to the laity, and Aaron is an emblem of that priesthood. His knife is a reminder that he offered the sacrifice in the temple on behalf of God's people, and his cup recalls

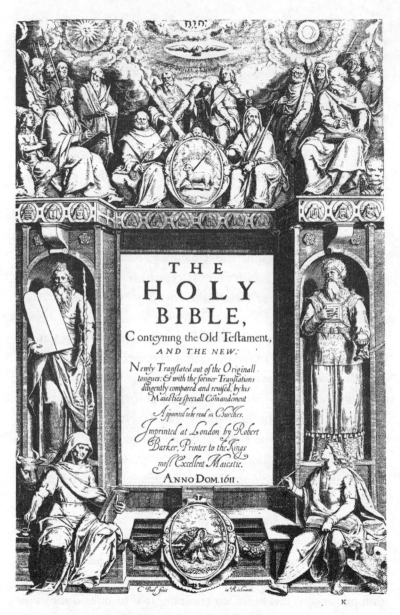

FIGURE 17. Title-page, 1611, King James Version.

that he sprinkled the blood on the altar. His prominent position is a rebuke to presbyterianism.

At the top of the design there is, as in 1602, a representation of the trinity. The Tetragrammaton is again at the top, but on this occasion the dove is above the lamb, which allows the emblem of Christ to be connected with the world below. The other figures can be identified by their traditional attributes. The four evangelists are all shown writing their gospels. Matthew, in the upper left, is accompanied by an angel holding an inkwell; Mark, in the upper right, is shown with a lion; Luke, in the bottom left, is portrayed with an ox; John, in the bottom right, is shown with an eagle holding his inkwell. To the right of Matthew sits Peter, who holds keys; between them Bartholomew stands with the tanner's knife with which he was to be flayed. To the left of Mark sits Paul, who holds a sword; between them stands Simon with a saw (he was to be killed by being cut in half with a saw). Above the lamb of God, the figure standing on the left is Andrew, holding the transverse cross of his martydom; the figure standing on the right is John the Apostle, who holds a chalice in his left hand (he is the same person as the evangelist in the lower right, but appears here with his attribute as an apostle); Luke, on the lower left, was not an apostle, and so does not appear above. Between Andrew and John the Apostle is the shaded figure of doubting Thomas, with a builder's square alluding to his activities in India; the shade represents the spiritual darkness of his doubt (John 20:25).

At the bottom centre there is a female pelican 'vulning' herself—that is, stabbing herself with her beak to feed her young with her own blood; this is an ancient image of Jesus voluntarily shedding his blood to redeem humankind. Here it is placed in a cartouche similar to the one that encloses the paschal lamb; together they represent the body and blood of Christ.

It is difficult to be confident about all of the figures in the upper corners, but in the back left, behind Bartholomew, are Jude, called Thaddaeus in the gospels (with the halberd used to kill him), and, probably, Philip (with a sword resembling a Latin cross), and, possibly, Matthias (with a lance); in the back right, behind Simon, are James the Less (with a fuller's club) and James the Greater (with pilgrim's hat and scallop shell, carrying a walking stick).

The most problematical figure is the bearded man in the top-right corner, standing in partial shade and facing towards the back. One possibility is that he may be Judas, who, in a minority tradition that originated in the third century with Origen, was counted among the redeemed; if that were correct, the shade would represent his spiritual darkness, and the lance would be an inference from the story in which he is said to have struck Jesus as a boy (according to an infancy narrative that survives in Arabic) in the same spot at which the soldier's lance pierced the body of the crucified Jesus. On the other hand, Judas seems never to have appeared on a title page, and the overwhelming consensus was that he was counted among the damned, so the figure is more likely be one of the apostles, in which case someone other than John must be represented twice; one possibility is Matthew, as the person standing behind Matthew seems to share his features.

These images reflect a curious mixture of Protestant and Catholic sensibilities. None of the human characters has a nimbus (halo), and the godhead is represented by symbols rather than pictorial representation; such features represent Protestant thinking. On the other hand, the figure of Peter is strikingly

Catholic: not only is he the sole possessor of the keys (whereas on the Coverdale cover all apostles have been issued with keys), but he is paired with Paul on either side of the godhead, which is the normal arrangement in Catholic altarpieces; similarly, many of the apostles carry the instruments of their eventual deaths, as recorded in post-biblical accounts that were valued by Catholics but ignored (or even scorned) by Protestants. Boel was presumably a Catholic (the previous year he had made engravings for a life of Thomas Aquinas), as is apparent from his elevation of Peter, but he was alert to Protestant reservations about pictorial representation.

Apart from the two title pages, pictorial design also appears in the initial letters that begin each chapter of the Bible. Most are simple floral designs, but a few are pictorial, and, of these, some are classical: Pan appears in the initial of Psalm 141 and 1 Peter 3, Daphne is shown in the initial of Romans 1, and Neptune is pictured in the initial of Matthew 1 and Revelation 1. These initials have troubled commentators, who are quick to argue that the translators did not approve of their use. Perhaps not, but the case is not straightforward. The initials portraying Daphne and Neptune had been used in the Bishops' Bible, and had attracted censure from some quarters, so their reuse must have been deliberate. In any case, there was no reason for the translators to disapprove. It is true that Daphne is naked, but so is Eve in the preliminary pages; Jacobeans were not Victorians, and were not markedly inhibited about the human body. Perhaps more importantly, classical figures were by the seventeenth century regarded in clerical circles not as antithetical to Christian figures, but rather as pagan foreshadowings. Pan was thought to foreshadow Jesus as the good shepherd, and his name, which means 'all' in Greek, to

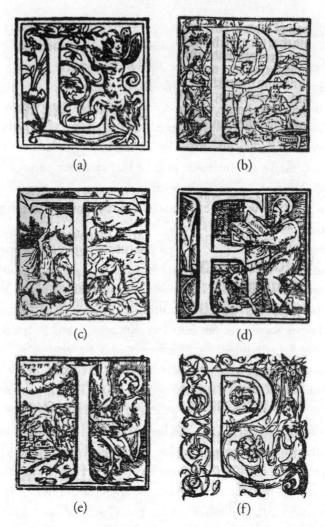

FIGURE 18. Six ornate initials from the 1611 King James Version. (a) L illustrated with figure of Pan (b) P illustrated with figure of Daphne (c) T illustrated with figure of Neptune and horses (d) F illustrated with figure of Luke and ox (e) I illustrated with figure of John and eagle (f) P illustrated with figure of woman with asp and vase.

hint at Christ as 'all'. Similarly, Daphne provides an image of
transfiguration and Neptune of resurrection. This is not to say
that these initials were placed to provoke a particular parallel at
a particular point, but rather that there was no reason to think
that they would have incurred the obloquy of the translators.
Two other pictorial initials, however, are deliberated placed. At
the beginning of Luke's Gospel the initial has a picture of Luke,
with an ox; this might allude to the sacrifice in the temple near
the beginning of the gospel. Similarly, the reuse of this initial at
the beginning of 1 Thessalonians 2 probably alludes to the
common belief that Luke accompanied Paul, Silas, and Timothy
to Thessalonica.

The initial that begins John's Gospel has his picture with an
eagle, a symbol that has traditionally been associated with the
heights to which he rises in the first chapter of his gospel. Other
initials contain figures (for example, the P at the beginning of 2
Thessalonians, Philemon, and 1 Peter) or faces (for example, the
beginning of Hebrews). There is a particularly puzzling initial P
(Ephesians, 1 Thessalonians) that contains the figure of a woman
with an asp at her breast and a vase on her head; one possibility is
that the figure is an image of Cleopatra (in one version of the
story the asp is hidden in a vase), in which case there may be an
allusion to Cleopatra's visit to Ephesus in 41 BC and to the Ptole-
maic strand in the past of Thessaloniki (Cleopatra's ancestor
Ptolemy I had sent Jewish artisans to assist in the construction of
the city).

The text framed by the recess in the wall on the title page says
(in modernized English);

> The Holy Bible, containing the Old Testament, and the New.
> Newly translated out of the original tongues, and with the

former translations diligently compared and revised by His Majesty's special commandment. Appointed to be read in churches. Imprinted at London by Robert Barker, Printer to the King's Most Excellent Majesty. Anno Dom. 1611.

The phrase that has received the most attention is 'appointed to be read in churches', which is chiefly remarkable for what it does not say. Whereas the Bishops' Bible proclaimed on the title page of every edition from 1585 to 1602 (the last) that it had been 'authorized and appointed to be read in churches', the KJV seems merely to have been appointed, a term that means little more than 'provided': the Bible known in England as the Authorized Version seems not to have been authorized. That does not mean, of course, that it was unauthorized. Formal authorization, if it had been sought and granted, would have been given by the King in the form of an Order in Council, and recorded in the Privy Council Registers now in the National Archives at Kew. The records are reasonably complete from 1540 to the present, but there is a gap in the early seventeenth century caused by a fire in 1619, so the Orders of 1611 do not survive. That said, if it had been authorized by an Order in Council, the KJV is likely to have proclaimed its authorization on its title page.

The phrase 'to be read in churches' is significant. The preliminaries of the KJV include a licence for the book to be printed 'Cum Privilegio Regiae Maiestatis' ('by authority of the king'), but that is a different matter. So, indeed, are small Bibles printed for family devotions or private study; the Church did not prescribe a Bible for use in the home. The phrase 'appointed to be read in churches' did not mean that churches were obliged to replace their Bishops' Bibles, but rather that, when the time came to replace the church Bible, the KJV would be purchased in its stead;

it also meant that the privilege of printing the large folio Bibles was the sole prerogative of the king's printer.

Printer's Errors

The first edition of the KJV was not perfectly printed, but in many respects it was more accurate than later editions that attempted to correct it, because the correction of errors seems inevitably to be accompanied by the introduction of new errors. The most obvious printer's error in the 1611 edition is the repetition of three lines in Exodus 14:10. The most common incorrectly printed word is 'and', which appears as 'aud' on twenty-eight occasions. The mistake is easily understood. Type had to be reused, so, when one page had been set, the type was released from its frame and redistributed into two cases, the upper case (for capitals) and the lower case. A lower-case 'n', when turned upside down, looks remarkably like a lower-case 'u', so the apprentice in charge of redistributing the type could easy throw an 'n' into the 'u' box; the result, when the compositor (typesetter) resumed his task, was 'aud'.

The scale of printer's errors is very small indeed, about 350 in all. The Book of Numbers, for example, has 'wece' for 'were' (1:31), 'soune' for 'sonne' (10:24), 'wilderuesse' (10:31), 'chldren' (14:8), 'vncleaue' for 'vncleane' (in the summary to chapter 19), 'Lord' for 'LORD' (20:7), 'Levit' with an inverted 'i' (29:1, margin), a missing comma after 'golde' (31:50; present in the catchword) and 'Jorden' for 'Jordan' (in the summary to chapter 32). The survival of this small number of errors does not reflect badly on the compositors, who did a good job, but rather on the proofreaders, who should have noticed them. There is, however, a smaller group of errors that can be attributed to the compositors, because the proofreaders would have had no way of knowing that they were errors. The identification of these errors has been a laborious process done repeatedly, initially by editors of later editions, and then, because editors did not compile lists, by scholars such as F. H. A. Scrivener and David Norton (see Further Reading).

Five printer's errors were corrected in the second folio edition of 1611: 'hoopes' was corrected to 'hooks' (Exodus 38:11), 'straight' to 'strait' (Isaiah 49:20), 'if he offer' to 'if ye offer' (Malachi 1:8), 'reiected' to 'recited' (Ecclesiasticus 44:5), and 'and in you' to 'and I in you' (John 15:4). Subsequent king's printer editions caught eight more, the Cambridge Bibles of 1629 and 1638 another thirteen, and a single error in the Apocrypha persisted until 1769, when 'threescore and seuenth' was finally corrected to 'threescore and seventeenth' (1 Maccabees 16:14).

Binding was not the responsibility of the king's printer, which had no in-house bookbinders. The evidence of surviving copies seems to imply that copies could be purchased in sheets, or sewn together, or in bindings arranged by the bookseller or commissioned by the purchaser. In October 1610 John Speed had secured a royal privilege that entitled him to insert a copy of the genealogies and a map of Canaan into every copy; these were incorporated into the book in the process of sewing and binding. Those who dislike Speed's genealogies and map insist that they are not part of the Bible, because they were inserted after the sheets left the king's printer. This exclusion rides roughshod over one of the supplementary rules that governed the translation ('that a very perfect genealogy and map of the Holy Land should be joined to the work'), and also raises the broader question of what may be said to constitute the Bible. This question is particularly acute for readers who believe that the KJV was either blessed by God or inspired by God. Is the essential core of the Bible the text as it was agreed by the revisers, or does it include the translation of that text into print? Does it include the preliminaries, the divisions into chapters and verses, the material in the chapter summaries and the margins? The translators prayed for divine guidance at the beginning of every meeting, and perhaps their prayers were answered. There is no evidence that any printer prayed before setting a page, and perhaps it shows, though the number of printer's errors was relatively low. Indeed, what would now be called 'production values' were remarkably high, and the quality of the first edition of KJV, judged purely as a printed book, comfortably exceeded that of any other book published in the seventeenth century.

6

THE SEVENTEENTH CENTURY

Bibles by the King's Printer

Until 1629 all English Bibles were printed by Robert Barker and his partners, Bonham Norton and John Bill. The publication of the King James Version (KJV) did not signal an immediate halt to the production of other Bibles, in that there were five more editions of Geneva New Testaments (the last was 1616) and seven more editions of the Bishops' New Testament (the last was 1619); thereafter the only English Bible published by the king's printer was the KJV. Barker was a talented printer but an untalented businessman, and in 1617 his financial difficulties obliged him to assign his rights as king's printer to Bonham Norton (whose daughter was married to Barker's son) and John Bill; from July 1617 to 7 May 1619 Bibles were published by Norton and Bill, whose names appear on the title pages. Litigation followed when Barker sought to recover a portion of the rights of king's printer, and the dispute ended in disaster. Barker was required to raise £8,000 to buy Norton's rights, and his finances never recovered. Norton was fined £6,000 for slander and libel; he could not pay, and was committed to the Fleet prison, where he died in 1635. As the dispute proceeded, the names on the title pages of Bibles printed by the king's printer changed. From 8 May 1619 to January 1621 the Bibles were printed by Barker and Bill; from January 1621 to 20 October 1629 by Norton and Bill; from 21 October 1629 to 5 May 1630 (when Bill died) by Barker and Bill.

In 1630 the death of Bill and the imprisonment of Norton should have signalled a fresh start for Robert Barker, but the following year disaster struck. An edition of the Bible with the imprint of Barker and Martin Lucas (John Bill's executor) omitted the 'not' from the version of the seventh commandment in Exodus 20, and so made adultery compulsory. It has long been thought that this could have been a disastrous printer's error, but Ian Gadd (see Further Reading) has recently noted that the court judgment also says that the edition printed the beginning of Deuteronomy 5:24 as 'the Lord our God hath shewed us his glory and his great asse' (instead of 'greatnesse'), which is surely mischief rather than error; one mistake may be an improbable accident, but two points to sabotage. In seventeenth-century English 'ass' was a respectable word meaning 'donkey', not a coarse word meaning 'buttocks', but the reading nonetheless verges on blasphemy. No copy of a Bible with the 'great asse' misprint is known to survive, though at least three copies (in Bloomington, Toronto, and Cambridge) have a blob of ink over what is likely to be 'great asse').

Although the evidence points to a malicious act, possibly by an ally of Norton, neither Barker nor Lucas pleaded sabotage as a defence when they were arraigned before the court of high commission on 8 May 1632. In October Barker and Lucas were heavily fined (£300), and a few months later the King intervened at the behest of Archbishop Laud, commanding that the fine 'be converted to the present buying of...Greek letters [type] and matrices' and ordering Barker and Lucas to print one Greek work

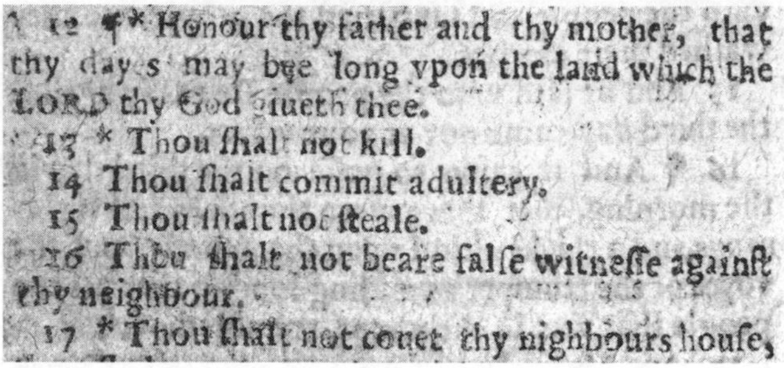

12 ¶* Honour thy father and thy mother, that
thy dayes may bee long vpon the land which the
LORD thy God giueth thee.
13 * Thou shalt not kill.
14 Thou shalt commit adultery.
15 Thou shalt not steale.
16 Thou shalt not beare false witnesse against
thy neighbour.
17 * Thou shalt not couet thy nighbours house,

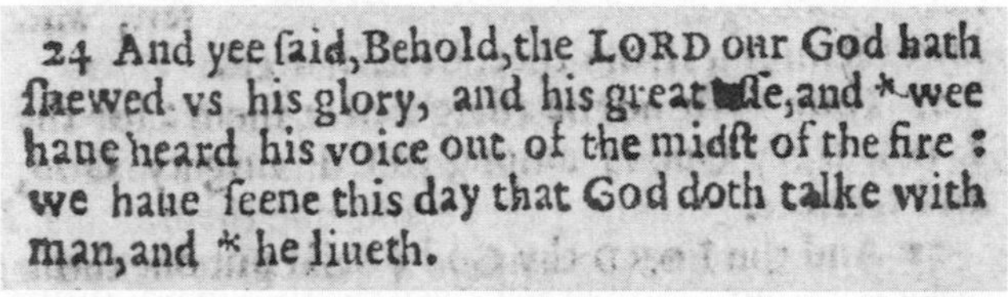

24 And yee said, Behold, the LORD our God hath
shewed vs his glory, and his greatnesse, and *wee
haue heard his voice out of the midst of the fire :
we haue seene this day that God doth talke with
man, and * he liueth.

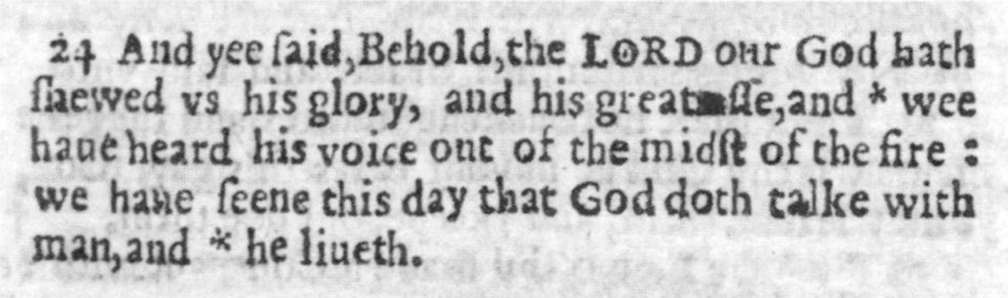

24 And yee said, Behold, the LORD our God hath
shewed vs his glory, and his greatnesse, and * wee
haue heard his voice out of the midst of the fire :
we haue seene this day that God doth talke with
man, and * he liueth.

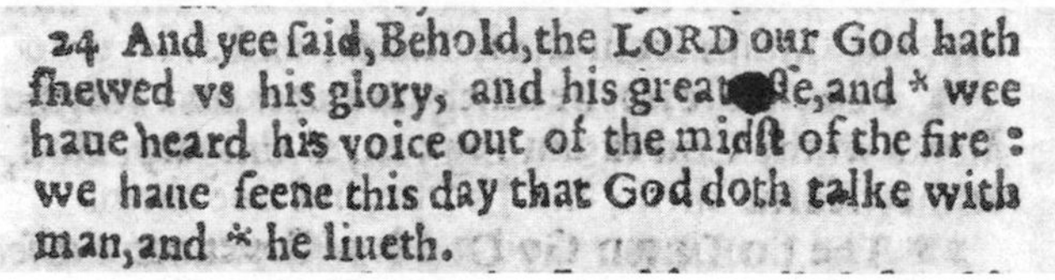

24 And yee said, Behold, the LORD our God hath
shewed vs his glory, and his greatnesse, and * wee
haue heard his voice out of the midst of the fire :
we haue seene this day that God doth talke with
man, and * he liueth.

FIGURE 19. 'The Wicked Bible' of 1631: (a) Exodus 20:14. Cambridge
University Library. Inkblots on three editions of Deuteronomy 5:24;
(b) Cambridge University Library; (c) The Thomas Fisher Rare Book
Library, University of Toronto; (d) The Lilly Library, Indiana University.

a year. All copies of the offending Bible (which is now known as the Wicked Bible) were ordered to be destroyed, as a result of which it is now a rare and valuable book. The eventual destination of the fine did not affect Barker's dire financial situation, and, although his name continued to appear on title pages, he spent the rest of his life in a debtors' prison. On 19 August 1644 he yielded his rights to the Bible patent to the Stationers' Company, which granted him a monthly pension of 10 shillings, but he died in prison.

In the seventeenth century, books came in various sizes, as did the paper from which they were made. The description of books as folios, quartos, and so on refers not to paper sizes, but to the foldings. If a printed page has been folded once, the result is a large book known as a folio, which has two leaves (four pages) per sheet. In descending size, a quarto has four leaves per sheet, an octavo eight leaves, a duodecimo twelve leaves, and sextodecimo sixteen leaves. The fact that paper size varied meant that the size of the books also varied, so, although all folios are comparatively big, booksellers distinguished between large folios and small folios. The Bible is a substantial book, so only the larger sizes were used for complete Bibles; separate New Testaments could be published in smaller sizes, though most were octavos.

The first edition of the KJV (the 'He' Bible) published by the king's printer was a large folio, as was the second (the 'She' Bible). Both were published in 1611, but the second edition was relaunched in 1613, so the date on the title page of the second edition may be 1611, 1612, or 1613. The second edition is a page-for-page reprint of the first, so when the compositor reached Exodus 14:10, in which three lines are repeated in the first edition, the compositor of the second corrected the error and then executed some fancy footwork to ensure that the page ended at the same point. Something seems to have happened to Boel's engraved title page (it may have been broken or lost, or he may have taken it to Spain with him), and a woodcut imitation of Boel's engraving was used instead.

The printing of the first edition of the KJV seems to have started before the copy-editing was finished (hence, for example, the lack of paragraph markings after Acts 20), but the high quality of the finished product implies that printing had not been hurried. The same cannot be said for the second edition of 1611, which shows signs of being a rushed response to the brisk sales of the first edition. One striking feature is that some copies consist of a mixture of pages from the first and second editions. Another sign of haste is the number of prominent misprints. The dedication, for example, refers to 'Chkist our Lord', and in some copies, 'that eateth' (Jeremiah 31:30) is printed as 'ehat tateth', an error that should have been noticed by any proof-reader, even one freshly returned from a pub lunch. The best-known error is the printing of 'Judas' instead of 'Jesus' in Matthew 26:36, a gaffe that has led to the 'She Bible' being referred to as the Judas Bible.

Some thirty readings from the second edition survive into modern KJV texts. Most are corrections of misprints, but at least one creates an error: the first edition read 'waters of gall' in Jeremiah 8:14, because the Hebrew form is plural; the second edition changed the text to 'water of gall', and this incorrect reading has yet to be expunged. There is a more problematical issue concerning the word 'shew' (the old form of 'show') in Hosea 6:5, which in the first edition reads 'therefore have I shewed them by the Prophets'; the second edition reads 'therefore have I hewed them by the Prophets', which is the reading that survives in modern editions of the KJV. But was 'shew' an error? It was not a misprint, as the annotated Bishops' Bible in the Bodleian shows, but rather a deliberate decision on the part of the translators. 'Hew' is an accurate translation of the Hebrew, but 'shew' may well reflect the reading of the Aramaic paraphrase known as the Jonathan Targum; if 'shew' is a mistake, it is one that reflects the judgement of the translators rather than the accuracy of the typesetters.

The two folios of 1611 (or 1611 and 1613) satisfied the immediate demand for large-folio Bibles, but a third edition in large type was published in 1617, a fourth in 1634, and a fifth in 1640. Additionally, there was a small folio published in 1613 with smaller type (seventy-two lines to the page rather than fifty-nine), and this was also intended for church use, particularly churches with little money to spare; a similar version in roman type followed in 1616. Smaller Bibles were required for use in family devotions, and still smaller ones for private study. In 1612, two quartos and two octavos were issued, one quarto and one octavo following the first edition, and the other pair the second edition. By 1614, at least fourteen quartos and octavos had been printed; the octavos were all printed in roman type, as were some of the quartos. These small Bibles had their share of errors, of which the one closest to the heart of authors is the version of Psalm 119:161 in some copies of the first octavo (1612), which reads 'printers have persecuted me' (instead of 'princes').

By the end of 1614 the market for small Bibles was temporarily sated, and production slowed to a more stately pace. In order to stimulate the market for the KJV, the king's printer was discouraged from printing folio and quarto editions of the Geneva Bible; thereafter Geneva Bibles were printed with false imprints, suggesting either that they were old editions or that they had been printed abroad. But, even as the Geneva Bible was being quietly suppressed, competition was arising from another quarter, that of Cambridge University Press.

Cambridge Bibles

The monopoly on the printing of Bibles (and prayer books) that the king's printer enjoyed had two possible exceptions, which were the universities of Oxford and Cambridge; both were exempted from monopoly restrictions. It was Cambridge that first developed the ambition to compete with the king's printer in the production of Bibles. Its claim was based on a charter granted by Henry VIII in 1534, but a test case in 1623 resulted in failure when the privy council refused permission for the university printer to produce Bibles. The legal position was reversed five years later, when in February 1628 a new monarch (Charles I) was content to reaffirm the charter of 1534. The printer moved quickly, and fourteen months later the university was granted permission to print the KJV.

The high quality of the first folio edition published by Cambridge in 1629 makes it highly unlikely that the editorial and production processes could have been squeezed into a period of less than two years, so it seems probable that work began earlier, perhaps with the election of a royal favourite, the duke of Buckingham, to the chancellorship of Cambridge University in June 1626. Buckingham's power within the privy council meant that it was unlikely to resist the requests of the university to print Bibles, especially as the financial plight of the king's printer meant that no bribes would be forthcoming from that quarter.

The Cambridge folio Bible of 1629 set a standard far higher than the declining standards of Bibles produced by the king's printer.

The university printers, Thomas and John Buck, produced an elegant Bible in roman type, and gave purchasers a choice of seven grades of paper. Moreover, the high production values of the edition mirrored a renewed scholarly commitment to the text. The edition introduced more than 200 changes to the text, most of which have since been embodied in the textual tradition. Many reflect an aspiration to make proper names consistent: the 1611 KJV had printed Olofernes and Holofernes, Sem and Shem, Japheth and Japhet, Caldees and Chaldees, but the editors of the Cambridge folio chose one form for each name and stuck with it.

Other changes reflect adjustments of singular and plural forms. In Song of Solomon 4:6, the 1611 KJV has 'I will get me to the mountains of myrrh and to the hill of frankincense'. In the Hebrew, Greek, Latin, Arabic, and Ethiopic texts then in use, 'mountain' is singular, as is appropriate to the parallel with 'hill', but, for reasons that are not altogether clear, the translators of 1611 chose to follow the Syriac text, and made it plural; its presence as a handwritten correction in the 1602 Bishops' Bible in the Bodleian Library shows that the decision was deliberate, not a printer's error. As it happens, the Syriac text also makes 'hill' plural, but the 1611 translators chose not to follow the Syriac, so the parallelism is lost. The Cambridge editors chose to use the singular forms, and their decision is still embodied in modern Bibles.

There appears to be only one occasion in the Cambridge Bible of 1629 when the editors chose to redraft a verse. The 1611 text of Job 4:6 (which is again written into the Bishops' Bible of 1602) is 'is not this thy fear, thy confidence; the uprightness of thy ways and thy hope?', which the Cambridge editors of 1629 changed to either 'is not thy fear, thy confidence; and the uprightness of thy ways, thy hope?' or '*is* not *this* thy fear, thy confidence; and the uprightness of thy ways, thy hope?' (both readings occur in copies of the 1629 Bible). Anyone who has translated from a dead language remote from English (and the ancient Semitic languages certainly qualify) knows that, when the syntax is not clear, the safest way ahead is to translate literally in the order in which the words occur in the original language. That is what the 1611 translators did, but at some cost to rendering the sentence comprehensible. The Cambridge editors had two attempts at improving on the 1611 translation; it is not clear which was their first and which their second attempt, but both are an improvement on the 1611 version, which merely baffles.

The second Cambridge folio edition, printed in 1638, marked a further advance; indeed, by the measure of scholarly probity (as opposed to fidelity to the 1611 version), it is probably the best of the Bibles produced in the seventeenth century. The pamphleteer William Kilburne later praised this edition as 'the authentic corrected Cambridge Bible, revised *mandato regio*, by the learned Doctor Ward, Doctor Goad of Hadley, Mr Boyse, Mr Mead &c and printed by the elaborate industry of Thomas Buck Esquire and Mr Roger Daniel'. The claim that the revision was conducted by royal command is not confirmed by the title page (such pages would include the phrase *ex mandato regio*) or by any other document. Roger Daniel (who was later to publish an edition of the Septuagint) and Thomas Buck were the printers. Samuel Ward and John Bois had both been important participants in the translation of 1611. Thomas Goade and Joseph Mede (see Appendix 1) were both wide-ranging biblical scholars with formidable linguistic skills. These scrupulous editors returned to Job 4:6, and changed the word order yet again, printing it as '*is* not this thy

fear, thy confidence, thy hope, and the uprightness of thy ways?'
This is the version that appears in modern editions of the KJV—it
follows Geneva, which has 'is not this thy fear, thy confidence,
thy patience, and the uprightness of thy ways?'

The Cambridge edition of 1638 remained influential until the
late eighteenth century, when an Oxford edition displaced it and
established the modern text. Some of the errors that it introduced,
however, still survive in modern KJVs. In Jeremiah 34:16, for
example, the 1611 text correctly printed 'whom ye had set at
liberty'; the 1638 Cambridge Bible introduced the misprint 'whom
he had set', which survived into editions of the KJV into the
twentieth century. One error in the 1638 edition that was corrected
at an early stage has become infamous. This was the reading of
Acts 6:3 ('wherefore, brethren, look ye out among you seven men
of honest report…whom ye may appoint over this business'), in
which 'we' has been substituted for the second 'ye'; conspiracy
theorists long insisted that this misprint was the result of a sinister
plot by the Anglican authorities to justify episcopacy.

Oxford Bibles

Oxford was the last of the three guardians of the text to publish
the KJV. The university had remained silent while Cambridge
attempted to secure the right to print Bibles, but the success of that
endeavour and the publication of the Cambridge Bible of 1629
prompted Oxford to reconsider its position. In 1632 William Laud,
the chancellor of the university (soon to be archbishop of Canterbury) secured letters patent giving Oxford the right to print Bibles.
In exchange for not exercising that right, the university accepted
compensatory payments at intervals for the next forty years.

¶ The firſt book of Moses,
called

GENESIS.

CHAP. I.

1 *The creation of heaven and earth, 3 of the light, 6 of the firmament, 9 of the earth ſeparated from the waters, 11 and made fruitfull, 14 of the ſunne, moon, and ſtarres, 20 of fiſh and fowl, 24 of beaſts and cattel, 26 of man in the image of God. 29 Alſo the appointment of food.*

*Pſal.33.6.
and 136.5.
Acts 14.15.
and 17.24.
Heb.11.3.

N * the beginning God created the heaven and the earth.

2 And the earth was without form and void, and darkneſſe *was* upon the face of the deep: and the Spirit of God moved upon the face of the waters.

*2.Cor.4.6.

3 And God ſaid, * Let there be light: and there was light.

4 And God ſaw the light, that *it was* good:

†Heb.between the light and between the darkneſſe.

†Heb. and the evening was, and the morning was, &c.

*Pſal.136.5.

Jerem. 10.12. and 51.15.

†Heb. expanſion.

and God divided † the light from the darkneſſe.

5 And God called the light Day, and the darkneſſe he called Night: † and the evening and the morning were the firſt day.

6 ¶ And God ſaid, * Let there be a † firmament in the midſt of the waters, and let it divide the waters from the waters.

7 And God made the firmament, and divided the waters which *were* under the firmament, from the waters which *were* above the firmament: and it was ſo.

8 And God called the firmament Heaven: and the evening & the morning were the ſecond day.

*Job 38.8.
Pſal.33.7.
and 136.6.

9 ¶ And God ſaid, * Let the waters under the heaven be gathered together unto one place, and let the drie-land appear: and it was ſo.

10 And God called the drie-land Earth, and the gathering together of the waters called he Seas: and God ſaw that *it was* good.

11 And God ſaid, Let the earth bring forth

†Heb. tender graſſe.

† graſſe, the herb yeelding ſeed, *and* the fruit-tree yeelding fruit after his kind, whoſe ſeed *is* in it ſelf, upon the earth: and it was ſo.

12 And the earth brought forth graſſe, *and* herb yeelding ſeed after his kind, and the tree yeelding fruit, whoſe ſeed *was* in it ſelf, after his kind: and God ſaw that *it was* good.

13 And the evening and the morning were the third day.

*Deut.4.19.
Pſal.136.7.
†Heb.between the day and between the night.

14 ¶ And God ſaid, Let there be * lights in the firmament of the heaven, to divide † the day from the night: and let them be for ſignes, and for ſeaſons, and for dayes, and yeares.

15 And let them be for lights in the firmament of the heaven, to give light upon the earth: and it was ſo.

16 And God made two great lights; the greater light † to rule the day, and the leſſer light to rule the night: *he made* the ſtarres alſo.

†Heb. for the rule of the day, &c.

17 And God ſet them in the firmament of the heaven, to give light upon the earth,

18 And to * rule over the day and over the night, and to divide the light from the darkneſſe: and God ſaw that *it was* good.

*Jer.32.35.

19 And the evening and the morning were the fourth day.

20 And God ſaid, * Let the waters bring forth abundantly the ||moving creature that hath † life, and fowl *that* may flie above the earth in the † open firmament of heaven.

*2.Eſdr.6.47.
||Or, creeping.
†Heb.ſoul.
†Heb. face of the firmament of heaven.

21 And God created great whales, and every living creature that moveth, which the waters brought forth abundantly after their kind, and every winged fowl after his kind: and God ſaw that *it was* good.

22 And God bleſſed them, ſaying, * Be fruitfull, and multiply, and fill the waters in the ſeas, and let fowl multiply in the earth.

*Chap.8.17.
and 9.1.

23 And the evening and the morning were the fifth day.

24 ¶ And God ſaid, Let the earth bring forth the living creature after his kind, cattel and creeping thing and beaſt of the earth after his kind: and it was ſo.

25 And God made the beaſt of the earth after his kind, and cattel after their kind, and every thing that creepeth upon the earth after his kind: and God ſaw that *it was* good.

26 ¶ And God ſaid, * Let us make man in our image, after our likeneſſe: and let them have dominion over the fiſh of the ſea, and over the fowl of the aire, and over the cattel, and over all the earth, and over every creeping thing that creepeth upon the earth.

*Chap.5.1.
and 9.6.
Wiſd.2.23.
1.Cor.11.7.
Epheſ.4.24.
Col.3.10.

27 So God created man in his own image, in the image of God created he him: * male and female created he them.

*Matth.19.4.

28 And God bleſſed them, and God ſaid unto them, * Be fruitfull, and multiply, and repleniſh the earth, and ſubdue it: and have dominion over the fiſh of the ſea, and over the fowl of the aire, and over every living thing that † moveth upon the earth.

*Chap.9.1.
†Heb.creepeth

29 ¶ And God ſaid, Behold, I have given you every herb † bearing ſeed, which *is* upon the face of all the earth, and every tree, in the which *is* the fruit of a tree yeelding ſeed: * to you it ſhall be for meat.

† Heb.ſeeding ſeed.
* Chap.9.3.

30 And to every beaſt of the earth, and to every fowl of the aire, and to every thing that creepeth upon the earth, wherein *there is* † life, *I have given* every green herb for meat: and it was ſo.

†Heb. a living ſoul.

31 And

FIGURE 20. Opening of Genesis, Cambridge 1638 edition, King James Version.

118

The first Oxford Bible was a quarto published in 1673 (New Testament) and 1675 (complete Bible). It is significant as a prelude to what was to become Oxford's Bible Press, which remained distinct from the Learned Press until the two were merged in 1906. As an edition of the Bible, the 1675 quarto appears to be a modest production. It has no preliminaries, not even the dedication to the king, and few distinguishing features apart from some eccentric spelling. There is, however, evidence of scholarly intervention in the text by John Fell, vice-chancellor of the university and later bishop of Oxford. Fell had secured the Sheldonian Theatre for use as a printing house, and an engraving of the Sheldonian featured on many of the title pages printed there. Fell's personal involvement is evident not only in the spelling (he seems to have disliked the letter 'y', and often substituted 'i', so eyes became 'eies' and days became 'daies'), but also in some of the scholarly details. The clearest example is the presentation of Matthew 12:23, which has a complex history. The Bishops' Bible had said 'Is not this that sonne of Dauid'; in the Oxford copy of the Bishops' Bible marked up for the KJV translators 'the' was substituted for 'that', but in the text of 1611 'not' was omitted, so the phrase read 'Is this the sonne of Dauid'. The 1638 Cambridge text (which Fell had studied) restores the 'not' (which does not change the meaning), but Fell decided that it was implied (even though there is no negative in the Greek) and so placed it in italics as a supplied word. This emendation does not survive in modern editions, but it was a good one, and is indicative of the care that Fell took. Harry Carter, the historian of Oxford University Press, is not eager to claim this Bible for the university, because Fell acted without the authority of the university, but this scholarly scruple may not be wholly justifiable. Even by Carter's austere

FIGURE 21. Title-page from the first Oxford edition of the King James Version, 1675.

reckoning, the second quarto of 1679 was a university publication, and indeed inaugurated Oxford's mighty Bible Press, which for the next two centuries was to overshadow Oxford's Learned Press, which published secular books.

The second Oxford quarto (1679) introduced a pioneering biblical chronology that was to become a point of contention in the nineteenth century, when physicists and geologists began to argue that the earth was millions of years old. The dates in this Bible are *anno mundi* (year of the Earth) rather than *anno Domini* (year of the Lord), so Adam's death (Genesis 5:3) is dated 130, the birth of Jesus 4000, and the crucifixion 4036. This important initative prompted William Lloyd, bishop of Worcester, to insert the more precise figure of 4004 BC into his scholarly edition of the Bible published by the king's printer in 1701; this date was used in subsequent Oxford Bibles.

The 1701 chronology was the work of James Ussher, archbishop of Armagh, whose capacious learning had rightly earned him the respect of scholars throughout Europe. In three magisterial Latin works published in the 1640s and 1650s Ussher had brought his knowledge of ancient languages, ancient calendars, and biblical scholarship to bear on the question of the date that the world had been created. He argued that the creation could be dated quite precisely to the evening preceding Sunday, 23 October 4004 BC, in the Julian calendar then in use in Protestant Europe. The year was in part an inference from the belief that, because Herod had died in 4 BC, Jesus must have been born in that year. The Hebrew calendar, which is based on lunar and solar cycles, led Ussher to conclude that the creation had coincided with the autumn equinox, and the idea that that was a Sunday was an inference from the assertion that God rested on the seventh day, which

FIGURE 22. James Ussher by William Faithorne, line engraving, 1656.

must have been a Saturday. As for the time of day, the Genesis account (reflecting the Jewish convention) asserts that 'the evening and the morning were the first day' (Genesis 1:5). Once this date had been established, Ussher was able to work forwards through biblical history, so the date of Noah's flood, for example, was fixed at 2849 BC.

Ussher's chronology lived on in early editions of Oxford's Scofield Bible (see Chapter 12), and still has advocates amongst Young Earth Creationists, but the precision of his calculation has long been the subject of mockery. It is true that modern scientific thinking has left Ussher pilloried as a buffoon, but this is an unjust verdict on a man who was both learned and wise. When Oxford University Press decided to incorporate his chronology in its Bibles, it was not being foolish, but rather honouring the insights of recent scholarship.

Oxford was a late starter, but its Bible Press grew at an astonishing speed. By 1683 the Bible Press was the largest printing

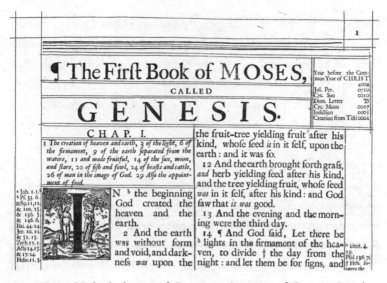

¶ The First Book of MOSES,

CALLED

GENESIS.

Year before the Common Year of CHRIST	4004
Jul. Per.	0710
Cyc. Sun	0010
Dom. Letter	B
Cyc. Moon	0007
Indiction	0005
Creation from Tisri	0001

CHAP. I.

1 *The creation of heaven and earth, 3 of the light, 6 of the firmament, 9 of the earth separated from the waters, 11 and made fruitful, 14 of the sun, moon, and stars, 20 of fish and fowl, 24 of beasts and cattle, 26 of man in the image of God. 29 Also the appointment of food.*

a Joh. 1. 1.
b Pf. 33. 6.
&89.11,12.
& 102. 25.
& 136. 5.
& 146. 6.
Ifai. 44. 24.
Jer. 10. 12.
& 51. 15.
Acts 14. 15.
& 17. 24.
Hebr. 11. 3.

IN [a] the beginning God created the [b] heaven and the earth.

2 And the earth was without form and void, and darkness was upon the fruit-tree yielding fruit after his kind, whose feed *is* in it felf, upon the earth : and it was fo.

12 And the earth brought forth grafs, and herb yielding feed after his kind, and the tree yielding fruit, whofe feed *was* in it felf, after his kind : and God faw that it *was* good.

13 And the evening and the morning were the third day.

14 ¶ And God faid, Let there be [h] lights in the firmament of the heaven, to divide † the day from the night : and let them be for figns, and

h Deut. 4.
19.
Pfal. 136. 7.
† Heb. between the

FIGURE 23. Ussher's dating of Creation. Opening of Genesis, London 1701 edition, King James Version.

house in England. The profits that it generated soon began to subsidize the university's academic and educational publications for the simple reason that Bibles sold well.

Reception

The king's printer, Cambridge, and Oxford all sold the KJV in the seventeenth century, but how did readers feel about it? The first printed reaction was a vitriolic tract by Hugh Broughton, who had long pressed for a new English translation but had been excluded from the project, despite his high standing as a Hebraist. There are many reasons why Broughton might have been excluded—he was cantankerous and opininated, he had fallen out with John Rainolds, he lived abroad in what is now the Netherlands—and the precise reason is not known. When the KJV was published, he received a copy in Middelburg, where later in 1611 he published an eight-page pamphlet called *A Censure of the Late Translation for our Churches*. In Broughton's view, the translation was so incompetent that it should be burnt. As for the inclusion of the Apocrypha, Broughton argued that 'lying fables and vain speech' should not 'come side by side with the holy books, nor under the same roof'. The only other dissenting voice was that of Ambrose Ussher, the younger brother of James Ussher. His complaint to the effect that the KJV was just a hastily prepared rehash of older translations contains an element of sour grapes, because, when the KJV was published, Ussher was well advanced in his own translation, which now lies unpublished in the library of Trinity College Dublin. It is now forgotten, but its language does provide a revealing contrast to the KJV: he uses contemporary personal pronouns ('you' instead of 'ye') and has a distinct preference for Anglo-Saxon words rather than Latin ones, so he uses 'lust' rather than 'concupiscence'; on the other hand, he tries to follow Hebrew word order in the Old Testament, and so his prose is sometimes clunky.

Those involved in the preparation of the KJV naturally took the view that the translation was a success. Samuel Ward was a puritan, but his report on the project to the Synod of Dort on 20 November 1618 was entirely upbeat, praising the translation for its accuracy. Puritans were broadly content with the translation, but there was unease about the inclusion of the Apocrypha. The strictures of the Westminster Confession of Faith (1647), which declared that 'the books commonly called Apocrypha, not being of divine inspiration, are no part of the Canon of Scripture; and therefore are of no authority in the Church of God, nor to be any otherwise approved, or made use of, than other human writings', meant that the Apocrypha were quietly omitted from editions of the KJV published during the Commonwealth and Protectorate.

In the course of the early seventeenth century, churches gradually replaced their Bishops' Bibles with KJVs, but this process was scarcely remarked upon. Instead, for several decades opposition mostly took the silent form of private purchasers buying the Geneva Bible, which continued to be imported from Amsterdam. The eventual solution to this difficulty was suppression, and after 1644 the Geneva Bible was neither printed not imported.

The execution of King Charles and the advent of Cromwell's godly republic in 1649 produced no call for a return to the Geneva translation, but a few editions of the KJV were equipped with notes from the Geneva Bible. There was, however, a move to revise the KJV. The earliest surviving call for a revision came from the Hebraist John Lightfoot in a sermon to the House of Commons preached in August 1645. His remarks centred on the issue of accuracy, and it was this issue that created the impetus for translation. At this stage the argument focused on the translation, but there was also concern about the number of misprints in printed Bibles; indeed, sometimes unspecific complaints about errors could apply either to mistranslations or to misprints. The project for a revision of the KJV was eventually initiated in 1657, when Parliament established a subcommittee 'to consider of the translations and impressions of the Bible' and to report their findings to the Grand Committee for Religion. Meetings were held to discuss the extent of the problems to be addressed, but in the event the project was never realized. The committee acknowledged that there were mistakes in translation, but nonetheless affirmed that the KJV was the best translation of the Bible into any language.

The KJV's most benign reader in the seventeenth century was the historian and clergyman Thomas Fuller, a beacon of tolerance in an intolerant age, who in 1655, writing of 1611, recorded that,

> after long expectation, and great desire, came forth the new translation of the Bible (most beautifully printed) by a select and competent number of divines appointed for that purpose; not being many, lest one should trouble another; and yet many, lest, in any, things might haply escape them.... So that their industry, skilfulness, piety, and discretion hath herein bound the Church unto them in a debt of special remembrance and thankfulness. These, with Jacob, rolled away the stone from the mouth of the well of life, so that now even Rachels, weak women, may freely come, both to drink themselves and to water the flocks of their families at the same.

This passage is remarkable not only for its generosity of spirit, but also for its singling out of women readers as particularly important.

Fuller goes out to identify two groups of detractors. First, Roman Catholics disliked the KJV for a variety of reasons, including, Fuller explains, the use of the margins to record alternative senses of words, a practice deemed to cast doubt on the certainty of the Scriptures. Second, 'some of the Brethren were not well pleased with this translation'; the Brethren (that is, the puritans) 'complained that they could not see into the sense of the Scripture for lack of the spectacles of those Geneva annotations'. Fuller quietly sets aside these objections and pronounces his gracious verdict on the translators of the KJV:

> Leave we then these worthy men, now all of them gathered to their Fathers and gone to God (however they were required on earth) well rewarded in Heaven for their worthy work. Of whom

as also of that gracious King that employed them we may say, wheresoever the Bible shall be preached or read in the whole world, there shall also this that they have done be told in memory of them.

Fuller's words constitute the first affirmation of the enduring importance of the KJV for the preaching of the gospel.

The last gasp of learned dissent came as the puritan government drew to a close: Robert Gell was the rector of a wealthy London parish who dabbled with radical theology but at the Restoration presented himself as wholly orthodox. His huge *Essay toward the Amendment of the Last English Translation of the Bible* (1660) is a collection of sermons that explore the shortcomings of the translation of the Pentateuch in the KJV by the measure of scholarly probity. He repeatedly cites Greek, Latin, Hebrew, Syriac, and Arabic sources to justify his corrections. Centuries later, one can still feel compassion for the congregation to which he preached.

After 1660 attacks on the KJV abated, and it was quietly adopted by Protestants of all persuasions. There were reservations in nonconformist circles about the inclusion of the Apocrypha and the use of ecclesiastical language (for example, 'bishop'). There was also dissatisfaction with the canonization of New Testament figures (St Matthew, St Luke, etc.) but not of godly Old Testament figures (there is no St Moses or St Job), whom many regarded as saints in the evangelical sense of the term, meaning those who are redeemed (as in 'when the saints go marching in'). There were also continued reservations about the accuracy of the printing, as every edition seemed to contain new typographical errors. The pamphleteer William Kilburne assembled a formidable list of printing errors in his short *Dangerous*

Errors in Several Late Printed Bibles (1660). He had no reservations about the translation itself, which he praised as 'the national and common Evidence of our Religion...an *Elysian flower* of Supremacie'. Surveying a range of Bibles, most but not all of which can now be identified, he noted errors such as 'found rulers' (Genesis 36:24; should read 'found the mules'), 'the LORD gave her corruption' (Ruth 3:15; should read 'conception'), 'your condemnation draweth nigh' (Luke 21:28; should read 'redemption'), 'slew their flesh' (Psalm 105:29; should read 'fish'), 'waters shall overthrow' (Isaiah 28:17; should read 'overflow'), 'no more than five loves' (Luke 9:13; should read 'loaves'), 'if my kingdom were of this word' (John 18:36; should read 'world'), 'leave my oul in hell' (Acts 2:27; should read 'soul'), 'that I might by all men save some' (1 Corinthians 9:22; should read 'means'), and 'therefore is my spirit over' (Psalm 143:4; should read 'overwhelmed'). If to such errors one adds Kilburne's long litany of omitted words and verses, it becomes clear that there was indeed a printing problem. The errors occurred in Bibles printed by the king's printer, and Kilburne argued that the monopoly, which had already been breached by Cambridge, should be discontinued. Unease about accuracy was to lead eventually to the publication of two scholarly editions (one by Cambridge, one by Oxford) in the late eighteenth century.

7

⊶⊷

THE EIGHTEENTH CENTURY

Baskett at Oxford

In the early eighteenth century the key figure in Bible publishing was the stationer and printer John Baskett, who in 1710 secured a half-share in the rights of the queen's printer (as the king's printer became during the reign of Queen Anne) in England and in 1712 was formally appointed to the post; he also bought a one-third share in the rights of the queen's printer in Scotland, and later leased the right (with two partners) to print Bibles and other books published by the University of Oxford. As Cambridge did not re-enter the market until 1743, Baskett was able to secure a monopoly, which meant that prices were high and quality low. The English monopoly was challenged by the Stationers' Company and the Scottish monopoly by one of his partners, but he resisted energetically, and in the course of his career launched almost forty lawsuits against those who dared to infringe his expensively acquired rights.

Baskett was to publish twelve editions of the King James Version (KJV) in the course of his career, of which the best known is the first, a two-volume imperial folio (15 inches × 22 inches) with fine engravings (1716 and 1717); the small print run included three luxurious vellum copies (of which two survive in the British Library in London and one in the Bodleian Library in Oxford). It is one of the most beautiful Bibles ever produced, surpassed in the elegance of its design, the beauty of its typeface, and the quality of its paper only by Baskerville's Bible for Cambridge (see below). Baskett's attention to the appearance of the text was not, however, complemented by careful attention to textual accuracy. Its many errors include a mistranscription of the parable of the vineyard, which in this version of Luke 20 was headed 'the parable of the vinegar'; it has been known ever since as the Vinegar Bible, and its reputation as a book of great beauty has been destroyed by its reputation for misprints. Baskett's Bibles were thereafter said to contain a 'Baskettful of errors'. The compromised quality of proof-reading at the Bible Press at Oxford stood in marked contrast to the production values of the Learned Press.

The Vinegar Bible was expensive to produce, and compounded Baskett's already considerable debts. He responded by mortgaging his rights and assets, and a protracted series of lawsuits arose as he tried to recover his property. He continued to print Bibles, but in 1731 the Syndics of Cambridge University Press leased their right to print Bibles to William Ged, the first printer in Britain to use stereotypes, which he described as a method of printing 'each page of a book upon a single plate, instead of a type for every letter, as used in the common way of printing'. Baskett issued a legal challenge to Ged, denying his right to print Bibles; the suit ground through the courts for years, but when it was finally concluded (sixteen years after Baskett's death in 1761), the court ruled in favour of Oxford, and Ged's publication rights were restricted. Baskett's son Mark continued to print Bibles in the 1760s, but his press became, as a contemporary phrased it, 'more

chief priefts and the fcribes came upon him, with the elders,	fcribes the fame hour fought to lay hands on him; and they feared the people: for they perceived that he had fpoken this parable againft them.
2 And fpake unto him, faying, Tell us, By what authority doeft thou thefe things? or who is he that gave thee this authority?	
3 And he anfwered and faid unto them, I will alfo afk you one thing; and anfwer me.	20 And they watched *him*, and fent forth fpies, which fhould feign themfelves juft men, that they might take hold of his words, that fo they might deliver him unto the power and authority of the governour.
4 The Baptifm of John, was it from heaven, or of men?	

FIGURE 24. Luke 20: 1716–17 edition, vol. 2 edited by John Baskett, with the erroneous running head 'Parable of the Vinegar'.

like an Ale House than a Printing Room', and the quality of the Bibles produced by his drunken employees left much to be desired.

Baskerville at Cambridge

John Baskerville was one of England's greatest type founders, and type was his passion as well as his profession. His association with the University of Cambridge began in 1758, when he was appointed university printer and granted permission to print two prayer books and a folio Bible. He did not, however, replace the existing university printer, Joseph Bentham, who continued to print prayer books and folio Bibles. The prospectus for Baskerville's Bible demonstrated that he was more interested in type than in textual accuracy. Prospective purchasers were, for example, offered a choice between borders with type ornaments on each page or simply 'plain lines'; clearly the preoccupation with decoration offended some potential buyers, and in a revised version of the prospectus Baskerville acknowledged that, 'as many Gentlemen have objected to every Kind of Ornament round the Page, the work will be printed quite plain, with the marginal notes all at the bottom'. The Bible that eventually ensued, the folio of 1763, is arguably the most elegant edition of the KJV ever produced. Baskerville aspired to produce a Bible that was 'more correct and beautiful' than any of its predecessors. It was certainly more beautiful, but by 'correct' he meant only free from typographical error; there was no attempt to rethink the text in relation to the original 1611 Bible, and, indeed, this folio, in common with Baskerville's other books, is characterized by textual inaccuracy. Baskerville was a brilliant designer, but he left production to others.

Parris at Cambridge

In 1740 the Syndics of Cambridge University Press declared their intention 'to serve the public with a more beautiful and correct edition than can easily be found'. The task was entrusted to F. S. Parris, a fellow of Sidney Sussex who would shortly become its master; he eventually became university librarian. In editing the text of the KJV, Parris concentrated on the correction of textual errors, italics, and cross-references, but also attended to changes in grammar and in the meanings of words. The new edition, which was published in 1743, established important editorial principles. In several instances, for example, he changed nouns from singular to plural, either because the Hebrew or Greek original demanded it, or because in context it made sense to do so. In Genesis 47:6, for example, he observed that the singular form 'man' made little sense in the phrase 'if thou knowest any man of activity among them, then make them rulers over my cattle', and so changed 'man' to 'men', which is what the Hebrew says; in the

M I C A H.

CHAP. I.

1 Micah sheweth the wrath of God against Jacob for idolatry: 10 he exhorteth to mourning.

THE word of the LORD that came to ᵃ Micah the Morasthite in the days of Jotham, Ahaz, and Hezekiah, kings of Judah, ᵇ which he saw concerning Samaria and Jerusalem.

2 *Hear, all ye people; ᶜ hearken, O earth, and †all that therein is: and let the Lord GOD be witness against you, the Lord from his holy temple.

3 For behold, ᵈ the LORD cometh forth out of his ᵉ place, and will come down, and tread upon the ᶠ high places of the earth.

4 And ᵍ the mountains shall be molten under him, and the valleys shall be cleft; as wax before the fire, and as the waters that are poured down ‡ a steep place.

5 For the transgression of Jacob is all this, and for the sins of the house of Israel. What is the transgression of Jacob? is it not Samaria? and what are the high places of Judah? are they not Jerusalem?

6 Therefore I will make Samaria ʰ as an heap of the field, and as plantings of a vineyard: and I will pour down the stones thereof into the valley, and I will discover the foundations thereof.

7 And all the graven images thereof shall be beaten to pieces, and all the hires thereof shall be burned with the fire, and all the idols thereof will I lay desolate: for she gathered it of the hire of an harlot, and they shall return to the hire of an harlot.

8 Therefore ⁱ I will wail and howl, ᵏ I will go stripped and naked. ˡ I will make a wailing like the dragons, and mourning as the ‖ owls.

9 For §her wound is incurable; for it is come unto Judah; he is come unto the gate of my people, even to Jerusalem.

10 ¶ ᵐ Declare ye it not at Gath, weep ye not at all in the house of ᵒ Aphrah; ⁿ roll thyself in the dust.

11 Pass ye away, †thou ‡ inhabitant of Saphir, having thy ᵒ shame naked: the inhabitant of ‖ Zaanan came not forth in the mourning of § Beth-ezel; he shall receive of you his standing.

12 For the inhabitant of Maroth ᵒ waited carefully for good; but ᵖ evil came down from the LORD unto the gate of Jerusalem.

13 O thou inhabitant of Lachish, bind the chariot to the swift beast: she is the beginning

of the sin to the daughter of Zion: for the transgressions of Israel were found in thee.

14 Therefore shalt thou give presents †to Moresheth-gath: the houses of ‡ Achzib shall be a lie to the kings of Israel.

15 Yet will I bring an heir unto thee, O inhabitant of Mareshah; ‖ he shall come unto Adullam the glory of Israel.

16 Make thee ᑫ bald, and poll thee for thy delicate children; enlarge thy baldness as the eagle: for they are gone into captivity from thee.

CHAP. II.

1 Against oppression. 4 A lamentation. 7 A reproof of injustice and idolatry. 12 A promise of restoring Jacob.

WO to them ᵃ that devise iniquity, and ᵇ work evil upon their beds! when the morning is light, they practise it, because it is in the power of their hand.

2 And they covet ᶜ fields, and take them by violence; and houses, and take them away: so they *oppress a man and his house, even a man and his heritage.

3 Therefore thus saith the LORD, Behold, against this family do I devise an evil, from which ye shall not remove your necks, neither shall ye go haughtily: for this time is evil.

4 ¶ In that day shall one take up a parable against you, and lament †with a doleful lamentation, and say, We be utterly spoiled: ᵈ he hath changed the portion of my people: how hath he removed it from me! ‡ turning away he hath divided our fields.

5 Therefore thou shalt have none that shall *cast a cord by lot in the congregation of the LORD.

6 ‖ § ᶠ Prophesy ye not, say they to them that prophesy: they shall not prophesy to them, that they shall not take shame.

7 ¶ O thou that art named the house of Jacob, is the spirit of the LORD *straitened? are these his doings? do not my words do good to him that walketh †uprightly?

8 Even ‡ of late my people is risen up as an enemy: ye pull off the robe ‖ with the garment from them that pass by securely, as men averse from war.

9 The §women of my people have ye cast out from their pleasant houses; from their children have ye taken away my glory for ever.

10 Arise ye, and depart; for this is not your rest: because it is polluted, it shall destroy you even with a sore destruction.

11 If a man *walking in the spirit and falshood,

ᵃ Jer. 26. 18. ᵇ Amos 1. 1. * Heb. Hear ye people all of them. ᶜ Deut. 32. 1. Isa. 1. 2. †Heb. the fulness thereof. ᵈ Isa. 26. 21. ᵉ Psal. 115. 3. ᶠ Deut. 32. 13. & 33. 29 Amos 4. 13. ᵍ Psal. 97. 5. Isa. 64. 1, 2. Amos 9. 5. Hab. 3. 6, 10. ‡Heb. a descent. ʰ ch. 3. 12. Isa. 11. 3. & 22. 4. Jer. 4. 19. ⁱ Isa. 20. 2, 3, 4. ˡ Job 30. 29. Psal. 102. 6. ‖ Heb. daughters of the owl. §Or, she is grievously sick of her wounds. ᵐ 2 Sam. 1. 20. ᵒ That is, dust. * Jer. 6. 26. †Or, thou that dwellest fairly. ‡Heb. inhabitress. ᵒ Isa. 20. 4. & 47. 1, 3. Jer. 13. 22. ‖ Or, the country of flocks. §Or, a place near. * Or, was grieved. ᵖ Amos 3. 6. †Or, for. ‡That is, a lie. ‖ Or, the glory of Israel shall come, &c. ᵃ Job 1. 20. Isa. 22. 12. Jer. 7. 29. & 47. 5. & 48. 37. ᵇ Hof. 7. 6. ᶜ Psal. 36. 4. ᶜ Isa. 5. 8. *Or, defraud. †Heb. with a lamentation of lamentations. ᵈ ch. 1. 15. ‡ Or, instead of restoring. ᶜ Deut. 32. 8, 9. ‖ Or, Prophesy not as they prophesy. †Heb. Drop, &c. Ezek. 21. 2. ᶠ Isa. 30. 10. Amos 7. 16. *Or, shortened. †Heb. upright. ‡Heb. yesterday. ‖ Heb. over-against a garment. §Or, wives. *Or, walk with the wind, and lie falsly.

FIGURE 25. Opening of Micah. Cambridge, 1763 edition, edited by Baskerville.

133

New Testament, 'the words of Jesus' (Matthew 26:75) becomes 'the word of Jesus', and 'the hands of the Angel' (Acts 7:35) becomes 'the hand of the angel'. Parris also restored definite articles that had been omitted in 1611, so, for example, 'the feast of Passover' (Exodus 34:25) becomes 'the feast of the passover', and 'the rest of the silver and gold' (Ezra 7:18) becomes 'the rest of the silver and the gold'. One of the New Testament additions of a definite article seems to shift the meaning slightly, as when 'thou art Christ' (Matthew 16:16) becomes 'thou art the Christ'. There are other instances in which Parris substituted an indefinite article for a definite one: 'the sonne of Abraham' (Luke 19:9) becomes 'a son of Abraham', and 'he sent the third' (Luke 20:12) becomes 'he sent a third'. On occasion he also changed a definite article to a possessive pronoun, so 'greater then [an old spelling of 'than'] the Lord' (John 15:20) becomes 'greater than his Lord', presumably to remove the ambiguity, and the description of Gamaliel as 'a doctour of Law' (Acts 5:34) is changed to 'a doctor of the law', presumably to avoid the suggestion that he had been awarded a degree by a university. This is, of course, only a partial solution: as 'doctor' meant 'teacher' in the seventeenth century, Parris might usefully have disposed of the word 'doctor'.

In the 1611 Bible possessives were indistinguishable from nominative forms, but in the second quarter of the eighteenth century apostrophes had begun to represent possessive forms. Parris therefore inserted possessive apostrophes throughout the text. Of Parris's changes in language designed to bring idioms up to date, the most striking (because it is in the mind of every reader of the KJV) is the change of 'no' to 'not' in the phrase that now reads 'and though I have all faith, so that I could remove mountains, and have not charity, I am nothing' (1 Corinthians 13:2); in saying

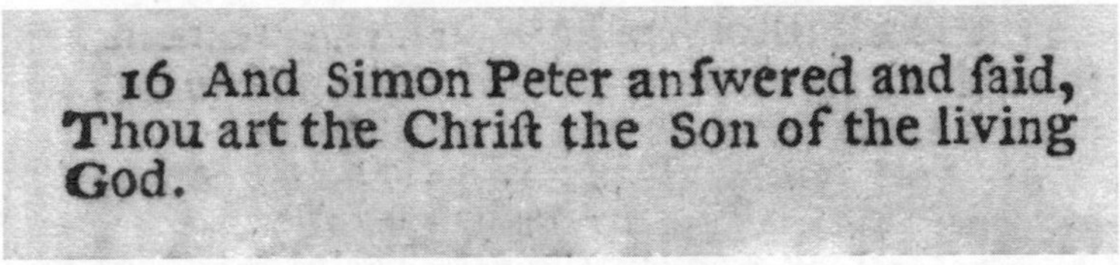

> **16** And Simon Peter anſwered and ſaid,
> Thou art the Chriſt the Son of the living
> God.

FIGURE 26. Matthew 16:16. Cambridge, 1743 edition edited by Parris.

'and have not charity' the modern reader is recalling Parris, not the 1611 KJV.

Parris also changed words to modern forms, so 'neesed' became 'sneezed' (2 Kings 4:35), 'had dedicate' became 'had dedicated' (2 Kings 12:18), 'crudled' became 'curdled' (Job 10:10), 'to be heat' became 'to be heated' (Daniel 3:19), 'ware' became 'aware' (Matthew 24:50, Luke 12:46), 'bide' became 'abide' (Romans 11:23) and 'inhabiters' became 'inhabitants' (Revelation 17:2); more radically he changed 'fourscore' to 'eightieth' in 1 Kings 6:1, because 'fourscore' was no longer acceptable as an ordinal number. Parris's judgement about when narrative becomes direct speech occasionally differs from that of the 1611 translators. In Jeremiah 1:13, for example, 1611 read 'And I said, I see a seething pot; and the face thereof *was* toward the north'; in that account, only 'I see a seething pot' is direct speech, but Parris changed the italicised *was* to *is*, and so included the rest of the sentence in the direct speech. He may (or may not) have been wrong to make the change, as the Hebrew is ambiguous.

Finally, Parris tackled the problem of the inconsistent use of 'ye' and 'you' in the 1611 text. As I explained in Chapter 4, the distinction between 'ye' (the nominative plural) and 'you' (the accusative plural) had been distinctly old-fashioned for decades before the KJV was prepared, but the distinction was nonetheless preserved in verses such as 'Blessed are ye, when *men* shall revile you' (Matthew 5:11). By the mid-eighteenth century the distinction was obsolete, and 'you' was used in all cases. Parris could have decided to modernize to contemporary usage, but the decision to eliminate 'ye' would have brought 'thee' and 'thou' down with it, and Parris was not that radical. He therefore chose the other course, which was to restore the distinction in places where the original translators had failed to observe it, so initiating the process whereby revisions of the KJV archaized as well as modernized the original text. Perhaps his resolution failed, or Parris simply ran out of time, because the principle was not fully implemented; indeed, it is much more in evidence in his text of Genesis than in later books.

The folio Bible that Parris produced for Cambridge University Press in 1743 was an important edition because of the principles on which it was edited. The full implementation of those principles, however, was not accomplished until an Oxford editor assumed the task and produced what is in effect the modern text of the KJV.

Blayney and the Triumph of Oxford

Benjamin Blayney is little known today, but he might rightly be regarded as the single most important individual in the history of the KJV, because the twenty-first-century text of the Bible is essentially Blayney's text. Blayney was a clergyman, a Hebraist, and an academic with a fellowship at Hertford College, Oxford. Blayney was asked by the University Press to prepare a corrected edition of the KJV. The impetus for this project was the work of Parris at Cambridge, and the instructions of the Oxford delegates specified that the Cambridge editions of 1743 and 1760 should be used as part of the scholarly underpinning of the new Oxford edition. These two editions were to be collated with the first edition and with Lloyd's folio of 1701. In stipulating that the first edition (described as 'the original or most authentic edition') should be an integral part of the process, the delegates were introducing an important principle, but there was a difficulty: they did not know which was the first edition. They therefore decided to consult Thomas Secker, the archbishop of Canterbury. The archbishop was uncertain, but thought that it was probably the roman-type folio of 1612.

Blayney volunteered to edit the edition (for which he was paid £350), and an account of his principles is embodied in his report to the vice-chancellor and the delegates, which was of sufficient public interest to be published in the *Gentleman's Magazine* in November 1769. The report courteously acknowledges the corrections made by Parris, and presents the new edition as a continuation of his endeavours. Blayney explains that he has lavished time on the chapter summaries, on the italics, on the running heads at the top of the columns on each page, and on corrections to the chronology of Bishop Ussher. He also translated proper names in the margins 'for the benefit of the unlearned'; this was a period at which Greek and Hebrew were taught in England's schools as well as universities, so anyone without this basic linguistic competence was deemed to be unlearned. The edition of Bishop Lloyd is taken to task for fanciful or inaccurate cross-references, which Blayney was able to correct by recourse to a Scottish edition 'of which the present vice-chancellor was kind enough to lend a copy'. The result of his labours, in Blayney's immodest estimation, was a text 'reformed to such a standard of purity, as, it is presumed, is not to be met with in any other edition hitherto extant'.

These observations, at once deferential and triumphalist, are almost entirely concerned with the apparatus surrounding the text of the Bible, which makes the report more interesting for its silences than for its assertions. It does not mention what the delegates had described in an Olympian phrase as 'modern variations in mere orthography', and it is silent on the subject of grammar, including word order and punctuation. Ironically, it is the changes in these unspoken areas that make Blayney's folio edition of 1769 the most important text since 1611, the edition that was to become the authoritative text for subsequent editions.

The sheer scale of the changes wrought by Blayney on the text can be seen in a copy of his edition owned and annotated by a clergyman called Gilbert Buchanan and now in the Cambridge University Library. Buchanan collated Blayney's folio with what he thought was a first edition of the KJV but was in fact the second edition known as the 'She Bible'. Thousands of changes to italics, spelling, punctuation, chapter headings, and cross-references are noted, and the cumulative effect is quite overwhelming.

The changes that Blayney wrought are for the most part an implementation of Parris's principles. On the numbers of nouns, for example, 'the names of other gods' (Exodus 23:13) becomes 'the name of other gods', and 'keepe me from the snare' (Psalm 141:9) becomes 'keep me from the snares'. In dealing with tenses, Blayney sometimes prefers grammatical coherence to fidelity to the original, so 'he calleth [present tense] unto him the twelve, and began' (Mark 6:7) becomes 'he called onto them the twelve, and began'; similarly, 'and said, Where have ye laid him? They say unto him' (John 11:34) becomes 'and said, Where have ye laid him? They said unto him'. He occasionally restores 1611 readings: 'fleshy tables of the heart' (2 Corinthians

David his father: and Jehoshaphat his son reigned in his stead.

25 ¶ And Nadab the son of Jeroboam began to reign over Israel in the second year of Asa king of Judah, and reigned over Israel two years.

26 And he did evil in the sight of the LORD, and walked in the way of his father, and in his sin wherewith he made Israel to sin.

27 ¶ And Baasha the son of Ahijah, of the house of Issachar, conspired against him; and Baasha smote him at Gibbethon, which *belonged* to the Philistines; for Nadab and all Israel laid siege to Gibbethon.

28 Even in the third year of Asa king of Judah did Baasha slay him, and reigned in his stead.

29 And it came to pass, when he reigned, *that* he smote all the house of Jeroboam; he left not to Jeroboam any that breathed, until he had destroyed him, according unto "the saying of the LORD, which he spake by his servant Ahijah the Shilonite:

30 Because of the sins of Jeroboam which he sinned, and which he made Israel sin, by his provocation wherewith he provoked the LORD God of Israel to anger.

31 Now the rest of the acts of Nadab, and all that he did, *are* they not written in the book of the chronicles of the kings of Israel?

32 ¶ And there was war between Asa and Baasha king of Israel all their days.

33 In the third year of Asa king of Judah began Baasha the son of Ahijah to reign over all Israel in Tirzah, twenty and four years.

34 And he did evil in the sight of the LORD, and walked in the way of Jeroboam, and in his sin wherewith he made Israel to sin.

CHAP. XVI.

1 *Jehu's prophecy against the house of Baasha.* 5 *Baasha dieth, and is succeeded by Elah.* 8 *Zimri slayeth Elah, and succeedeth him.* 11 *He executeth Jehu's prophecy against Baasha's house.* 15 *Omri, made king by the army, besiegeth Zimri in Tirzah, who in despair burneth himself.* 21 *The people being divided, Omri's faction prevaileth against Tibni.* 23 *Omri buildeth Samaria.* 25 *After a wicked reign,* 27 *he dieth, and is succeeded by Ahab.* 29 *Ahab's excessive wickedness and idolatry.* 34 *Joshua's curse fulfilled upon Hiel the builder of Jericho.*

THEN the word of the LORD came to Jehu the son of Hanani against Baasha, saying,

2 Forasmuch as I exalted thee out of the dust, and made thee prince over my people Israel; and thou hast walked in the way of Jeroboam, and hast made my people Israel to sin, to provoke me to anger with their sins;

3 Behold, I will take away the posterity of Baasha, and the posterity of his house; and will make thy house like the house of Jeroboam the son of Nebat.

4 Him that dieth of Baasha in the city shall the dogs eat; and him that dieth of his in the fields shall the fowls of the air eat.

5 Now the rest of the acts of Baasha, and what he did, and his might, *are* they not written in the book of the chronicles of the kings of Israel?

6 So Baasha slept with his fathers, and was buried in Tirzah: and Elah his son reigned in his stead.

7 And also by the hand of the prophet Jehu the son of Hanani came the word of the LORD against Baasha, and against his house, even for all the evil that he did in the sight of the LORD, in provoking him to anger with the work of his hands, in being like the house of Jeroboam; and because he killed him.

8 ¶ In the twenty and sixth year of Asa king of Judah began Elah the son of Baasha to reign over Israel in Tirzah, two years.

9 And his servant Zimri, captain of half *his* chariots, conspired against him, as he was in Tirzah, drinking himself drunk in the house of Arza † steward of *his* house in Tirzah.

10 And Zimri went in and smote him, and killed him, in the twenty and seventh year of Asa king of Judah, and reigned in his stead.

11 ¶ And it came to pass, when he began to reign, as soon as he sat on his throne, *that* he slew all the house of Baasha: he left him " not one that pisseth against a wall, || neither of his kinsfolks, nor of his friends.

12 Thus did Zimri destroy all the house of Baasha, " according to the word of the LORD, which he spake against Baasha † " by Jehu the prophet,

13 For all the sins of Baasha, and the sins of Elah his son, by which they sinned, and by which they made Israel to sin, in provoking the LORD God of Israel to anger " with their vanities.

14 Now the rest of the acts of Elah, and all that he did, *are* they not written in the book of the chronicles of the kings of Israel?

15 ¶ In the twenty and seventh year of Asa king of Judah did Zimri reign seven days in Tirzah. And the people *were* encamped " against Gibbethon, which *belonged* to the Philistines.

16 And the people *that were* encamped heard say, Zimri hath conspired, and hath also slain the king: wherefore all Israel made Omri, the captain of the host, king over Israel that day in the camp.

17 And Omri went up from Gibbethon, and all Israel with him, and they besieged Tirzah.

18 And it came to pass, when Zimri saw that the city was taken, that he went into the palace of the king's house, and burnt the king's house over him with fire, and died,

19 For his sins which he sinned in doing evil in the sight of the LORD, in walking in the way of Jeroboam, and in his sin which he did, to make Israel to sin.

20 Now the rest of the acts of Zimri, and his treason that he wrought, *are* they not written in the book of the chronicles of the kings of Israel?

21 ¶ Then were the people of Israel divided into two parts: half of the people followed Tibni the son of Ginath, to make him king; and half followed Omri.

22 But the people that followed Omri prevailed against the people that followed Tibni the son of Ginath: so Tibni died, and Omri reigned.

23 In the thirty and *first* year of Asa king of Judah began Omri to reign over

FIGURE 27. Buchanan's annotated copy of the 1769 edition by Blayney.

3:3) had since 1617 been misprinted as 'fleshly tables of the heart', but Blayney restored 'fleshy'. One particularly insightful correction of an error that is almost certainly the fault of the printer rather than the translators is the shift of a comma: 'For in this we grone earnestly, desiring' (1611) is corrected to 'For in this we groan, earnestly desiring' (2 Corinthians 5:2). And, just as Parris corrected an ordinal number, so Blayney substituted 'first' for 'one' (1 Kings 16:23). In the prophetic passage about the wheel in the middle of the wheel, he changed 'they returned not when they went' to the clearer 'they turned not when they went'. He also modernized archaic idioms, so 'was a building' becomes 'was building' (2 Chronicles 16:6). On 'you' and 'ye', Blayney fully implemented the principle that Parris had started to implement.

Blayney prepared a quarto for private reading at the same time as the folio for public reading, but, as he explains in the report to the delegates, the printing of the Folio was so flawed that it had to be done again. In Blayney's view,

> the editor thinks he has just reason to congratulate himself on the opportunity hereby given him of discovering and correcting some few trivial inaccuracies, which in spite of all his vigilance had escaped his notice in the quarto edition. So that the folio edition is rendered by this somewhat the more perfect of the two, and therefore fit to be recommended for a standard copy.

And so it was. His text was clearly an advance on Parris's and, after a decent interval, Cambridge quietly adopted it.

The first editions of Blayney's and Parris's Bibles are now comparatively rare books, because the warehouses of the London booksellers who held the wholesale stock (Thomas Payne for Oxford and Benjamin Dodd for Cambridge) both fell victim to serious fires. Parris's text was destined to fade into scholarly obscurity, but Blayney's set the standard for centuries to come. A comparison of Blayney's text of 1769 with the twenty-first-century British text of the KJV reveals very few changes indeed, apart from a handful of names that have reverted to the spellings of earlier editions. In the Old Testament the only innovation since 1769 has been the change from LORD to 'Lord' in Nehemiah 1:11; in the New Testament the only change has been the introduction of the archaic spelling of 'Zacchæus' (replacing 'Zaccheus'). As Cambridge University is now the queen's printer (having bought Eyre and Spottiswoode, the previous holder of the privilege), and Cambridge uses the Blayney text for both its own and its queen's printer editions, all British editions of the KJV are now identical in the Old and New Testament. In the text of the Apocrypha, however, there is a difference. Since Blayney's edition, four changes have been introduced, of which three have been adopted by both presses: 'Ioribas' has become 'Joribus' (1 Esdras 8:44), 'doth' becomes 'do' in Tobit 4:10 (so treating 'alms' as a plural), and 'generation' has become plural in Ecclesiasticus 4:16. The fourth change, and the one that differentiates the modern texts, relates to the placing of an apostrophe: at Baruch 1:4 the Cambridge and queen's printer texts treat 'king' as a plural, and so print 'the kings' sons'; the Oxford text treats 'king' as a singular, and so prints 'the king's sons'. These are changes that reflect policy, but there have also been corrections of more than 100 printing errors in Blayney's text, of which the most serious was the omission of a clause ('And no craftsman, of whatsoever craft he be, shall be found any more in thee') in Revelation 18:22. A few of Blayney's errors still pop up in modern editions: at Joshua 19:2, for example, Blayney printed 'and Sheba' instead of 'or Sheba', and the misprint has proved to be remarkably difficult to extirpate.

Beyond establishing the text of the modern Bible (a sufficient claim in itself), Blayney's text may have had an influence on the way English is written and printed. In the eighteenth century, nouns were written with initial capital letters (as is still the case with German), so in *Gulliver's Travels* (1726) the Brobdingnagian king denounces the human race as 'the most pernicious Race of odious little Vermin that Nature ever suffered to crawl upon the Surface of the Earth', and Article One of the United States Constitution of 1787 refers to 'the whole Number of free Persons, including those bound to Service for a Term of Years'. Blayney, following Parris, rebelled against this practice, possibly to save space in his double-columned text, and his abandonment of capital letters (except for proper nouns) became standard practice in Bibles. Such was the influence of this edition of the KJV that the practice of capitalizing common nouns disappeared from English. It is true that in the nineteenth century reverential capitals began to appear in nouns and pronouns relating to God, but they never made serious inroads into KJVs, and are no longer in general use. We owe our lower-case common nouns to Blayney's edition of the Bible.

Reception

The origins of the literary adulation of the KJV in the late eighteenth century lie in the religious convictions of the seventeenth century, when the Greek and Hebrew originals were praised for their eloquence and the value of the KJV was judged by its accuracy. The few aesthetic judgements of the period were restricted to the physical book: Thomas Fuller praised the KJV as 'beautifully printed', but made no comment about the beauty of its prose beyond observing that it 'agreeth with the common speech of our country'. Little enthusiasm for the prose is expressed in the post-Restoration period, because the KJV is deemed to be mired in the old-fashioned and often incorrect prose of the early part of the century. The attitude can be clearly discerned in comments about Shakespeare. The diarist John Evelyn, for example, dismissed *Hamlet* as an old play that 'disgusts this refined age'. John Dryden, who insisted that 'the language, wit and conversation of our age are improved and refined above the last', said of Shakespeare that

> it must be allowed to the present age that the tongue in general is so much refined since Shakespeare's time that many of his words and more of his phrases are scarce intelligible. And of those which we understand, some are ungrammatical, others coarse.

In 1731 John Husbands published a collection of poetry (mostly his own) with an enormous introductory essay on 'natural' primitive poetry, of which the Hebrew Bible was his principal example. Such is the literary merit of the Hebrew Bible, he argues, that its beauty can be glimpsed 'under all the disadvantage of an old prose translation'. Just as *Hamlet* can be dismissed as an old play, so the KJV can be waved aside as an 'old prose translation'. Many a twenty-first-century parent will recognize this withering use of 'old'; the KJV had become terribly 'last century'.

The first clear anticipation of the shift in attitude that would occur mid-century came in Jonathan Swift's *A Proposal for Correcting, Improving and Ascertaining the English Tongue* (1712), in which Swift proposed the creation of an English Academy (modelled on the Académie Française) to regulate the English language. Perhaps unsurprisingly for a clergyman, he believed that it was the clergy of the Church of England who had created a model language for the lay community. In this tract he argues that,

> if it were not for the Bible and Common Prayer Book in the vulgar Tongue, we should hardly be able to understand any Thing that was written among us an hundred Years ago: Which is certainly true: For those Books being perpetually read in Churches, have proved a kind of Standard for Language, especially to the common People. And I doubt whether the Alterations since introduced, have added much to the Beauty or Strength of the English Tongue, though they have taken off a great deal from that Simplicity which is one of the greatest Perfections in any Language.... No Translation our Country ever yet produced, hath come up to that of the Old and New Testament: And by the many beautiful Passages...I am persuaded that the Translators of the Bible were Masters of an English Style much fitter for that Work, than any we see in our present Writings, which I take to be owing to the Simplicity that runs through the whole.

Swift wanted to resist linguistic change, and his idea was to use the language of the KJV as a bulwark against linguistic innovation. Such an enterprise was doomed to failure, as such change, like the tide, cannot be halted, but modern readers who shiver at the occurrence of a split infinitive or the misuse of the apostrophe will surely recognize the sentiment. Swift's elevation of the language of the KJV as a model for English may have been futile, but it was a stepping stone on the road to proclaiming the KJV as the greatest work of prose in the English language.

Swift had allies, but the KJV continued to have detractors throughout the century, principally because its language was deemed to be obsolete and uncouth. Matthew Pilkington's *Remarks upon Several Passages of Scripture* (1759), for example, mounted an argument to the effect that the 'improprieties, obscurities and inconsistencies' in the English of the Old Testament reflect lapses in understanding of the Hebrew text on the part of the translators. His examples of obscurities are hard to resist: who can now understand 'In measure when it shooteth forth, thou wilt debate with it: he stayeth his rough wind in the day of the East wind' (Isaiah 27:8) or 'Woe to the women that sew pillows to all armholes, and make kerchiefs upon the head of every stature to hunt souls' (Ezekiel 13:18)? They are both faithful renderings of the Hebrew text, but they are not sufficiently translated to be understood. Similarly, Pilkington's list of obsolete words include many that continue to puzzle readers of the KJV: advisement (1 Chronicles 12:19), bestead (Isaiah 8:21), bewray (Isaiah 16:3), blains (Exodus 9:9), holpen (Isaiah 31:3), purtenance (Exodus 12:9), silverlings (Isaiah 7:23), wist (Luke 2:49), wotteth (Genesis 39:8); others, such as 'aliant' and 'wastness', disappeared in Blayney's modernization of the text.

The culmination of these attacks on the language of the KJV was contained in the introduction and appendices to *A New and Literal Translation of all the Books of the Old and New Testament; with Notes, Critical and Explanatory* (1864), which was a new translation by a self-taught Quaker, Anthony Purver. In 'Axiom II' ('a translation should be well or grammatically expressed in the language it is made in') of his 'Introductory Remarks', Purver attacks the 'obsolete words and uncouth ungrammatical expressions' of the KJV, arguing that the language of the seventeenth century is scarcely intelligible to his generation. In the fourth and fifth of the eight appendices to his introduction, Purver offers a sample of words that are 'barbarous, base, hard, technical, misapplied or new-coined'. The list is a testament to the vicissitudes of the lexical stock of English, in that, while it does include words and forms that would now be regarded as 'scarcely intelligible' (for example, aliant, bewray, marishes, wotteth), it also condemns words and forms that have since returned to everyday usage (for example, amends, ate, banner, confiscation, dismayed, dismissed, seethe, unwittingly). In the event, Purver's was a lonely voice in the wilderness, and both his translation and his strictures on the KJV have been forgotten. He was a remarkable man whose erudition was an easy match for scholars who had enjoyed a conventional education, but the tide had turned, and the chorus of praise for the KJV was, for the time being, sufficiently strong to drown out dissenting voices.

The publication of Blayney's modernized text in 1769 proved to be the event that stilled criticism of the language of the KJV as obsolete. Thereafter, Swift's lonely vision of 1712 re-emerged as a commonplace view, and the KJV came to be regarded as a model of English prose. The headmaster Vicesimus Knox, who is best known for his books on education and conduct, saw the study of literature as a means of promoting taste, manners, and morality. The second edition of his *Essays, Moral and Literary* (1782) contained a new essay 'on the impropriety of publicly adopting a new translation of the Bible', in which Knox acknowledged that the Hebrew text that had been the basis for the KJV had been revised in the light of scholarly investigation. He argued, however, 'that the present translation derives an advantage from its antiquity greatly superior to any which could arise from the correction of its antiquities'. The argument that he advances introduces two points that are still to be heard today. First, he praises the beauty of the KJV and introduces the word 'majestic' to describe its style:

I cannot help thinking that the present translation ought to be retained in our churches for its intrinsic beauty and excellence. We have had one specimen of a new translation of the Bible by a very learned and ingenious Bishop. It is exact and curious, but I will venture to say that it approaches not the majesty, sublimity and fire of the old translation.... That translation abounds with passages exquisitely beautiful and irresistibly transporting. Even where the sense is not very clear, nor the construction of ideas obvious at first sight, the mind is soothed and the ear ravished with the powerful yet unaffected charms of the style.

Second, Knox acknowledges the popular belief that the KJV was divinely inspired: 'Some devout and well-meaning people... profess to believe that our translation was written with the finger of the Almighty, and that to alter a tittle of it is to be guilty of blasphemy.' Such belief is the remote progenitor of the King James Only Movement that emerged in the United States in the 1970s (see Chapter 13).

Knox was headmaster of a boys' school, but he also championed the idea of a literary education for girls. This theme was taken up by Mary Wollstonecraft, whose *Female Reader* (1789) uses the KJV as an important exemplar of 'a pure and simple style'. Wollstonecraft is important for another reason, because she is indicative of the growing separation between religious and literary reverence for the KJV. She had abandoned the Anglicanism of her youth in favour of a heterodox theology devised by herself. The paradox, which was developed in the nineteenth century, was that readers who had abandoned belief in God created substitutes to fit God-shaped holes in their spiritual lives. The reverential language used to describe the works of Shakespeare and the KJV were indicative of a kind of idolatry.

8

⚬⚬⚬⚬

THE NINETEENTH CENTURY

The Challenge to the Monopoly

At the beginning of the nineteenth century, the right to print the King James Version (KJV) in England was still exclusively held by the three privileged publishers: the king's printer, Oxford University Press, and Cambridge University Press. There was, however, growing opposition to monopolies from advocates of free trade. The secular focus of the free trade movement was the Corn Laws, a series of protectionist measures aimed at supporting the agricultural sector. In 1839 a national Anti-Corn Law League was formed, championing the view that the Corn Laws increased the price of 'the poor man's bread'. This view found a religious expression in dissenting circles, where opposition to tariffs and monopolies led in spiritual matters to opposition to the monopoly of the Church of England and advocacy of free trade in Bibles; the latter sentiment fuelled opposition to the monopoly of the privileged publishers. Just as bread should be cheap, so should the bread of life be affordable. In 1860 a divided Parliamentary Select Committee decided by a narrow margin to renew the Bible monopoly in England, but the battle had already been lost in America, where independence had rendered the monopoly meaningless, and in Scotland, where the

Bible monopoly was abolished in 1839. In England the monopoly continues to be renewed (most recently until 2039), but in practice the privileged publishers of the KJV now include HarperCollins, who publish under licence from the Scottish Bible Board but sell Bibles in England as well as in Scotland.

The Text

Blayney's text of 1769 had produced a version of the KJV about which most scholarly readers were content until the mid-nineteenth century, but there was one sector that felt aggrieved: the KJV purists. One such group, which styled itself the 'Committee for the Restoration and Protection of the Authorized Version', consisted of learned dissenting ministers (mostly Congregationalists) led by Thomas Curtis. The group wrote a series of letters to the bishop of London, Charles James Blomfield, and the two universities, and these letters, together with their responses, were published in 1833 as *The Existing Monopoly, an Inadequate Protection of the Authorised Version of Scripture*. The decision to target Blomfield was determined by a century-old order from King George I that 'correctors of the press' responsible for the printing of the Bible 'shall be appointed from time to time by the Archbishop of Canterbury and Bishop of London'; the choice of Blomfield over William Howley, the archbishop of Canterbury (with whom there was a brief exchange), was probably a reflection of Blomfield's standing as a textual scholar of Greek classical texts.

Curtis argued that the text of the Bible 'has developed at least 10,000 critical and intentional departures from King James' version'. The question of which changes are critical is a matter for individual judgement, but there are certainly many thousands of intentional changes to spelling and punctuation, and to the apparatus in the margins and the chapter summaries. In addition to these changes, most of which can be attributed to Parris and Blayney, Curtis identified an alarming number of misprints. At least one of the mistakes in the Blayney text identified by Curtis's group has persisted to the present day, in that the final phrase of Judges 11:19, which in 1611 was correctly given as 'unto my place', was printed in Blayney's text as 'into my place'. The error has been corrected in the *New Cambridge Paragraph Bible* (on which see Chapter 9) published in 2005, but not in standard editions of the KJV. Such casting of stones is, of course, a perilous business: Curtis misprints the reference as Judges 11:9. Curtis argued that the changes that had been wrought upon the text were unauthorized, and that in some cases they broke the original rules. The marginal note on Genesis 36:39 ('after his death was an aristocracy'), for example, was taken to violate the injunction against marginal notes.

Curtis was a vigorous polemicist, and his targets were well chosen. Correspondence with the Cambridge spokesman revealed that the Press was not working from an authoritative text and that the existence of Parris's edition had been forgotten. Enquiries at Oxford produced similarly vague and disconcerting answers. There was a general reliance on Blayney's text, but there was also some unease about the marginal notes and chapter headings in Blayney, so the Oxford Bible of 1817 (reprinted regularly thereafter), sponsored by the Society for the Propagation of Christian Knowledge and edited by George D'Oyly (theologian and polemicist) and Richard Mant (bishop of Down and Connor), had combined Blayney's text with a modernized version of the 1611 marginal notes and chapter headings, to which Mant and D'Oyly added a commentary drawn from the Anglican tradition.

The delegates of Oxford University Press took Curtis's complaints seriously. First, they instructed one of their printers to collate the current edition with the 1611 text; the conclusion drawn from this project was that 'departures from the edition of 1611 are of no importance whatever'. By way of proving the point, the delegates commissioned 'an exact reprint, in roman letter, of the Authorised Version printed in the year 1611', arguing that this was 'the most effectual method of enabling themselves and others to judge how far the complaints were well-founded'. It seems bizarre to have published a Bible to prove a point, but the Bible itself, which was published in 1833, is a wonderful production. Its letter-by-letter exactness even extends to printing inverted letters. The only loss is of artwork in the initials: just as the original black-letter type was replaced by roman, so the original woodcut initials were replaced by bland nineteenth-century letters. It is a corrected version of this edition, with the original initials restored, that the Press is publishing to mark the quatercentenary in 2011.

Curtis was a relentless lobbyist, and his campaign was in part successful. He brought the two university presses together and persuaded them that higher production values were essential if Bibles were to be printed accurately. He failed, however, to rein-state an early text, and the unintentional result of his labours was the adoption of a corrected version of Blayney's Bible as the standard British text.

The American Text

Another unintended effect of Curtis's lobbying was the creation of a separate American text of the KJV. Until the outbreak of the Revolutionary War, English-languages Bibles were all KJVs imported from Britain. The trade embargo imposed on the rebellious colonists by the British government, however, cut off the supply of Bibles, and so gave the impetus to the printing of Bibles in America. First off the mark was Robert Aitken, a Scottish bookbinder, printer, and publisher who had emigrated in 1771 from Paisley to Philadelphia. Aitken issued four editions of the KJV New Testament between 1777 and 1781, and in 1782 he published America's first complete Bible in English. Printing standards were high, which drove up the price, and the return of the supply of imported Bibles meant that the Aitken Bibles did not sell, and the edition was a financial failure, despite Congressional approval and the endorsement of General George Washington. The edition is now rare, and copies are now sold for more than $150,000.

Thereafter KJVs imported from England dominated the market. This pattern changed, however, when the American Bible Society (ABS, founded in 1816), the mightiest force in American Bible publishing, decided to prepare its own text. From the outset members of the ABS were concerned about the textual accuracy of the Bibles that it was distributing, and Curtis's pamphlet fuelled such anxieties. In 1847 the ABS decided to address the problem by creating a standard American text of the KJV. The process proved to be protracted. An edition was published (in a large quarto format) in 1856. This edition proved to be controversial, in part because of its chapter summaries, and in due course new committees were convened to consider revisions and publish yet another standard text.

There is a fascinating account of the process whereby the ABS attempted to stabilize the text in its *Report on the History and Recent Collation of the English Version of the Bible, Presented by the*

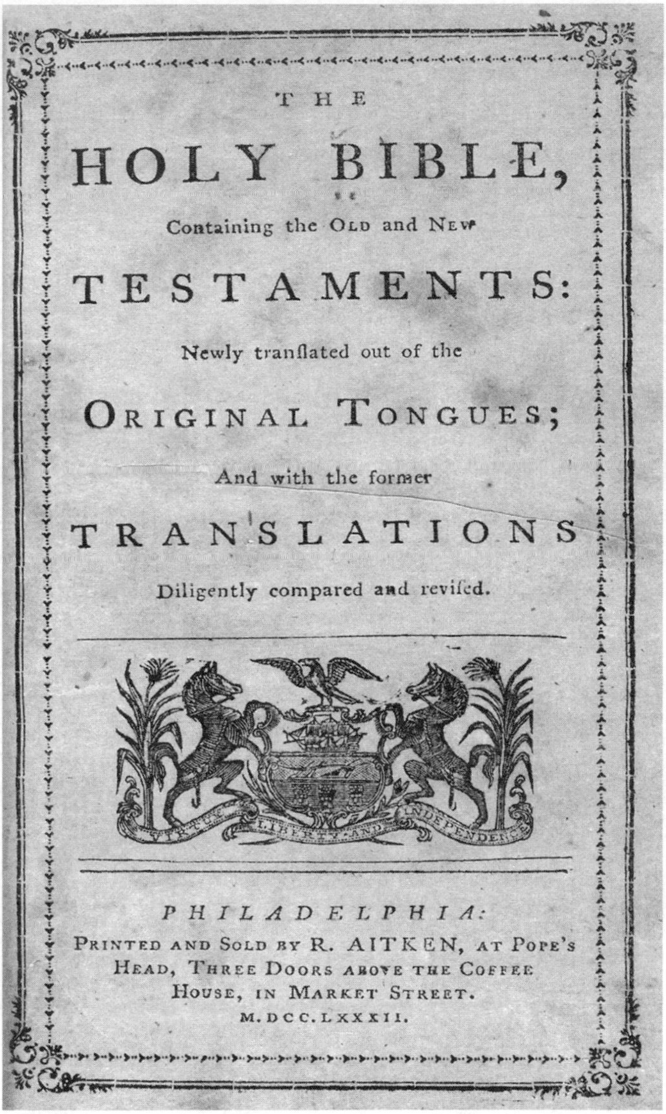

THE

HOLY BIBLE,

Containing the Old and New

TESTAMENTS:

Newly tranſlated out of the

ORIGINAL TONGUES;

And with the former

TRANSLATIONS

Diligently compared and reviſed.

VIRTUE LIBERTY AND INDEPENDENCE

PHILADELPHIA:

Printed and Sold by R. AITKEN, at Pope's Head, Three Doors above the Coffee House, in Market Street.

M.DCC.LXXXII.

FIGURE 28. Title page from the first American edition of the complete King James Version, published by Robert Aitken in 1782.

Committee on Versions to the Board of Managers of the American Bible Society (New York, 1851). The scholarly foundation of the process was a collation of six KJVs: its own earlier edition, the editions of Oxford and Cambridge, the editions of the king's printers in London and Edinburgh, and the text of 1611. The collation, which was undertaken by a Presbyterian minister called James McLane, produced almost 24,000 variations in the texts, including punctuation but excluding apparatus in the margins and chapter summaries. At the end of their *Report* the members of the Committee declared, in defiance of the discrepancies that they had identified, that 'the English Bible, as left by the translators, has come down to us unaltered in respect of its text, except in the changes of orthography which the whole English language has undergone'. Apart from orthography (that is, spelling) and misprints, they concluded, 'the text of our present Bibles remains unchanged, and is without variation from the original copy as left by the translators'.

Were members of the Committee asleep on the job? Or perhaps not of the requisite calibre? It is true that they did not bring to the task the daunting learning of the American committees of the Revised Version assembled by Philip Schaff in 1871 (see Chapter 11), but they were competent students of the Bible, and the group included Edward Robinson, the most distinguished biblical scholar of his generation. The difficulty lay not in the individuals involved, but in the methodology with which they discharged their task. The Oxford text was Blayney's, and the other nineteenth-century British texts were in varying degrees derivatives of Blayney's text. The 1611 text was accorded no special authority, so, when the principle that 'the uniform usage of any three of the copies shall be followed' was applied, the 1611 text was outvoted by Blayney and its clones. The variations between the texts, in the understanding of the Committee, could be attributed to printing errors, and its task was to eliminate those errors by the process of collation.

The result is a text that broadly reflects Blayney's and its cousins, but with important differences occasioned by three factors: scholarly scruple, the impetus to consistency, and the desire to use modern spelling. In the case of the first, the Committee acknowledges a few changes, all centuries-old textual cruces, that constitute a reversion to the 1611 text, so setting aside the principle of following the consensus: in Joshua 19:2, for example, the ABS text follows 1611 in reading 'or Sheba' instead of 'and Sheba'; in Ruth 3:15, ABS reads 'he went' over 'she went', so preferring the literal sense to the contextual sense (it was Ruth who went, not Boaz); in Song of Solomon 2:7, ABS reads 'nor awake my love, till he please' (instead of 'she please'), this time preferring the contextual sense to the literal (the Hebrew verb is feminine). The pursuit of consistency led to a regularization of indefinite articles ('a' and 'an'), though some anomalies remain, especially in the vexed area of a definite article before a word beginning with 'h': in Genesis 25:25 Esau has skin 'like an hairy garment', but in Genesis 27:11 he is said to be 'a hairy man'. The third intention, to use modern spelling, is the most obvious difference between the British and American texts of the KJV, because the former uses eighteenth-century spelling and the latter nineteenth-century spelling, so in the ABS text 'astonied' becomes 'astonished', 'asswaged' becomes 'assuaged', 'ought' becomes 'aught', 'aul' becomes 'awl', and 'bason' becomes 'basin'. The American text of the KJV is altogether more modern than its British cousin.

The Mormon Version

The most audacious version of the KJV in America was the work of Joseph Smith, the founder of the Church of Jesus Christ of Latter-Day Saints, which is also known as the Mormon Church; this version is commonly known as the Joseph Smith Translation or the Inspired Version. Although commonly referred to as a translation, Smith's version is a KJV with interpolations, revisions, and paraphrases that were, as he explained, divinely inspired. Smith completed the work before his murder in 1844, but it remained unpublished even after Brigham Young had led his followers from Manchester (New York State) to Salt Lake City (Utah). In 1866 Smith's widow gave the manuscripts to the Reorganized Church of Jesus Christ of Latter-Day Saints (now known as the Community of Christ), which published it the following year. The Community of Christ recognizes the Inspired Version as a canonical text, but the Church of Latter-Day Saints does not, instead according it the status of an enlightened commentary; some 600 of the altered or additional verses are included as notes in the Saints' edition of the KJV. More recently, the Latter-Day Saints collaborated with the Community of Christ on *Joseph Smith's New Translation of the Bible: Original Manuscripts* (2004), which contains all 3,410 new or altered verses. In the view of those who hold the Inspired Bible to be canonical, its contents are a divinely inspired restoration of the Bible to its original content and meaning; new material includes content that was deleted by scribes and commentary by Prophet Smith. Here, for example, is the beginning of Genesis in the Inspired Version:

And it came to pass, that the Lord spake unto Moses, saying, Behold, I reveal unto you concerning this heaven and this earth; write the words which I speak. I am the Beginning and the End; the Almighty God. By mine Only Begotten I created these things. Yea, in the beginning I created the heaven, and the earth upon which thou standest. And the earth was without form, and void; and I caused darkness to come up upon the face of the deep. And my Spirit moved upon the face of the waters, for I am God. And I, God, said, Let there be light, and there was light.

The KJV account of the creation lies at the heart of the passage, which is supplemented by new material that draws on the distinctive idiom of the KJV (for example, 'and it came to pass').

The Mormon Version of the KJV has not exercised significant influence beyond adherents of its various branches, but it has served to maintain the centrality of the KJV in a strand of the Christian faith that has millions of adherents.

Distribution

The nineteenth century saw the establishment of Bible societies that aspired to place a Bible in the hands of as many people as possible. The first Bible society in the English-speaking world was the British and Foreign Bible Society (BFBS), which was formed in London in March 1804. Part of its purpose was to supply Bibles in a range of languages (initially Welsh), but it also distributed KJVs, which at that stage still included the Apocrypha. The BFBS founded branches (called auxiliaries) elsewhere in Britain and abroad. In America the Pennsylvania Bible Society was founded only four years later, in 1808, and the Chicago Bible Society was formed in 1840.

In the first instance the Bible societies were truly non-denominational, and represented a broader constituency than is the case now, because they have long been identified with evangelical Protestantism (though the Chicago Bible Society also works through the Roman Catholic and Orthodox churches). In the early years the English-language Bibles distributed by the societies were KJVs, which then included the Apocrypha. In a series of fissures occasioned by the presence of the Apocrypha, many of the auxiliaries broke away and formed independent Bible societies. In the case of Scotland, the Glasgow and Edinburgh societies consolidated to form the Scottish Bible Society; the case of the American Bible Society is more complex, in that it eventually commissioned its own edition of the Apocrypha, but, despite its very considerable merits (it is better edited than its British counterpart), it never achieved much visibility, because the ABS became more evangelical. When the BFBS stopped printing the Apocrypha in 1826, the decision led to the secession of the European Bible societies. The presence of a small number of unitarians among the evangelical officers of the BFBS alienated some members, and in 1831 some 2,000 evangelical trinitarians gathered in London and founded the Trinitarian Bible Society. It is this society that has remained faithful to the KJV, though it is careful to point out that its advocacy is based on the conviction that the KJV is the best translation, a position quite distinct from that of advocates of the view that the KJV is in some sense an inspired translation.

The Roman Catholic Church became increasingly uneasy about these societies, and in 1844 Pope Gregory XVI issued an encyclical on Bible societies, which, he asserted, were 'concerned primarily that the reader becomes accustomed to judging for himself the meaning of the books of Scripture, to scorning divine tradition preserved by the Catholic Church in the teaching of the Fathers, and to repudiating the very authority of the Church'; this was to remain the position of the Catholic Church until 1965, when Pope Paul VI promulgated the constitutional document *Dei Verbum* ('the Word of God'), which cautiously proposed an accord with the Protestant Bible societies.

In the intervening century the societies had become ever more identified with evangelical Protestantism. They distributed millions of Bibles in a large number of languages, but the central strand of their work was the distribution of millions of KJVs. It was in this period that the KJV became the most printed book in history. In the fifty years from its foundation to 1854, for example, the BFBS (which was the biggest customer of the privileged presses) distributed 28,000,000 Bibles; by 1884 the number had risen to more than 100,000,000. The work of the Bible societies was supplemented by the commercial activities of Bible publishers, some of which sold Bibles through door-to-door salesmen; unlike many such salesmen, sellers of Bibles were welcomed into homes. Some of the Bibles that they sold were for individual reading and, if suitably bound, for carrying to church, a habit that lives on in evangelical circles. Others were large Bibles intended for use in family devotions and for the recording of family events. The latter purpose was often served by inserted pages (between the testaments or at the beginning) headed 'Births', 'Marriages', and 'Deaths' or simply 'Our Family'; such Bibles rightly became prized possessions.

Illustrated Bibles

In the early years of printing, woodcuts and (at a later stage) copperplate engravings were used to illustrate books, including

Bibles. As early as 1478, two Bibles printed in Cologne contained more than 100 woodcut illustrations. This tradition continued in the early years of the Reformation. The publication in sections of Martin Luther's translation (1522–34) utilized the talents of several graphic artists, including Lucas Cranach the younger, whose designs reflect a High Renaissance style. The Swiss printing centres, Basle and Zurich, produced illustrated Bibles, the illustrators of which included Hans Holbein the younger. His best-known Bible illustrations appeared in a picture Bible prepared by Johannes Treschel, the *Historiarum veteris testamenti icones* (Lyons, 1538). Holbein's woodcuts were also used in or influenced illustrations of English translations by William Tyndale and Miles Coverdale, as well as the Great Bible in the 1530s and 1540s. Thereafter, however, book illustration (including Bible illustration) largely ceased, living on only in title pages.

In the centuries that followed, book illustration was a rare exception to a continuous expanse of print, though it survived in emblem books, popular literature, and children's books. With few exceptions (which include John Medina's engravings for the 1688 edition of John Milton's *Paradise Lost*), books with a religious dimension were not illustrated. Bibles were no exception to this rule. The 1611 editions of the KJV had illustrated preliminary matter (notably the title pages and genealogies), but the text was not interrupted by illustrations.

Gradually the preliminary matter disappeared from editions of the KJV, which became a book consisting entirely of words. One reason for this phenomenon is that the KJV is a Protestant Bible, and Protestantism shares with Judaism and Sunni Islam an iconoclastic impulse, a mistrust of images; the art of Catholic and Orthodox Christianity (and of Shi'a Islam) shows few such inhibitions. In the Protestant tradition there is a particular aversion to divine images, which, as in the case of the golden calf of Exodus, raise the spectre of idolatry, a sin associated by many Protestants with images in Catholic churches.

The overturning of the view began with the work of Benjamin West, a celebrated American artist in England (now remembered for the *Death of General Wolfe*). In 1779 West was commissioned by George III to paint thirty-six scenes on the *History of Revealed Religion* for St George's Chapel at Windsor Castle. In the event, the project was never completed, and the canvasses were never hung in the chapel, but West completed eighteen canvasses (notably the *Last Supper*, now in the Tate Britain in London). The commission excluded the depiction of saints and the Virgin to avoid any accusation of popery, but nonetheless overturned the prohibition against pictorial images in English churches.

In the nineteenth century illustrated Bibles began to appear. In England, John Kitto produced *The Pictorial Bible*, which was in the first instance published anonymously in monthly parts and subsequently published in three volumes (1836–8). The subtitle (*The Old and New Testaments According to Authorized Versions. Illustrated with Steel Engravings and Woodcuts Representing Landscape Scenes, and Subjects of Natural History, Costume and Antiquities*) reassures the reader that there will be no pictures that might be considered idolatrous.

The subsequent history of one copy of this Bible, however, takes the process of illustration to an altogether higher level. The Bible in question is an edition of Kitto's Bible illustrated by the process variously known as 'grangerizing' and 'extra-illustration'; the eponym of the former term was James Granger, an English clergyman who in 1769 had published a biographical history of

We are disposed to think that it rather describes such a head-dress as is still seen among the Arabian females. It consists of a large handkerchief, or shawl, or piece of linen or cotton (usually black, but in some parts white, or of some dark colour), which, after covering the head, falls some way down the back; the corners being brought round in front, to cover the throat and bosom; and generally the lower part of the face to the tip of the nose; being in fact the customary veil of the class of women by whom it is used. As shown in our cut, it is not unlike what our translators must have understood to have been intended by the word which they translate "wimples" in the next verse.

'Muffler.' Lady of Modern Egypt, showing the common Face-Veil, with one form of the walking wrapper ("Wimple") mentioned in v. 24.

"Wimple." Another form of the walking wrapper mentioned under v. 24.

Woman Wearing the Tob, mentioned in the note on "Wimples."

"Hoods," v. 23. Hood-Veil of an Arab Female.

"*Vails*."—We believe this to be the head-veil which the ladies of Western Asia and Egypt usually wear within-doors. It is usually a long strip of white muslin, embroidered with threads of coloured silk and gold; or of coloured crape, ornamented with gold thread, lama, and spangles. It rests upon the head, and falls down the back, forming

746

FIGURE 29. Page illustrating Isaiah 3 taken from John Kitto's *Pictoral Bible*, 1835.

England 'adapted to a methodological catalogue of engraved British heads'. The left-hand pages in this volume were left blank with the intention that they should be used for readers' notes, but what happened in practice was that readers glued engravings from their own collections onto the blank pages; this is the practice known as 'grangerizing', even though Granger himself never grangerized a book.

The most famous of grangerized books is known somewhat inaccurately as the Kitto Bible; it is owned by the Huntington Museum in California. The core of the Bible is an unidentified edition of Kitto's Bible, probably published in about 1850. That Bible was published in three volumes, but the extra-illustrated version consists of sixty large volumes; it is the world's largest Bible. The leaves of Kitto's Bible are interspersed with a collection of some 30,000 engravings, woodcuts, drawings, watercolours, and printed leaves from early Bibles; the collection includes woodcuts by Dürer, etchings by Rembrandt, and engravings by William Blake. The engravings are an astonishingly comprehensive set of biblical illustrations (some scenes, such as the expulsion from Eden, are represented by more than fifty prints), one of the largest now in America. The compiler was one 'J. Gibbs', whose name is on the printed title page of each volume. Gibbs has recently been securely identified as James Gibbs, a London bookbinder and print-seller; he must have spent at least thirty years assembling the Bible. In 1872 the set passed through the hands of the bookseller J. W. Bouton to Theodore Irwin of Oswego, New York; Irwin continued to enrich the Bible, notably by adding William Blake's watercolour painting of *The Conversion of Saul* to volume 86. Irwin sold his library to J. Pierpont Morgan, but retained the Kitto Bible; his son eventually sold it to Henry Huntington.

The precise purpose of the Kitto Bible is not clear, but it was certainly more than a mechanism for collecting art. At its heart is the KJV. Gibbs often underlined the verses that are illustrated in the interleaved pages, and used the illustrations to connect related biblical passages. The KJV was used as a way of organizing the art, but it also seems to be the case that the art was used as a way of reading the KJV. The extra-illustrated Kitto Bible exists in only one copy, so, although it remains the world's greatest illustrated Bible, it is essentially a private Bible. Its counterpart in the public realm is *Harper's Illuminated Bible*.

In America a precedent for illustrations in serious books had been set by the publication of John James Audubon's *The Birds of America* (4 vols, 1827–38), which was copiously illustrated by sumptuous aquatinted and hand-coloured plates. In the popular market the most important publisher was Harper Brothers of New York, which published both magazines (notably the superbly illustrated *Harper's Weekly* and *Harper's Bazar*, now spelt *Bazaar*) and books. It was this company that published *Harper's Illuminated Bible* in New York in 1846. The text of the KJV was lavishly illustrated with more than 1,400 wood-engravings, which had been designed by John Gadsby Chapman, the American artist who is now best known for the fine painting of the *Baptism of Pocahontas* in the Rotunda of the Capitol in Washington, DC. The style is indebted to the religious paintings of Benjamin West.

Harper's Illuminated Bible is one of the most important Bibles to have been printed in America. There are more than 1,000 floriated initials, each of which has a different design: there are, for example, 353 different engravings of the letter 'A'. There are also 185 large illustrations (approximately 5 inches × 7 inches). The

THE PARABLE OF ST. LUKE. THE GOOD SAMARITAN.

THE GOOD SAMARITAN.

kings have desired to see those things which
ye see, and have not seen *them;* and to hear
those things which ye hear, and have not
heard *them.*
25 ¶ And behold, a certain lawyer stood
up, and tempted him, saying, [i]Master, what
shall I do to inherit eternal life?
26 He said unto him, What is written in
the law? how readest thou?
27 And he answering, said, [k]Thou shalt love
the Lord thy God with all thy heart, and
with all thy soul, and with all thy strength,
and with all thy mind; and [l]thy neighbour
as thyself.
28 And he said unto him, Thou hast answered right: this do, and [m]thou shalt live.
29 But he, willing to [n]justify himself, said
unto Jesus, And who is my neighbour?
30 And Jesus answering, said, A certain
man went down from Jerusalem to Jericho,
and fell among thieves, which stripped him
of his raiment, and wounded *him,* and departed, leaving *him* half dead.
31 And by chance there came down a certain priest that way; and when he saw him,
[o]he passed by on the other side.
32 And likewise a Levite, when he was at
the place, came and looked *on him,* and passed by on the other side.
33 But a certain [p]Samaritan, as he journey-
ed, came where he was: and when he saw
him, he had compassion *on him,*

A.D. 32.

i Matt. 19, 16, & 22, 35.

k Deut. 6, 5.

l Lev. 19, 18.

m Lev. 18, 5. Neh. 9, 29. Ezek. 20, 11, 13, 21. Rom. 10, 5.

n ch. 16, 15.

o Ps. 38, 11.

p John 4, 9

‖ See Matt. 20, 2.

q John 11, 1, & 12, 2, 3.

r 1 Cor 7, 32, &c.

s chap. 8, 35. Acts 22, 3

34 And went to *him,* and bound up his
wounds, pouring in oil and wine, and set him
on his own beast, and brought him to an inn,
and took care of him.
35 And on the morrow, when he departed,
he took out two ‖pence, and gave *them* to
the host, and said unto him, Take care of
him: and whatsoever thou spendest more,
when I come again, I will repay thee.
36 Which now of these three, thinkest
thou, was neighbour unto him that fell among
the thieves?
37 And he said, He that shewed mercy on
him. Then said Jesus unto him, Go, and do
thou likewise.
38 ¶ Now it came to pass, as they went,
that he entered into a certain village: and a
certain woman, named [q]Martha, received him
into her house.
39 And she had a sister called Mary,
[r]which also [s]sat at Jesus' feet, and heard his
word.
40 But Martha was
cumbered about much
serving, and came to
him, and said, Lord,
dost thou not care
that my sister hath
left me to serve alone?
bid her therefore that
she help me.
41 And Jesus an-

72

FIGURE 30. The Parable of the Good Samaritan taken from *Harper's Illuminated Bible*, 1846.

quality of the book is high, thanks in large part to the skill of the engraver, Joseph Alexander Adams, who in this project was the first engraver in America to use the electrotype process from woodcut engravings. The Bible was expensive to produce (Adams, for example, was paid $60,000), so it was sold, often by street hawkers, in fifty-four monthly sections for 25 cents each; the return on each section helped to finance the next. Some 50,000 copies were printed each month, but only about 100 complete sets are known to have survived.

In England, the Methodist publisher John Cassell produced a four-volume Bible sold as *Cassell's Illustrated Family Bible* (1859–63), again using the text of the KJV; this edition successfully circumvented the monopoly enjoyed by the privileged publishers. The text was lavishly illustrated and printed in a variety of formats, and was sold in parts costing as little as a penny. On the back of its success in England Cassell opened an office in the United States, where sales were also huge. Installments sold at the rate of 300,000 a week, and bound volumes sold for many years thereafter. When this project was securely launched, Cassell entered another sector of the market by buying the English-language rights to Gustave Doré's illustrated French translation of the Vulgate, which was the finest of nineteenth-century illustrated Bibles.

Gustave Doré was a French illustrator, painter and sculptor who set himself the task of illustrating the masterpieces of world literature, including English works such as Milton's *Paradise Lost* and Poe's *The Raven*. Cassell produced a folio edition of the KJV with Doré's illustrations, published in parts from 1866 to 1870; in Britain the sixty-four parts were sold for 4 shillings each, and in America the thirty parts were sold for $2 each. Smaller spin-offs from this large and expensive edition were soon published, and Doré's illustrations became immensely popular. In the early 1880s a selection of the 240 illustrations was sold without a biblical text as *The Doré Bible Gallery*. An exhibition of the *Doré Gallery Collection* held in 1896 at the Art Institute of Chicago attracted more than 1.5 million visitors in nine months. Perhaps the best-known of these illustrations is *The Deluge*, which depicts a family climbing onto a rock (already occupied by a tiger and its cubs) in a futile attempt to save themselves from the rising waters. The father has placed four of his children on the rock, and a fifth floats lifeless in the water. In his muscular arm he holds his wife above the waters. What is most striking for a modern viewer imbued with the notion that Victorians were prudish is that the figures are naked and that the body of the mother is displayed in a pose that emphasizes her youthful figure. The illustration is an image of divine wrath, but a less savoury part of its appeal seems to lie in sexual titillation. The same illustration was used in *The Child's Bible* of 1870, where it perhaps induced fear, even horror.

Reception

The nineteenth century was the last great age of learning, or (more precisely) the last age of great learning. James Murray (editor of the *Oxford English Dictionary*), for example, had left school at 14, but his attainments in twenty-five languages included an ability to read Hebrew, Greek, and Syriac at sight and a modest compe-tence in Aramaic, Arabic, and Coptic; when he moved to Oxford there was a plan for him to take the first university post that fell vacant, in any subject (the first suggestion was a professorship of botany). Murray was one of many Victorian autodidacts who

THE DELUGE.

FIGURE 31. Gustave Doré's *The Deluge.*

learned the biblical languages: the atheist Charles Bradlaugh, founder of the National Secular Society, taught himself Hebrew, and the prison writings of the Chartist Thomas Cooper included a book on how to learn Hebrew. Such competence was also relatively common among those who had attended a good school: at

Christ's Hospital (the 'Bluecoat School'), for example, the generation of Coleridge, Lamb, and Leigh Hunt all learned Hebrew as well as Greek and Latin. Not everyone was educated (universal education awaited an Education Act of 1870, which ensured provision for all children aged 5–12, and another of 1880, which made attendance compulsory to the age of 10), but those who were well educated knew far more than their twenty-first-century counterparts, in part because bodies of knowledge from Greek verbs to Latin plant names were drilled into them. Debates about translations of the Bible were therefore much better informed than in our own monolingual age, and advances in textual scholarship with respect to the Greek and Hebrew texts were a subject of more general debate than is the case now; similarly, the burgeoning knowledge of the Holy Land in antiquity—flora and fauna, clothing and customs—was a subject of popular as well as academic interest, because it facilitated a greater understanding of the Bible. Those who faulted the KJV did so on the grounds that it did not reflect these new understandings.

An essay called 'Protestantism' published by the English writer Thomas de Quincey in 1847 is a good example. In the course of a complex argument about the limits of translation and precise nature of biblical inspiration, De Quincey argues that neither Catholicism nor Protestantism is free of idolatry.

> We Protestants charge upon…the Roman Catholics *Mariolatry*; they pay undue honours, say we, to the Virgin. They, in return, charge upon us *Bibliolatry*, or a superstitious allegiance—an idolatrous homage—to the words, to the syllables, and to the very punctuation of the Bible. They, according to *us*, deify a woman; and we, according to *them*, deify an arrangement of printer's types.

De Quincey's censure of the 'veneration' of the Bible (a word chosen for its pejorative Catholic associations) is focused on idolatrous attitudes to the KJV. He is uncomfortable with any sort of idolatry, but adamant that a translation, however competent, is only an approximation. He describes the claim that 'every idea and word which exists, or has existed, for any nation, ancient or modern, must have a direct interchangeable equivalent in all other languages' as delusory, and so concludes that 'Bibliolatry depends on ignorance of Hebrew and Greek'; in a nineteenth-century context, that was a seriously insulting remark.

Such attitudes do not imply that the KJV did not have the standing of a sacred book, but in educated circles the grounds on which it was so regarded were increasingly literary rather than scholarly. The KJV may not have reflected current scholarly understandings, but it was increasing regarded as the high-water mark of the English language. It was in this period that readers began to speak of the 'majesty' of the KJV, and of its cadences. The rise of such epithets relates in part to the shift in reading practices in the intervening centuries. In the sixteenth century, being able to read without moving the lips was uncommon. In the eighteenth century, silent reading moved from the preserve of the few to a widespread phenomenon, and by the nineteenth century it was the norm; then, as now, reading aloud was associated with children learning to read. Writing reflected this new reality, in that poetry, which had long been read aloud, was in increasing measure replaced by the new genre of the novel, which was meant to be read silently. The KJV was written to be read aloud in churches and homes, and so has rhythms appropriate to that mode of reading; that is why, to a modern ear (and a nineteenth-century ear), it sounds more like poetry than like the prose of a novel.

The standing of the KJV as the supreme work of English prose became a Victorian commonplace. Thomas Babington Macaulay famously declared that, 'if everything else in our language should perish', the KJV 'would alone suffice to show the whole extent of its beauty and power'. The sentiment is uttered with such epigrammatic power that it seems ungracious to point out that it is not true, because, for all its beauty and power, the vocabulary and grammatical range of the KJV are limited, for the simple reason that the translators aspired to a clear and consistent translation. Indeed, one of the glories of Macaulay's prose is his masterful deployment of the subordinate clause, which is not a feature of the KJV.

Two of the clearest examples of the separation of literary value from religious truth come from a Victorian atheist and a Victorian Catholic. The atheist was Thomas Huxley (who coined the term 'agnostic' to describe his disbelief) and the Catholic was Frederick William Faber, a convert from the Anglican priesthood. Huxley's comments are contained in an essay of 1870 on the subject of religious teaching in schools. The KJV clearly posed a challenge. He concludes, however, that he is 'in favour of reading the Bible, with such grammatical, geographical, and historical explanations by a lay-teacher as may be needful, with rigid exclusion of any further theological teaching than that contained in the Bible itself'. Huxley's reasons for this conclusion are a hymn of praise for the KJV. 'Consider', he says, that

> for three centuries, this book has been woven into all that is best and noblest in English history; that it has become the national epic of Britain, and is as familiar to noble and simple, from John-o'Groats House to Land's End, as Dante and

Tasso once were to the Italians; that it is written in the noblest and purest English, and abounds in exquisite beauties of mere literary form; and finally, that it forbids the veriest hind who never left his village to be ignorant of the existence of other countries and other civilisations, and of a great past, stretching back to the furthest limits of the oldest nations in the world.

These are the words of a man whose reading of the KJV as a child had marked him forever:

> some of the pleasantest recollections of my childhood are connected with the voluntary study of an ancient Bible which belonged to my grandmother. There were splendid pictures in it, to be sure; but I recollect little or nothing about them save a portrait of the high priest in his vestments. What come vividly back on my mind are remembrances of my delight in the histories of Joseph and of David; and of my keen appreciation of the chivalrous kindness of Abraham in his dealing with Lot. Like a sudden flash there returns back upon me, my utter scorn of the pettifogging meanness of Jacob, and my sympathetic grief over the heartbreaking lamentation of the cheated Esau, 'Hast thou not a blessing for me also, O my father?' And I see, as in a cloud, pictures of the grand phantas-magoria of the Book of Revelation.
>
> I enumerate, as they issue, the childish impressions which come crowding out of the pigeon-holes in my brain, in which they have lain almost undisturbed for forty years. I prize them as an evidence that a child of five or six years old, left to his own devices, may be deeply interested in the Bible, and draw sound moral sustenance from it. And I rejoice that I was left to deal with the Bible alone; for if I had had some theological 'explainer' at my side, he might have tried, as such do, to lessen my indignation against Jacob, and thereby have warped my

moral sense for ever; while the great apocalyptic spectacle of the ultimate triumph of right and justice might have been turned to the base purposes of a pious lampooner of the Papacy.

Beneath the anti-Christian polemic there runs a strong current of passion for the KJV, a passion that includes its ability to capture the moral imagination of a child.

The similarly adulatory praise of Frederick William Faber became as well known (and oft-quoted) as that of Huxley, and for the same reason: they were deemed to demonstrate that someone who had abjured Protestantism could still feel the power of the KJV. In an essay of 1853 Faber argued that the beauty of the KJV had bound Britain to the heresy of Protestantism:

> Who will say that the uncommon beauty and marvellous English of the Protestant Bible is not one of the great strongholds of heresy in this country? It lives on in the ear like a music that can never be forgotten, like the sound of church bells which the convert hardly knows how he can forgo. Its felicities seem often to be things rather than mere words. It is part of the national mind and the anchor of the national seriousness. Nay, it is worshipped with a positive idolatry, in extenuation of whose grotesque fanaticism its intrinsic beauty pleads availingly with the man of letters and the scholar. The memory of the dead passes into it. The potent traditions of childhood are stereotyped in its verses. The power of all the griefs and trials of a man is hidden beneath its words. It is the representative of his best moments, and all that there has been about him of soft, and gentle, and pure, and penitent, and good, speaks to him forever out of his English Bible. It is his sacred thing which doubt never dimmed and controversy never soiled. It has been to him all along as the silent, but o

how intelligible voice of his guardian angel; and in the length and breadth of the land there is not a Protestant, with one spark of religiousness about him, whose spiritual biography is not in his Saxon Bible. And all this is an unhallowed power!

More than 150 years later, Faber's words still have the power to move, despite the fact that he is decrying as unhallowed the power of the KJV to enter the inner life of its readers. Seldom has a combatant in the confessional wars of Christianity so revered his enemy.

In the course of the nineteenth century some admirers of the English Bible stepped beyond the easy assertion that the KJV was inspirational to the more extreme view that it was inspired. Theologians developed a taxonomy of inspiration, which could be verbal, plenary, moral, or dynamic. Verbal inspiration is the belief that every word was dictated by God; plenary inspiration is the idea that the collective meaning of the words is infallibly true; moral inspiration is the view that the moral and religious teaching of the Bible is true, but that the words are no more than human conveyors of divine truth; dynamic inspiration is the belief that the human writers were endowed with divine authority but that the words were not dictated mechanically. The argument was for the most part conducted with reference to the Hebrew and Greek texts, but a small band of enthusiasts made claims that anticipated those of the King James Only Movement of the late twentieth century (see Chapter 13). With respect to the KJV, some advocates of inspiration argued that each word of the translation contained the word of God, while others argued that each word was the word of God. The former view implies that each English word contains within it a divine meaning that transcends the limitations of language, and the latter implies that God had in some sense communicated the English of the KJV to the translators.

Advocates of the view that the KJV is inspired noted that the sessions of the Jacobean translators had begun with prayer for divine guidance, and argued that that guidance had been given. Some also argued that the translators had been chosen by God. The cleric and classical scholar James Scholefield, who advocated the revision of the Bible, nonetheless asserted that the translators were 'raised up by the providence of God and endowed by His Spirit to achieve for England her greatest blessing in the authorised version of the Scriptures'. Those words were published in 1832, and regularly republished. Twenty years later, across the Atlantic, the clergyman Alexander Wilson McClure published *The Translators Revived: A Biographical Memoir of the Authors of the English Version of the Holy Bible* (1853), a pioneering study of the original translators in which he cautiously moves in the direction of an assertion that the translators were inspired. He insists that the KJV, 'though not absolutely perfect, nor incapable of amendment in detached places, is yet so well done, that the Christian public will not endure to have it tampered with'. He nonetheless feels 'constrained to claim for the good men who made it the highest measure of divine aid short of plenary inspiration itself', carefully insisting that the translators were not 'inspired in the same sense as were the prophets and apostles, and other "holy men of old", who "were moved by the Holy Ghost" in drawing up the original documents of the Christian faith'. Despite this insistence on a distinction between the inspiration of the writers of the original Scriptures and the writers of the KJV, McClure goes on to elide the distinction:

we hold that the Translators enjoyed the highest degree of that special guidance which is ever granted to God's true servants in exegencies of deep concernment to his kingdom on earth. Such special succors and spiritual assistances are always vouchsafed, where there is a like union of piety, of prayers, and of pains, to effect an object of such incalculable importance to the Church of the living God. The necessity of a supernatural revelation to man of the divine will, has often been argued in favor of the extreme probability that such a revelation has been made. A like necessity, and one nearly as pressing, might be argued in favor of the belief, that this most important of all the versions of God's revealed will must have been made under his peculiar guidance, and his provident eye. And the manner in which that version has met the wants of the most free and intelligent nations in the old world and the new, may well confirm us in the persuasion, that the same illuminating Spirit which indited the original Scriptures, was imparted in rich grace to aid and guard the preparation of the English version.

Such conflation was not unusual. Another example would be the classical scholar Benjamin Jowett, a liberal Christian from an evangelical background, who is reported to have said that those who prepared the Revised Version (on which see Chapter 11) had 'forgotten that, in a certain sense, the Authorised Version is more inspired than the original'. We cannot lean too heavily on this utterance, partly because it is reported speech, but also because 'in a certain sense' enters an undisclosed qualification and because the tone verges on the playful. As with McClure, however, the gesture towards the notion that the KJV was inspired is not a theological assertion, but rather a measure of the reverence with which it was regarded.

9

THE CAMBRIDGE
PARAGRAPH BIBLES

Two Cambridge Bibles

The two greatest scholars of the text of the King James Version (KJV) are F. H. A. Scrivener (in the nineteenth century) and David Norton (in the early twenty-first century). Cambridge University Press chose Scrivener to prepare the Cambridge Paragraph Bible of 1873, and Norton for its successor of 2005. By the measure of textual scholarship, there are no better editions of the KJV, even though modernization of the text comes at a cost. Their one wholly avoidable fault is the title, which seems designed to frighten away potential buyers by highlighting a comparatively minor feature of these editions; the public is never going to be excited by the prospect of buying a book about paragraphs.

The KJV, following Robert Estienne and the Geneva Bible, arranged the chapters of the Bible into numbered verses, with each verse being laid out as what would now be thought of as a paragraph—that is, a new line and an indentation. There are paragraphs in the KJV, however, and they are indicated by the paragraph marker known as a paraph (¶). The first break with the traditional layout was a New Testament (with a revised text) laid out in paragraphs, which was published by John Wesley in 1755. The first edition of the KJV to be published in paragraphs was published in 1838 by the Religious Tract Society; this edition replaced the paraphs with the customary modern layout. This precedent was subsequently followed by the Revised Version and most subsequent translations. Scrivener moved the chapter and verse numbers to the margins, rearranged the text of the prose into paragraphs, and presented the text of what he deemed to be poetry in verse form. The paragraphing may have been conducive to reading (or might have been were the design not so crowded), but was an anachronism.

The Cambridge Paragraph Bible is, however, much more than a KJV divided into paragraphs. Its editor, F. H. A. Scrivener was a Greek manuscript specialist and a formidable textual editor; he was later to serve on the New Testament Company charged with preparation of the Revised Version. His introduction to the Cambridge Paragraph Bible was reprinted in a slightly revised form as *The Authorized Version of the English Bible (1611): Its Subsequent Reprints and Modern Representatives* (1884), and is still in print. Scrivener was a textual conservative, and a believer in the Textus Receptus (the Greek text on which the New Testament text of the KJV was based), and that made him an admirer of the KJV.

In the mid-1860s Scrivener turned his formidable textual firepower on the KJV, which he studied with an eye trained to detect tiny variations in Greek texts. His objective was to construct a 'critical [i.e. "analytical"] edition of the Authorized Version of the English Bible, having reference to its internal character rather than to its external history, and indicating the changes for good or ill introduced into the text of 1611 by subsequent reprints'. He catalogued the 'changes for good or ill' in three appendices.

A. list of wrong readings of the Bible of 1611 amended in later editions
B. variation between the two issues, both bearing the date of 1611
C. list of original readings of the Bible of 1611 restored, later alterations being withdrawn.

The first appendix, of wrong readings of the Bible of 1611 amended in subsequent editions, runs to fifty-five packed pages. It pays particular attention to the Cambridge folio editions of 1629 and 1638, which were prepared with scrupulous attention to detail at a time when many of the original translators were still alive. These folios offer many corrected readings that were duly incorporated into Bibles for centuries to come.

The second appendix catalogues the variations between the two 1611 folios, the 'He' Bible and the 'She' Bible (discussed in Chapter 5), and the third records the restored 1611 readings in the Cambridge Paragraph Bible. These lists constitute the first serious attempt to record the textual history of the KJV, and, although there are occasional mistakes and oversights, the scholarly standard is very high. This is not, however, the whole story, because Scrivener ventured beyond restoration to an attempt to create an ideal text, one that the translators might have achieved had they been fully true to their principles. In Hebrews 10:23, for example, he changed 'the profession of our faith' to 'the profession of our hope' (the reading of the Bishops' Bible) on the grounds that 'faith' is likely to be a misprint occasioned by 'faithful' later in the verse; similarly, his understanding of the Greek led him to change 'strain at a gnat' (Matthew 23:24) to 'strain out a gnat'. And, although the translators had decided that the Johannine Comma (1 John 5:7) was genuine, Scrivener thought that they were wrong, and placed the verse in italics to show that he regarded it as an interpolated sentence rather than Holy Writ.

Despite these occasional flaws, the quality of Scrivener's text in the Cambridge Paragraph Bible is high, but its impact was low, and it never threatened the supremacy of Blayney's text. In the late twentieth century the syndics of Cambridge University Press decided to produce a New Cambridge Paragraph Bible, which afforded an opportunity to refine Scrivener's text in the light of an additional century of scholarship. The reason for this decision was in part technical. In the 1990s plates were produced from film (a process now superseded by computer to plate technology), and by 1994 the film from which Cambridge printed its KJVs was deteriorating. The need to create a new film offered an opportunity to insert corrections or even to create a new text. Two possibilities were considered: adapting the text of the Cambridge Concord Bible (a cautiously modernized text prepared in the 1950s) or using Scrivener's text. The scholarly impulses of the syndics of Cambridge University Press (the equivalent of the delegates at Oxford) run deep, and so a collation of these two editions (no small task) was undertaken in order to enumerate and understand the differences between them. This investigation raised doubts about both editions, and the Press decided to commission David Norton to prepare a new edition. He proved to be the ideal choice.

The ungainly title of the New Cambridge Paragraph Bible implies more continuity with Scrivener than is the case, even though it builds on Scrivener's scholarship. The most obvious difference is in design: Scrivener's version is cramped and difficult to read at length, but Norton's is spacious and reader friendly. Two principles informed the process of revision: mistakes that had crept into the text of the Bible had to be expunged in favour of correct readings, and the spelling and punctuation had to be modernized. These principles are similar to Scrivener's, but the process of implementation has been more scrupulous.

The first principle, that of correcting mistakes, may seem straightforward, but it is not, in part because it is not always easy to identify a printing error with confidence, but also because the thinking behind the decisions of the KJV translators is imperfectly understood. The two important documents that afford insight into the processes used by the 1611 companies have both been used: the notes of John Bois (in Corpus Christi College, Oxford) and the Bishops' Bible annotated by the translators (now in the Bodleian Library), which represents the work of four of the six companies. The former document was unknown to Scrivener, and the latter was not properly understood. Although the annotations in the Bishops' Bible still await scholarly analysis (in part because some of the annotations are trapped in the binding), Norton has used them adeptly. He has also benefited from the Corpus Christi College document, which is well understood because of the brilliant analysis by the American scholar Ward Allen in the 1960s. Norton also improves significantly on Scrivener on the matter of mistakes, because he restricts his corrections to mistakes made by printers, whereas Scrivener ventured into what he understood to be mistakes made by translators.

The second principle embodied in the New Cambridge Paragraph Bible is that spelling and punctuation should be modernized, so continuing the incremental process of modernization that stalled with Blayney's edition in the late eighteenth century. The process of modernization raises questions about which elements should be preserved from the 1611 version of the KJV. What distinguishes the New Cambridge Paragraph Bible from its modernized predecessors (notably Blayney's text) is that the process of modernization is systematic rather than haphazard, and that it is rooted in a set of principles based on a good command of Early Modern English. This edition is therefore the best example of what can be achieved by modernizing the KJV, and of what perils lie in wait for the modernizer.

Spelling

In 1611 spelling was not fixed. Shakespeare's surname was variously spelt Shakespere, Shakspeare, Shakspere, Shaksper, and even Shaxberd, and in his six surviving signatures Shakespeare never used the same spelling twice. The compositors who set the KJV each had distinctive preferred spellings, and also used different spellings of the same word. Often these variations were needed to achieve lines of type that were justified on the right as well as the left. Consider Exodus 25:10 and Exodus 25:23.

The two verses that are illustrated have 'a half', 'an halfe', and 'a halfe'; 'cubits' and 'cubites'; 'and' and '&'; 'breadth' and 'bredth'. The differences in spelling mean nothing. On the other hand, 'shall' and 'shalt' are more than different spellings, because 'shalt' is an obsolete form, not a variant spelling. Here is how the verses appear in the New Cambridge Paragraph Bible:

> [10] And they shall make an ark of shittim wood: two cubits and a half shall be the length thereof, and a cubit and a half the breadth thereof, and a cubit and a half the height thereof.
> [23] Thou shalt also make a table of shittim wood: two cubits shall be the length thereof, and a cubit the breadth thereof, and a cubit and a half the height thereof.

10 ℭ* And they shall make an Arke of Shittim wood: two cubites and a halfe shalbe the length thereof, and a cubite and an halfe the breadth thereof, and a cubite & a halfe the height thereof.

23 ℭ* Thou shalt also make a table of Shittim wood: two cubites shall bee the length thereof, and a cubite the breadth thereof, and a cubite and a halfe the height thereof.

FIGURE 32. Exodus 25:10 and Exodus 25:23, 1611 edition.

This is an exemplary piece of editing on modernizing principles. The variant spellings that the original compositors used in order to accommodate the words in the narrow compass of the column have all been modernized, but 'shalt' has been retained, because it is a form rather than a spelling.

From preserving obsolete forms it is a small step to retaining obsolete words and constructions. The phrase 'most straitest' (Acts 26:5) illustrates both issues. The double comparative was wholly acceptable (compare, for example, 'more fairer than fair' in Shakespeare's *Love's Labour's Lost*), but has now disappeared from the language. And, although the word 'strait' survives as a noun (principally in place names, such as the Bering Strait), it has been obsolete as a comparative adjective since the early nineteenth century. The phrase 'most straitest' could be translated as 'strictest', but it cannot be modernized. The effect, in the New Cambridge Paragraph Bible as in other modernized versions, is a hybrid of old and new forms, in this case 'after the most straitest sect of our religion I lived a Pharisee'.

The same considerations have forced the retention of forms such as 'ye' and 'thou' and oddities such as 'agone' (1 Samuel 30:13), 'inhabiters' (Revelation 8:13, 12:12) and 'magnifical' (1 Chronicles 22:5). These are harmless archaisms, in that their meanings are clear, but there are other examples in which readers might be puzzled, such as 'dureth' (that is, 'ensures' (Matthew 13:21)) and 'neesings' (that is, nostrils (Job 41:18)). The most difficult cases of all are those in which leaving the original word intact can deceive the reader. Leviticus repeatedly speaks of washing 'the inwards and the legs' (for example, at 1:13), and the baffled reader might assume that the reference is to the mouth, where food travels inwards. In fact it is the word that led to the modern slang term 'innards', but using that term would be inappropriate to the legal context, and using 'entrails' would be an act of translation rather than modernization.

Finally, there is a question of what counts as modern usage. 'Among' and 'amongst' are both used in the KJV, but 'among' is used far more often than 'amongst'. In the eighteenth century 'amongst' was purged, and only two examples escaped to live on into modern editions (Genesis 3:8 and Genesis 23:9). The New Cambridge Paragraph Bible restores all ninety-five uses of 'amongst' in the belief that choosing between 'among' and 'amongst' is not a modernization issue, because both forms continue in use. This is true in educated British English, where 'among' is preferred before a consonant and 'amongst' before a vowel, but either can be used before 'the': Peter Rabbit famously lost 'one of his shoes among the cabbages and the other shoe amongst the potatoes'. In educated American English, however, 'amongst' has virtually disappeared, and has acquired, in the words of one dictionary, 'a rather dusty-genteel quality'. For Americans, 'amongst' is indeed a modernization issue.

Punctuation

The prospect of a discussion of punctuation may make the reader's eyes glaze over, but the issue has long been a battleground, and cannot be ignored, though it can be treated with merciful brevity. The core issues are that punctuation affects meaning and that seventeenth-century punctuation was primarily a guide to reading aloud.

The debate about meaning can be illustrated by reference to the Hebrew and Syriac versions of the Bible, in which punctuation (consisting of vowel signs and accent markings) preserved the sense of texts consisting entirely of consonants; the Massoretic Text of the Bible (that is, the text with punctuation provided by the Massoretes) is the bedrock of modern scholarship, but the authority of this punctuation has long been an issue. Is the punctuation inspired by God, in which case the entire Massoretic text must be of divine origin? Or is it the work of men, in which case alternative readings deriving from the Greek version of the Old Testament (the Septuagint) might be brought into play? A parallel argument obtains in the case of the KJV, where the waters are muddied by the conventions of seventeenth-century printing.

If one compares the manuscript of a seventeenth-century poem with a contemporary printed version of the same poem, it

quickly becomes apparent that the manuscript is hardly punctu-
ated at all. Many poets regarded matters such as punctuation and
capitalization and accents as a matter for the printer. This raises
the question of the extent to which the translators of the 1611
Bible took an interest in punctuation, which was in many respects
a recent innovation. In modernizing punctuation, is an editor
modernizing the work of the translators or of the compositors
who set the type? The New Cambridge Paragraph Bible incorp-
orates some bold decisions, of which the most dramatic example is
1 Maccabees 5:13, which in the 1611 text reads 'Yea all our brethren
that were in the place of Tobie, are put to death, their wives and
their children; Also they have carried away captives, and borne
away their stuffe'. The New Cambridge Paragraph Bible reads
'Yea, all our brethren that were in the place of Tobie are put to
death: their wives and their children also they have carried away
captives, and borne away their stuff'. In the first version, the
wives and children die; in the second, they are taken captive.

The second issue is that the use to which punctuation marks
are now put is more precise than in the early seventeenth century,
when punctuation was often rhetorical rather than grammatical.
The KJV was for the most part read aloud, and the punctuation
is sometimes intended to mark breathing points (as it is in the
lyrics of songs) rather than to conform to grammatical convention. The fluidity of punctuation also reflected the fact that some
punctuation marks were new arrivals. The comma, for example,
had been imported from continental Europe in the 1520s, and had
gradually replaced the virgule (an oblique stroke that would now
be called a slash); similarly, the semi-colon arrived in England in
the 1570s. In some cases, the way in which specific punctuation
marks were used has changed. The colon, for example, was used

for a pause stronger than that of a semi-colon but weaker than that of a full stop or period, so there was a clear hierarchy: full stop, colon, semi-colon, comma. In modern English, however, this use of the colon has disappeared, and it is now used (as it is in my previous sentence) to signal the delivery of something promised (in this case a list). Similarly, the apostrophe was used in the seventeenth century to indicate an elided letter, and had no particular role in possessive forms. Some modern punctuation marks did not exist. The markers of direct speech known in England as inverted commas and in America as quotation marks, for example, were not in use until the eighteenth century, so in the original KJV it is not always clear when narrative has modulated into direct speech and when that direct speech ends. There are no easy solutions to such editorial dilemmas.

In choosing to modernize the punctuation, the New Cambridge Paragraph Bible enters into controversial territory, simply because of the scale of the required change and the countless fine judgements that are required. That said, the process is elegantly accomplished, and in many cases the lightening of eighteenth-century punctuation has the happy effect of restoring the punctuation of 1611.

Paragraphs and Poetry

The boldest editorial policy of the Cambridge Paragraph Bibles was the decision to divide the prose into paragraphs and to present the poetry in verse lines. The art of paragraphing with the level of sophistication demonstrated in these Bibles is a product of the eighteenth century, possibly inaugurated by the master stylist Henry St John, Lord Bolingbroke, and does not arise naturally from the Hebrew, Greek, or KJV texts of the Bible, which do not collect groups of sentences that cohere around a single idea or theme. The KJV does use the paraph to mark breaks, sometimes at the end of passages to be read; on other occasions, such as the separate paragraphs for each of the four first verses of Exodus 23, it is hard to discern the purpose of the translators. In the Cambridge Paragraph Bibles the task has been done twice, because the paragraph is an evolving form. Scrivener paragraphed the KJV as if it were a Victorian novel, so his paragraphs, for a modern reader, seem to be inordinately long. David Norton has reparagraphed the Bible, 'chiefly guided by my own sense of the text'. As the modern idea of the paragraph is not the same as the ill-developed seventeenth-century idea, this is an act of interpretation rather than modernization; it is intelligently and sensitively done, but it is not the KJV.

The presentation of poetry is similarly problematical, because it is not entirely clear that the passages designated as poetry can reasonably be described as poetry in the original Hebrew. It is sometimes claimed that up to a third of the Old Testament is poetry, including Psalms, Proverbs, Lamentations, large tracts of Job and Ecclesiastes and shorter passages in the prophetical books. But is it poetry? The Hebrew has no rhyme, no assonance, no accentual rhythm, and no quantitative rhythm (sequences of short and long syllables), though scholars determined to find such effects have produced what may be a few examples. The principal ground for thinking of certain passages as poetry is the use of parallelism. The song of Deborah and Barak, for example, includes the phrase 'he asked water, and she gave milk' (Judges 5:25); the KJV adeptly captures the balancing structure, but the translation of a rhetorical effect does not mean that either the original or the translation need be poetry: prose also conveys such effects. In the absence of any discernible metrical patterns in ancient Hebrew poetry, it may seem imprudent to draw a clear line between prose and poetry in the Old Testament. Formal prose is still prose, and a culture that makes no distinction between poetry and prose is inevitably unaware of the distinction, rather like Monsieur Jourdain in Molière's *Le Bourgeois gentilhomme,* who is famously delighted to discover that he has been speaking prose all his life without knowing it.

Omitted Material

The question of what should be included in an edition of the 1611 Bible is problematical, because it raises the question of what constitutes the KJV. The most austere answer would be that a modern editor would produce only the translation, including chapter and verse numbers. The New Cambridge Paragraph Bible offers this and more, in that it also includes the dedication to the king, the preface written by Miles Smith on behalf of the translators, and the marginal notes. There is much here to applaud, especially the *tour de force* of the annotation of Smith's 'The Translators to the Reader', in which immensely obscure quotations are relentlessly traced to their sources. The difficulty is that much of the original editorial material is omitted.

One loss was occasioned by the decision not to reproduce the original chapter summaries and headings, which in some cases had been used to circumvent the injunction against interpretative marginal notes. In the chapter summary for Daniel 11, for example, the passage from verse 30 onwards is said to predict 'the tyranny of the Romans', who were not to invade Palestine until well after the book of Daniel was written. Similarly, Psalm 2 is headed 'the kingdom of Christ'. Other examples (discussed in Chapter 4) include the extensive theological commentary in the chapter summaries and headnotes of the Song of Solomon. The loss of this material, which was an integral part of the KJV, forfeits the use of an important guide to the translators' understanding of the text.

There is also the issue of the prefatory matter, which in 1611 included an engraved title page, a liturgical calendar, an almanac, a table for the calculation of Easter, a timetable for readers throughout the year, a licence for the book to be printed, thirty-six pages of genealogies, and a map and gazetteer of Canaan. This material shows how this Bible was used, and its loss is to be lamented. Some of it was also specified in the instructions: according to the report to the Synod of Dort, the publishers were instructed 'that a very perfect genealogy and map of the Holy land should be joined to the work'. And so it should.

Finally, there is the issue of italics. In the 1611 version of the KJV, italics were used extensively (and unevenly) to indicate additional words supplied by the translators to render the text more comprehensible. In the first edition italicized words were printed inconspicuously amongst the authoritative black-letter type used for words directly translated from the ancient languages. There are many difficulties associated with the italicized words for modern readers, in part because the use of italic has changed (in 1611 it de-emphasized words, and now it emphasizes them). Scrivener valiantly tried to correct all the errors in italics in the first edition, but the gain in accuracy may have been secured at the cost of misunderstanding for his Victorian readers. David Norton took the bold decision not to distinguish supplied words in his text. The shedding of italics represents a loss, in that a distinction that was important to the translators is no longer visible.

These are not simple issues, and the decisions embodied in the Cambridge Paragraph Bibles can all be defended. There is, however, a contrary case for a more generous view of what constitutes the Bible. The analogy of editing Shakespeare may be helpful. Shakespeare wrote his plays in scenes, and did not divide them into acts (that was done in the printing shop), but modern editors retain the act divisions; similarly, the lists of characters were not drawn up by Shakespeare, but are nonetheless included in modern editions. Such materials, together with stage directions that may not be Shakespeare's, are routinely included; it could be argued that a similar approach should be taken to editing the KJV.

The Bible for the Twenty-First Century?

The New Cambridge Paragraph Bible sets a scholarly standard for an edition of the KJV that is unlikely to be surpassed for generations. In terms of consistency and scholarly probity, it is second to none; the former quality has probably been achieved by the use of computerized search and replace functions, which have made a huge contribution to scholarly editing, and the latter is a reflection of David Norton's principled approach to editing and his ability to sustain rigorous standards throughout a long and complex text. The decision to modernize spelling may be helpful, but the modernizing of punctuation is more problematical, as were the decisions to use paragraphs for prose and the conventions of verse to represent what may or may not be poetry.

The shedding of italics and chapter summaries (and most of the preliminary material) may make the text look more modern, but it moves the text a long way from its origins in the version of 1611. The text (shorn of its textual notes and 'The Translators to the Reader') was published in 2006 by Penguin, which sells to the literary market, and is being published in 2011 by the Folio Society, which caters to the fine-book market. The scholarly version published by Cambridge University Press will be an important collector's Bible, but it seems unlikely ever to dislodge Blayney's Oxford text.

10

∽∾∽

THE BIBLE IN AMERICA

The Bible Culture of America

In 2006 the British comedian Ricky Gervais began his accept-
ance speech at the Golden Globe awards ceremony in Holly-
wood by explaining that 'I'm from a little place called England—we
used to run the world before you'. Beneath the joke is an acknow-
ledgement that, while Britain may have ruled the waves in the
nineteenth century, it is America that is the world's only super-
power in the early twenty-first century. And, just as the principal
centre of the English language has shifted from England to
America, so the centre of gravity of the King James Version (KJV)
has gradually moved across the Atlantic. Population size is clearly
a factor, but beyond that there is an important cultural difference:
in the post-war period England has become a largely secular
country, and church attendance is very low indeed, whereas the
United States has one of the highest church-attendance rates in
the world. Moreover, large parts of the religious culture of contemporary America are Bible centred. There are many modern Bible
translations available in modern America, but the KJV retains a
special place. Indeed, in no other country has the KJV had such
a central and prolonged presence in the religious life of the nation.

193

The final third of this book is therefore in significant part an American story. I therefore begin this chapter with an account of the history of America's distinctive Bible culture in the hope that it will provide a context for the American dimension in the chapters that follow, and then turn to the fortunes of the KJV in America.

Until 1776 English-speaking America consisted of thirteen British colonies, of which twelve were Protestant (Maryland was the exception). The New England colonies (now Connecticut, Maine, Massachusetts, New Hampshire, Rhode Island, and Vermont) were settled by English puritans who may have brought Geneva Bibles with them, but there is no evidence that this was the case: the famous Mayflower Geneva Bible of 1588 now in the Harry Ransom Library at the University of Texas is a fake. Whether or not the colonists brought Geneva Bibles with them, they soon settled on the KJV, which was from the mid-seventeenth century the only available English-language Bible. The Middle Colonies (now Delaware, New Jersey, New York, and Pennsylvania) welcomed migrants of many Protestant persuasions (Baptists, Congregationalists, Dutch Reformed, Presbyterians, Quakers, and so on), and, as English emerged as the dominant language, so the KJV became the Bible of the colonists. An emerging Protestant identity, which strengthened the conviction of early colonists that God was assisting the colonial enterprise, was consolidated during the Seven Years War, in which British colonial Protestants were pitted against French Catholics.

In the eighteenth century, rationalism became an important force in European Christianity, and, although it existed in America (where rationalists often became Unitarians), the movement was eclipsed by the two Great Awakenings. The first Awakening was spearheaded by the evangelical Methodist George Whitefield, whose revivalist preaching tour of New England and the Middle Colonies from 1739 to 1742 was characterized by an emphasis on personal conversion experiences. The KJV, which had been designed for reading aloud, was ideal for dissemination through sermons, and Whitefield took full advantage of this quality to embed the KJV in his highly emotional sermons. Conversionist preaching was not new, as it had been introduced a generation earlier to the Congregationalists (by Jonathan Edwards), the Dutch Reformed Church (by Theodorus Jacobus Freylinghuysen), and the Presbyterian Church (by Gilbert Tennent), but the sheer scale of Whitefield's ministry was unprecedented. Resistance to the first Great Awakening was led by Charles Chauncy (son of his namesake, the president of Harvard), who argued that the revivalist emphasis on the necessity of an emotional conversion experience excluded many Christians. In the event, the tide of American religious history favoured Whitefield and the revivalists, and the Awakening soon spread to the Southern Colonies of Virginia, Georgia, and the Carolinas, where Samuel Davies preached for the Presbyterians, Shubal Stearns for the Baptists, and a band of circuit riders for the Methodists; all used the KJV in their preaching.

The second Great Awakening, which extended from the 1790s to the 1820s, was in its origins a reaction to American deism. This was a rationalist movement that rejected belief in miracles and in the divinity of Jesus; deists denied that the Bible was a divine revelation and mocked the notion of biblical inerrancy. The leader of the deist movement was Elihu Palmer, its manifestos were Ethan Allen's *Reason the Only Oracle of Man* (1784) and Thomas Paine's *The Age of Reason* (1794), and its most prominent sympathizers were Benjamin Franklin and Thomas Jefferson. The high point of the movement occurred during the French Revolution, when a form of deism, the Cult of the Supreme Being (*Culte de l'Être suprême*), briefly became the official religion of France.

The Christian counter-attack was led by Timothy Dwight (president of Yale, and grandson of Jonathan Edwards) and his protégé Lyman Beecher. These were not backwoods preachers, but highly educated evangelicals whose resistance to deism was well informed, and who also had a marked ability to convey complex ideas in popular language. The favoured media of some of the key preachers of the second Awakening were the revival meeting and the camp meeting, and again the rhythms of the KJV made it ideally suited to such environments. The feature that distinguished the second Awakening from the first was the belief in a morally reformed Christian republic. Temperance groups opposed alcohol and gambling, and sabbatarian groups sought to keep Sunday special by restricting transport and mail delivery. The principal effect of the second Awakening was the ascendancy of evangelical Christianity, which was the dominant force in both white and African American religious cultures. Indeed, by 1835, Alexis de Tocqueville could observe that 'there is no country in the world where the Christian religion retains a greater influence over the souls of men than in America'.

The Awakenings had in common a millenarian emphasis that was articulated through the language of the KJV. In a phrase that has passed into the language, believers searched for 'signs of the times' (Matthew 16:3), using the visionary apocalyptic texts of Daniel, Ezekiel, and Revelation as indications of the 'end times', which would be presaged by the appearance of the antichrist. The identification of the antichrist shifted with the times.

In colonial America, when English puritan beliefs were transported across the Atlantic, the antichrist was identified with the papacy. This is a belief that has survived in some circles up to the present day, though there have been other candidates: during the Revolutionary War, for example, the antichrist was deemed to be King George III. Another branch of this millenarianism contained the seeds of the religious articulation of American exceptionalism, the belief that America has been chosen by God for a special role in the world. Puritan colonists in Connecticut, Massachusetts, New Haven, and Plymouth saw their 'errand into the wilderness', as it was called in Samuel Danforth's sermon of 1670, as a recapitulation of the refrain of Jesus in Matthew 11: 'What went ye out into the wilderness to see?' Danforth assured his listeners that the colonists enjoyed the 'promise of divine protection and preservation'. From such beginnings there emerged the belief that, just as God protected the children of Israel in the wilderness, so under a new covenant he would protect his new chosen people in the wilderness of America. This providential reading of American settlement fitted into an eschatological framework that would now be called postmillennialism, which is the belief of preachers such as Jonathan Edwards that the second coming of Jesus would follow the evangelization of the world. Revivals were, therefore, seen as portents of the second coming described in the prophetic passages of the New Testament (e.g. Matthew 23 and Mark 13). In the early nineteenth century, millenarian groups such as the Shakers (the United Society of Believers in Christ's Second Coming) and the Mormons (the Church of Jesus Christ of Latter-Day Saints) formed communities that prepared for the second coming.

In 1833 the Baptist lay preacher William Miller published a pamphlet in which he calculated that Christ would return in 1843; he later recalculated the date as 22 October 1844, but, when nothing happened on that day (which became known as the Great Disappointment), those of his followers who did not defect became Seventh-Day Adventists. Miller and his allies rejected the postmillennialism of the period in favour of premillennialism, the belief that the second coming of Jesus would precede the millennium. In this respect the Millerites were part of a larger premillennial movement whose origins can be traced to the Plymouth Brethren in England. The most important form of premillennialism was dispensationalism, which will be discussed in Chapter 12 in the context of its principal vehicle, the Scofield Reference Bible.

The expectation of the imminent return of Christ, when the trumpet will sound and the faithful will be lifted into the sky (the 'rapture'), became (and remains) a central belief in American evangelical culture. The publication of *The Late, Great Planet Earth* (by Hal Lindsey and Carole Cartson) in 1970 created an expectation that Christ was likely to return in the 1980s. In 1995 the first of a long series of 'Left Behind' novels (by Tim LaHaye and Jerry Jenkins) was published, and this series (sixteen adult books, forty books in the series for teenagers, audio dramatizations for radio, graphic novels, CDs, DVDs, and so on) dramatizes the fate of those who are left behind to face the tribulation after the rapture. The evangelist Jerry Falwell declared that the series had been more influential than any book in modern times other than the Bible.

In the late nineteenth century, a fundamentalist movement emerged from evangelical Protestantism. The origins of the term 'fundamentalism' can be discerned in the proclamation of a Bible conference held in Niagara in 1895, when 'five points of fundamentalism' were affirmed: the verbal inerrancy of the Bible, the divinity of Christ, the virgin birth of Christ, the substitutionary theory of the atonement (according to which Christ voluntarily substituted himself to bear the punishment that was due to sinful humankind), and the bodily return of Christ. The term came into popular use through a series of tracts published between 1910 and 1915 entitled *The Fundamentals*. Quotations were all taken from the KJV.

Fundamentalists supplemented the universal evangelical belief in the need for a personal conversion experience with a distinctive belief in the infallibility of the Bible (often the KJV) and in dispensational millennialism. The fundamentalist movement declared its chief opponent to be 'modernism', and its modernizing targets included liberal theology (especially the social gospel and liberal 'higher criticism'), secularism, and Darwinian evolution. The battle against evolution soon took centre stage, and there were campaigns to remove evolutionary biology from science teaching in American schools. The Scopes 'monkey' trial of 1925, which had opened with the request of the prosecution for the court to take judicial notice of the Book of Genesis in the KJV, ended in failure for the anti-evolutionists, but the movement soon recovered, and in the interwar years a vast network of seminaries (notably Dallas Theological Seminary), Bible institutes (notably Moody Bible Institute in Chicago), Christian colleges, Christian publishers, and Christian radio stations disseminated the fundamentalist perspective.

In the post-war years, part of the fundamentalist movement began to shed its separatist instincts, and instead aspired to create a national revival. This created a distinction between the group, still known as fundamentalists, who set their face against any engagement with science and 'modernism', and a larger group, known as New Evangelicals, who are fully engaged with contemporary culture; the distinction is not always clear to outsiders, because both groups habitually call themselves 'Christians', a term used in a restrictive sense to denote those who have undergone a conversion experience. Billy Graham, the most prominent of the New Evangelicals, filled football stadiums with his crusades, and his successors used television to evangelize.

In the late 1970s, evangelicals began to engage with the political process, initially in support of conservative views. The aspiration to create a Christian America encouraged these evangelicals to carry their traditional beliefs in patriotism, the freedom of the individual, and unconstrained capitalism into the political arena. In 1979 the evangelist Jerry Falwell established the Moral Majority, which aspired through the election of Ronald Reagan as President to champion its 'pro-life, pro-family, pro-moral, and pro-America' agenda and to oppose gay rights, abortion, and socialism. The Moral Majority was disbanded in 1989, but religious politics soon coalesced around the Christian Coalition ('Defending America's Godly Heritage'), which was founded by the evangelical broadcaster Pat Robertson to campaign on issues such as prayer in schools and equal curriculum space for creationism (latterly in the form of intelligent design) alongside Darwinian evolution. Those within the movement who retained sympathy for the pre-war separatist tradition created large numbers of private Christian schools, and transformed home schooling from the preserve of eccentrics to an important popular movement.

The Christian Coalition declined in influence, but the broader movement of which it is a part, variously known as the Religious Right or the Christian Right, increased its influence in the Republican Party, and its presence attracted some prominent Southern Democrats ('Dixiecrats'). The election of George W. Bush represented more than an example of dynastic American politics; it also signalled the ability of the Religious Right to place one of its own in the White House. Mr Bush was fully alert to the importance of this evangelical bloc, so in 2000 he addressed the staff and students of Bob Jones University, which is the oldest and most influential fundamentalist university in the United States; its regulations stipulate that the KJV must be used in its classrooms and its religious services.

The election of Barack Obama in 2008 was on one level a defeat for the Religious Right, but Democratic voters, many of whom had never previously voted, included a significant number of evangelical Christians, because churches helped to mobilize voters. Writing in the early 1990s, Mr Obama had described his tearful reaction to Jeremiah Wright's sermon on 'The Audacity of Hope' in terms of the ability of black churches to articulate the hopes and aspirations of African Americans. By the time he recalled that experience on the campaign trail in 2008, he had transformed it into an evangelical conversion narrative. John McCain attended a Southern Baptist church, but had no conversion narrative, so Mr Obama had stronger evangelical credentials; this was one of many factors that contributed to his victory. The balance of power had shifted from the Republicans to the Democrats, but, at the level of religious politics, little had changed, in that George Bush's conversion narrative had appealed successfully to Christian voters in earlier elections. Mr Obama did not succeed in bringing a significant number of white evangelicals onside in the course of his campaign, but he took the opportunity afforded by an unlikely friendship with Rick Warren, pastor of an evangelical megachurch in California, to invite Mr Warren to deliver the invocation at the inaugural ceremony. This invitation was on one level the opening of the campaign for re-election in 2012, as the constituency that Mr Warren represents is a powerful electoral force.

The election of Mr Obama was a reminder that the KJV is not the exclusive prerogative of the religious right. Indeed, there is some evidence of a parallel tradition on the left, but it is harder to discern, in part because prominent white evangelicals on the political left, such as Tony Campolo and Ron Sider, are very much a minority, but also because the voice of African Americans is not always as easy to hear as that of white Americans. There is, however, one clear instance of African American allegiance to the KJV, one that may represent the tip of the proverbial iceberg. The instance is Martin Luther King's 'I have a dream' speech of 28 August 1963, delivered from the steps of the Lincoln Memorial in Washington. The speech is rich in allusion, invoking the Declaration of Independence, the Emancipation Proclamation, and the US Constitution. The power of its language, however, lies in significant part in its evoking of the KJV. Consider, for example, this passage:

> I have a dream today. I have a dream that one day every valley shall be exalted, every hill and mountain shall be made low, the rough places will be made plain, and the crooked places will be made straight, and the glory of the Lord shall be revealed, and all flesh shall see it together. This is our hope. This is the faith with which I return to the South.

And here is Isaiah 40:4–5 in the KJV:

> Every valley shall be exalted, and every mountain and hill shall be made low: and the crooked shall be made straight, and the rough places plain. And the glory of the Lord shall be revealed, and all flesh shall see it together: for the mouth of the Lord hath spoken it.

Dr King was quoting from memory, and so transposed several phrases, but the translation that he is recalling is clearly the KJV.

The association of Martin Luther King with the KJV was eventually manifested in the publication in 1987 of the Martin Luther King Jr Remembrance Edition of the KJV with speeches by Dr King. This Bible has not been well received in conservative circles; one website denounces it in these words:

> Some apostate Bible publisher thought they'd cash in big by marketing *The Martin Luther King Remembrance Edition* Bible. It is a trustworthy *King James Version*, which makes it even more insulting to God. How dare anyone exploit the Word of God to honor such a wicked, Christ-rejecting, unrepentant man as Martin Luther King. Few Americans realize that Martin Luther King Jr was *a Communist*, involved in at least 60 known Communist front organizations.

The ferocity of such attacks is disconcerting, but they are useful reminders that King is still regarded as a villainous figure in some quarters (hence the long resistance to the establishment of Martin Luther King Day by Republicans such as John McCain), and that appropriation of the KJV can be contentious. More cheeringly, it is also a reminder that the KJV is the Bible of many African Americans. Indeed, there are special editions for the African American market, such as the *Original African Heritage Study Bible: King*

James Version and the *Holy Bible: King James Version: African American Jubilee Edition*. There are also bespoke editions for the conservative market. In 2009, in its modernized form (the NKJV), the KJV became the text of the *American Patriot's Bible*, 'the one Bible that shows how "a light from above" shaped our nation.... This extremely unique Bible shows how the history of the United States connects the people and events of the Bible to our lives in a modern world.' The KJV remains the Bible of choice for many Americans, and is not the preserve of one political or racial group.

Presidential Bibles

Both President Bush and President Obama chose to be sworn in with a KJV, and their choices reflect an important strain in American culture. George Bush, like his father, chose the Washington Bible, and Barack Obama chose the Lincoln Bible. Both Bibles have distinguished histories.

In 1789 General Washington became President Washington, and on 30 April he took his oath of office on a 1767 edition of the KJV printed in London by Mark Baskett, the king's printer. The Bible belonged (and still belongs) to the Freemasons, who have been generous in allowing it to be used for public occasions, including the Masonic cornerstone ceremonies and their centenaries for the Capitol, the White House, and the Statue of Liberty. The connection between this inaugural Bible and George Washington continued with its use in Washington's funeral in 1799 and the launching of the aircraft carrier USS *George Washington* in 1992. In the nineteenth century, this Bible was used in the funerals of Andrew Jackson, Zachary Taylor, and Abraham Lincoln. In the twentieth century, four presidents chose to place their hands on the Washington Bible as they took their oaths of office. The first was Warren Harding (1921), who was, like Washington, a Mason. This Bible was subsequently used by Dwight Eisenhower (1953), Jimmy Carter (1977), and George Bush Senior (1989); both Harding and Carter chose to place their fingers on Micah 6:8 ('He hath shewed thee, O man, what is good; and what doth the LORD require of thee, but to do justly, and to love mercy, and to walk humbly with thy God?'). In 2001 George W. Bush planned to use the same Bible, but it rained on inauguration day, so he had to use a family Bible instead. The justly famous Washington Bible is normally on display in the Federal Hall National Memorial in New York, on the site (but not in the original building) of Washington's inauguration.

The second inaugural Bible of historic significance is the one used by Abraham Lincoln at his first inauguration in 1861; it is a KJV published by Oxford University Press in 1853. The Bible remained in Lincoln's family until 1928, when it was presented to the Library of Congress in Washington, so until recently it did not have the public profile of the Washington Bible. That changed in 2009 with the inauguration of Barack Obama, who chose to take the oath of office on the Lincoln Bible, in part because of the association of Lincoln with the Emancipation Proclamation, a pair of executive orders (1862 and 1863) that began the process whereby slavery was abolished in the Thirteenth Amendment of 1865.

The Bible in American Public Life

Abraham Lincoln's religious convictions are not clear, but in his Gettysburg Address he provides one of greatest examples of the centrality of the KJV to American culture, in that its lofty

THE

HOLY BIBLE,

CONTAINING THE

OLD AND NEW TESTAMENTS:

TRANSLATED OUT OF

𝕿𝖍𝖊 𝕺𝖗𝖎𝖌𝖎𝖓𝖆𝖑 𝕿𝖔𝖓𝖌𝖚𝖊𝖘:

AND WITH THE FORMER TRANSLATIONS DILIGENTLY
COMPARED AND REVISED,

BY HIS MAJESTY'S SPECIAL COMMAND.

———

APPOINTED TO BE READ IN CHURCHES.

OXFORD:

PRINTED AT THE UNIVERSITY PRESS.

Sold by E. GARDNER and Son, at the Oxford Bible Warehouse,
Paternoster Row, London;
And by J. and C. MOZLEY, Derby.

| Minion 24's. | M.DCCC.LIII. | Cum Privilegio. |

FIGURE 33. Title-page, Lincoln Bible.

sentiments are articulated in the language of the KJV. Its opening words, 'Four score and seven years ago our fathers', echo 'The days of our years are three score years and ten' (Psalm 90:10). 'Brought forth' is a common locution in the KJV, but Lincoln's words resonate specifically with the repeated assertion that God 'brought forth' Israel from the bondage of Egypt, and the use of the same idiom to announce childbirth: Mary 'brought forth a son', just as 'our fathers on this continent brought forth a new nation'. The central verse of the conversionist preaching of the nineteenth century, 'For God so loved the world that he gave his only begotten Son, that whoever believeth in him should not perish, but have everlasting life' (John 3:16), is echoed in phrases such as 'shall not perish', 'new birth', and 'here gave their lives that that nation might live'. In his second inaugural address, delivered a month before his assassination, Lincoln observed the tragic fact that in the American Civil War both sides 'read the same Bible'; for Protestants on both sides, that meant the KJV:

> Both read the same Bible and pray to the same God, and each invokes His aid against the other. It may seem strange that any men should dare to ask a just God's assistance in wringing their bread from the sweat of other men's faces, but let us judge not, that we be not judged....The Almighty has His own purposes. 'Woe unto the world because of offenses; for it must needs be that offenses come, but woe to that man by whom the offense cometh.' If we shall suppose that American slavery is one of those offenses which, in the providence of God, must needs come, but which, having continued through His appointed time, He now wills to remove, and that He gives to both North and South this terrible war as the woe due to those by whom the offense came, shall we discern therein any

THE BIBLE IN AMERICA

departure from those divine attributes which the believers in a living God always ascribe to Him?

In these noble words, which are suffused with the language of the KJV (and include a quotation from Matthew 18:7), Lincoln shows that he is fully alert to the use both sides could make of the Bible. On the contentious issue of slavery, southern proponents could and did cite 'of the children of the strangers that do sojourn among you, of them shall she buy . . . and they shall be your possession' (Leviticus 25:45); northern opponents of slavery, on the other hand, could and did cite 'Stand fast in the liberty wherewith Christ hath made us free, and be not entangled again with the yoke of bondage' (Galatians 5:1). Biblical images of emancipation had obvious appeal to African Americans, in whose culture the KJV became deeply embedded, notably in the tradition of spirituals that celebrated Moses leading the Israelites from bondage in Egypt, Daniel's escape from the lions' den, Jonah's escape from the belly of the whale, and the notion of peace in a Christian heaven.

America is a homogeneous country with many religions, but it is dominated by a political and cultural establishment that is Protestant, often evangelical, and sometimes fundamentalist. The Bible, which is often the KJV, is read from countless pulpits every Sunday, in huge numbers of Bible study groups, and in the privacy of individual homes. The Bible is central to the fabric of large swathes of American society, and millions of citizens attempt to live by its precepts. Indeed, many millions of conservative Protestants habitually carry Bibles with them: the Bible carried to church (traditionally in a soft black leather binding) tends to be a complete Bible, while the small Bible carried in pocket or handbag tends to be a New Testament. Every year tens of millions of Bibles are sold in the retail market, and similar numbers are given away by Bible societies. Sales have always been buoyant, but after 9/11 sales figures rose sharply as Americans grasped their biblical faith.

The Bible continues to be a focal point of public debate in America. Just as in the nineteenth century the Bible was the common point of reference for arguments about issues such as Sunday observance (including the prohibition against mail delivery), alcohol consumption, gambling, divorce, and prostitution, so in the twenty-first century the Bible is invoked in debates about homosexuality, abortion, gun control, and the comparatively muted discussion of capital punishment. On the last of these, in 2009 a Texas jury recommended the death penalty for a man who had killed someone with a gun barrel. In the jury room Bibles had been passed around with salient passages highlighted, and one juror read aloud the passage that sealed the murderer's fate: 'And if he smite him with an instrument of iron (so that he die) he is a murderer: the murderer shall surely be put to death' (Numbers 35:16); the citation is from the KJV. In due course, the murderer was indeed put to death.

In the legal arena the principal areas of contention are the teaching of evolution and the right to display the Ten Commandments in public buildings. In 2002 a board of education in Georgia required stickers to be placed on high-school biology textbooks warning young readers that evolution is a theory rather than a fact; in 2005 the stickers were removed by judicial order. In 2004 a Pennsylvania school board authorized the teaching of intelligent design, but the following year the district court invoked the First Amendment (which prohibits Congress from enacting laws 'respecting an establishment of religion'), ruling that 'teaching intelligent design in public school biology classes violates the Establishment Clause of the First Amendment to the Constitution of the United States... because intelligent design is not science and "cannot uncouple itself from its creationist, and thus religious, antecedents"'.

The dispute about the Ten Commandments began in Alabama, where in 2001 Roy Moore, the chief justice of the state's supreme court, commissioned a large monument for the rotunda of the state courthouse; on the top of the monument the Ten Commandments were inscribed (in the KJV), and on the sides were mounted quotations from the Constitution, the Declaration of Independence, and the founding fathers. A federal judge ordered that the monument be removed, and, when Moore refused, he was dismissed as chief justice by the Alabama Court of the Judiciary; he has now turned to politics and is seeking election as a Republican, arguing that, from the founding fathers onwards, the Bible has been the basis of American justice. In this context the choice of the KJV for the text of the Ten Commandments is significant. In nineteenth-century America, the reading of the KJV in public schools had been challenged by Roman Catholics who argued that Catholic children should be allowed to read the Douai–Reims translation; Protestant objections to this request made it clear that the KJV was the true Bible and that it lay at the heart of America's Protestant identity. Similarly, in twenty-first-century America, verses from the KJV carved on a stone in an Alabama courthouse have developed into a debate about the posting of the Ten Commandments in schools and public buildings throughout the United States.

The Bible is central to the vision of a God-fearing English-speaking America whose public morality has a Christian dimension. This is not a vision shared by all Americans, nor is the KJV always the Bible of choice, but in formal contexts, of which presidential inaugurations and courthouse monuments are but two, the sonority and elegant archaisms of the KJV seem wholly apt. For such reasons, the KJV retains a special place in the affections of many Americans, and in the public life of the nation.

11

~oxxo~

THE REVISED VERSION

The Need for a Revision

In 1862 the Scottish publisher Robert Young, whose concord-
ance to the King James Version (KJV) still sits within reach on
the shelves of many students of the Bible (including mine),
published the Bible known from its spine title as *Young's Literal
Translation*. Young was a self-taught student of languages whose
linguistic portfolio extended beyond the usual Germanic and
Romance languages to include Finnish, Gaelic, Gujarati, and the
languages of the Bible, of which his command of Hebrew was
outstanding. His translation is chiefly remarkable for two features.
First, he attempted, in the words of his preface,

> to secure a comparative degree of uniformity in rendering the
> original words and phrases. Thus, for example, the Hebrew
> verb *nathan*, which is rendered by the King James' translators
> in *sixty-seven* different ways...has been restricted and reduced
> to *ten*...and so with many others. It is the Translator's ever-
> growing conviction, that even this smaller number may be
> reduced still further.

This ideal was to be realized in the next decade by Julia Evelina
Smith, a remarkable American translator who in 1876 produced a

translation in which every Hebrew and Greek word was translated by the same equivalent English word.

Secondly, Young decided to preserve the tenses of biblical Greek and Hebrew. He insisted that his version was intended to complement rather than compete with the KJV, but, on the subject of tenses in Hebrew, he accused the translators of ignorance:

> King James' translators were almost entirely unacquainted with the two distinctive peculiarities of the Hebrew mode of thinking and speaking... [namely] that the Hebrews were in the habit of using the past tense to express the *certainty* of an action taking place, even though the action might not really be performed for some time, and that the Hebrews, in referring to events which might be either *past* or *future*, were accustomed to act on the principle of transferring themselves mentally to the period and place of the events themselves, and were not content with coldly viewing them as those of a bygone or still coming time; hence the very frequent use of the *present* tense.

The result reads oddly: 'In the beginning of God's preparing the heavens and the earth, the earth hath existed waste and void... and God saith, "Let light be" and light is.' Parallel to this literal fidelity to tenses is a lexical policy with similar aspirations, so 'eternity' is replaced with 'age-during', which yields sentences such as 'And these shall go away to punishment age-during, but the righteous to life age-during' (Matthew 25:46); the result fails to charm. Young's version is easier to respect than to read, and it now remains in use as a Bible for consultation rather than a reading version. Its assault on the competence of the KJV revisers may have been unwarranted, but it struck home, and was a stimulus to revision of the KJV.

Proposals for Revision

Proposals for a revision of the KJV were advocated and opposed from the mid-nineteenth century. The scholarly impetus for revision rested on the need to incorporate important advances that had been made with respect to the Greek text that lay behind the translation of the New Testament. The Greek text that underlay the KJV (and other Reformation Bibles such as Luther's) is known as the Textus Receptus (Latin: 'the received text'), which had a history stretching back to Byzantium. By the mid-nineteenth century, German scholarship had created a corpus of Greek manuscripts earlier than the Textus Receptus, and an eclectic edition of these manuscripts formed the basis of the scholarly adjustments in the Revised Version (RV). Scholarly resistance to revision was based on the view that the formation of an enhanced corpus of manuscripts was not sufficiently advanced to warrant a revision; theological resistance lay in the doctrinal implications of the newly recovered corpus. Most of the 6,000 variants between the two texts are so minor that they disappear in translation, but a few are significant differences. Mark 9:29 in the KJV, for example, reads 'This kind can come forth by nothing, but by prayer and fasting'; it was clear to the RV revisers that 'and fasting' was a late addition, and not part of the original Greek text, so they render the line 'This kind can come out by nothing, save by prayer'. The difference may seem slight, but fasting is a practice in some churches and not in others, so the withdrawal of a verse that supports the efficacy of fasting is no small matter.

The momentum of the wish for revision proved to be irresistible. In 1868 Henry Alford, the dean of Canterbury, issued a call for a revision and formulated principles that might guide the revisers. In 1870 Samuel Wilberforce, bishop of Winchester (and son of the slavery abolitionist), proposed to the upper house of the Convocation of Canterbury that a committee be established to

> report upon the desirableness of a revision of the Authorized Version of the New Testament, whether by marginal notes or otherwise, in all those passages where plain and clear errors, whether in the Hebrew or Greek text originally adopted by the translators, or in the translations made from the same, shall, on due investigation, be found to exist.

Connop Thirlwall, bishop of St David's, successfully proposed an amendment to include the Old Testament in the proposal. The Convocation of York was invited to participate, but declined; the proposal was therefore carried forward by the province of Canterbury. The first report of the committee proposed a very cautious revision. They insisted that they did 'not contemplate any new translation of the Bible, or any alteration of the language, except when in the judgment of the most competent scholars such change is necessary'. The intention of the revisers was 'to introduce as few alterations as possible into the text of the Authorized Version'. This is one of many occasions on which the revisers demonstrated an extraordinary reverence for the KJV. As the Church of England thought of itself as the custodian of the KJV, the committee recommended that the revisers all be Anglicans, though they would be free to take expert advice from scholars of any denomination or nationality.

A second committee of Convocation was charged with turning these principles into procedures. In doing so, they overturned one of the principles, insisting that nonconformists be included among the revisers; they even issued an invitation to John Henry

Newman, the leading English Roman Catholic scholar, but he declined. In the event, the committees were dominated by Anglicans, but there were also representatives of the Scottish Presbyterians, Baptists, Congregationalists, Methodists, and Unitarians. Samuel Tregelles of the Plymouth Brethren accepted an invitation to join the New Testament committee, but the onset of blindness prevented him from attending any meetings. The presence of a Unitarian (George Vance Smith) on the New Testament committee created unease that reached crisis point when members were invited to participate in the celebration of the eucharist in Henry VII's chapel, Westminster Abbey, where they were meeting (in the Jerusalem Chamber). Smith's participation was condemned by Anglican extremists as an 'act of desecration', feeding 'that which is most holy to the dogs', and Bishop Wilberforce successfully proposed a motion to the upper house of the Canterbury Convocation recommending the expulsion of anyone 'who denies the Godhead of our Lord'. The motion was rejected in the lower house, and Smith was able to continue, though he often found himself as the sole dissenter from the consensus.

Convocation also decided to establish separate committees (which they called 'companies' in deference to the Jacobean revisers) for the Old and New Testaments; the Apocrypha was for the time being left aside. In 1871 it was decided to invite American Christians to participate in the process, and in due course they approached Philip Schaff, a high-church American who habitually described himself as 'a Swiss by birth, a German by education, and an American by choice'. Schaff's early years in America had not been easy, because he was subjected to two trials for heresy by the German Reformed church, but he was acquitted on both occasions, and gradually established an international reputation from his base at Union Theological Seminary in New York. He accepted the invitation, and quickly organized American committees for the revision of the Old and New Testaments. The American committees, which met in Bible House, New York (headquarters of the American Bible Society, then in Astor Place), were interdenominational; membership included Episcopalians, but the Episcopal Church declined to participate in the American revision. Schaff was alert to the sensitivity of the project, and so sought to reassure American Protestants:

> The people need not apprehend any dangerous innovations. No article of faith, no moral precept, will be disturbed, no sectarian views will be introduced. The revision will so nearly resemble the present version, that the mass of readers and hearers will scarcely perceive the difference; while a careful comparison will show slight improvements in every chapter and almost in every verse. The only serious difficulty may arise from a change of the text in a few instances where the overwhelming evidence of the oldest manuscripts makes a change necessary; and perhaps also from a change in the italics, the metrical arrangement of poetry and the sectional of prose and from new headings of chapters, which, however, are no part of the Word of God, and may be handled with greater freedom.

Transatlantic cooperation was not easy in the nineteenth century, especially as the two sets of committees intended to work as a single unit. The division of the committees by an ocean had the advantage, however, of ensuring that there were two independent views of the text. The British and American committees worked to the same timetables, and exchanged drafts in confidence. The committees then attempted to harmonize any differences, and the results of this process were exchanged. Although there was one important point on which the two sides agreed to disagree—the American translation of the Tetragrammaton was 'Jehovah', while the British retained 'the LORD'—the two versions are largely identical. There was, however, an appendix listing American words and phrases that had not been incorporated into the text (for example, 'wheat' instead of British 'corn'), and eventually these variants were embodied in the American text.

Members of the British and American committees are listed in Appendix 1 (pp. 296–303).

Procedures for Revision

Eight rules were devised to govern the process of revision:

1. To introduce as few alterations as possible into the text of the Authorized Version consistently with faithfulness.
2. To limit, as far as possible, the expression of such alterations to the language of the Authorized or earlier versions.
3. Each Company to go twice over the portion to be revised, once provisionally, the second time finally.
4. That the text to be adopted be that for which the evidence is decidedly preponderating; and that when the text so adopted differs from that from which the authorized version was made, the alteration be indicated in the margin.
5. To make or retain no change in the text, on the second final revision by each Company, except two-thirds of those present approve of the same; but on the first revision to decide by simple majorities.
6. In every case of proposed alteration that may have given rise to discussion, to defer the voting thereon till the next meeting, whensoever the same shall be required by one-third of those present at the meeting, such intended vote to be announced in the notice of the next meeting.

7. To revise the headings of chapters, pages, paragraphs, italics, and punctuation.
8. To refer, on the part of each Company, when considered desirable, to divines, scholars, and literary men, whether at home or abroad, for their opinions.

These rules echo those of the first edition of the KJV. The first rule of the RV recapitulates the first rule of the KJV, which was 'The ordinary Bible read in the church, commonly called the Bishops' Bible, to be followed, and as little altered as the truth of the original will permit'. In this sense, the work of the Victorian revisers reflects the aspirations of the 1611 translators, which 'was not to make a new translation...but to make a good one better'.

The ambition to improve the KJV rather than replace it was laudable inasmuch as improvement was defined in terms of taking into account the biblical scholarship of the nineteenth century. The problem that the English New Testament committee faced was a lack of consensus on the standing of the new corpus of Greek manuscripts. The principal antagonists were all formidable scholars. Frederick Scrivener, a textual conservative who was later to become the editor of the Cambridge Paragraph Bible (see Chapter 9), was a champion of the 'Byzantine text', which was close to the Textus Receptus of the KJV. Fenton Hort and Brooke Foss Westcott represented the opposite position, which was that Vatican and Sinaitic codices (see p. 269) offered superior readings of the Greek text. Hort was a particularly insistent debater, and it was said that he spoke for three of the ten years during which the committee met. In the event, it was the views of Westcott and Hort that prevailed, and translations of traditional readings were consigned to the margins. As the chairman of the American Committee proclaimed, 'the Greek text followed by these Revisers is of far higher authority than that known and followed by the King James' revisers. Their Greek text was based on manuscripts of the later parts of the Mediaeval Ages, but ours has been perfected by the discovery of far more ancient manuscripts.'

The change in the Greek text that underlay the translation was so important that Oxford University Press agreed to publish a scholarly account of the new readings. The editor was Edwin Palmer, whose *Greek Testament with the Readings Adopted by the Revisers of the Authorised Version* was published in 1881 as a companion to the Revised Version of the New Testament. Palmer's preface explains that the revisers

> did not esteem it within their province to construct a continuous and complete Greek text. They adopted, however, a large number of readings which deviated from the text presumed to underlie the Authorised Version, and they put a list of these readings into the hands of the Delegates and Syndics of the Oxford and Cambridge University Presses, in order that they may be brought in one way or another before the public. The Delegates of the Oxford Press have thought it most convenient to introduce them into a continuous Greek text, and to set at the foot of each page the readings which they displace, together with those readings which are noticed in the margin of the Revised Version.

In 1882 this text was reprinted (again by OUP) together with parallel KJV and RV texts in *The New Testament of our Lord and Saviour Jesus Christ, being the Authorised Version Set forth in 1611 Arranged in Parallel Columns with the Revised Version of 1881 and with the Greek Text Followed in the Revised Version, to which are Added the Readings Followed in the Authorised Version and the Readings Noted in the Margin of the Revised Version*. With respect

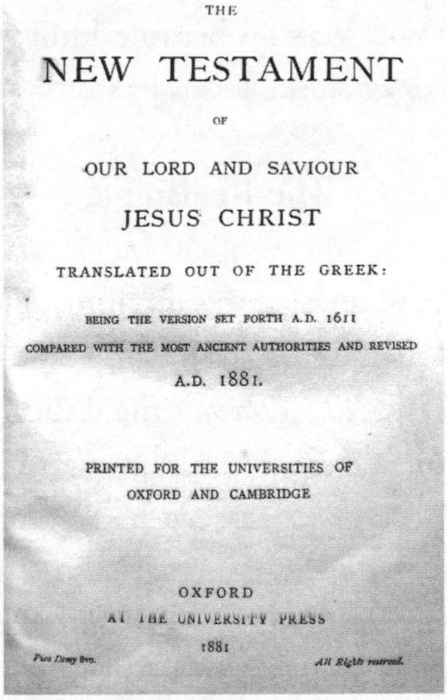
THE
NEW TESTAMENT
OF
OUR LORD AND SAVIOUR
JESUS CHRIST
TRANSLATED OUT OF THE GREEK:
BEING THE VERSION SET FORTH A.D. 1611
COMPARED WITH THE MOST ANCIENT AUTHORITIES AND REVISED
A.D. 1881.
PRINTED FOR THE UNIVERSITIES OF
OXFORD AND CAMBRIDGE
OXFORD
AT THE UNIVERSITY PRESS
1881
All Rights reserved.

FIGURE 34. Title-page of the Revised Version of the New Testament, Oxford, 1881.

to the New Testament, this edition was Oxford's answer to the Cambridge Paragraph Bible of 1873, which had been based on the Textus Receptus.

The Revised Version of the New Testament was published in 1881 and the Old Testament (in four volumes) in 1885. The Apocrypha was more problematical, because of its suspect standing in the eyes of many Protestants, especially in the United States. In the event three small companies were assembled from the English New Testament Committee and a fourth from the English Old Testament Committee, and the Americans took no part in the revision of the Apocrypha, which was published as a separate volume in 1895.

The Revised Version, Standard American Edition, which is now known as the American Standard Version, was not published until 1901 because of copyright issues. Thereafter the British version of the Revised Version became known to Americans as the English Revised Version.

The Revision

The second rule of the revisers was 'to limit, as far as possible, the expression of such alterations to the language of the Authorized or earlier versions'. Indeed, such was the standing of the KJV that the revisers had little alternative. Language that in 1611 had been a formal version of everyday speech had become archaic by the 1870s, but reverence for the language of the KJV had reached such a peak that modernizing it was out of the question. The revisers were, however, obliged to change words and phrases and sentences in the light of recent scholarship, but could not present these changes in contemporary English, which would have struck a discordant note in a text dominated by Jacobean English. They therefore took the decision to imitate Jacobean English, so producing the literary equivalent of mock-Jacobean architecture and 'Ye Olde Tea Shoppe'. And, as change was driven by scholarly scruple, there was a strong collective impulse towards literalism. There were also deleterious grammatical and lexical changes. The formulation of grammatical rules in the eighteenth century (when it became immoral to end a sentence with a preposition) and their refinement in the nineteenth century (when splitting an infinitive became a sin) had rendered some of the grammar of the KJV incorrect, so it was quietly corrected. And, whereas the KJV and its Protestant predecessors favoured a plain vocabulary that was Old English in origin, the RV revisers tended to deploy a Latinate vocabulary that at times resembles that of the Douai–Reims Bible; the result was increased sonority and increased distance from the language of ordinary readers. Consider, for example, the final clause in Romans 6:19, which in the KJV read 'even so now yield your members servants to righteousness, unto holiness'. In the RV, the clause reads 'even so now present your members *as* servants to righteousness unto sanctification'. 'Yield' and 'holiness' both derive from Old English; 'present' and 'sanctification' are both of Latin origin. Indeed, 'sanctification' comes from ecclesiastical Latin, where it has a technical meaning that has been carried over into English. Many readers would be baffled by sanctification, but all would understand holiness. The result of all these changes, alas, is that the language of the RSV is flat; lovers of well-wrought prose esteem the KJV but cast a cold eye on the RSV.

Reception of the New Testament

On the day of its publication, the Revised Version of the New Testament sold 300,000 copies, and on a single day in May 1881 Oxford University Press sold more than a million copies. Such was the excitement that passages were serialized in newspapers. The success of the launch was a publisher's dream, but adulation proved to be short lived. The Revised Version was well received in academic circles, but failed to win the affection of the church-going public, and incurred the enmity of conservatives, who disapproved of the use of the Greek text by Westcott and Hort rather than the Textus Receptus of the KJV. The most vociferous opponent was John William Burgon, dean of Chichester, who is now remembered for his description of Petra as 'a rose-red city half as old as time' (when he later visited Petra, he was disappointed to find 'nothing rosy'). Burgon was a tireless opponent of progressive causes, notably the advancement of women; their place, he argued, like Sarah's, was in the tent. He therefore opposed the admission of women (and Roman Catholics and Jews) to public bodies and to universities. When the Church of Ireland was disestablished in 1869, he declared the action to be 'the nation's formal rejection of God'.

In 1875 Burgon accepted Prime Minister Disraeli's offer of the deanery of Chichester. He was by this time an established biblical scholar, and had published a treatise arguing for the authenticity of the last twelve verses (the 'long ending') of Mark's gospel. When the Revised Version of the New Testament was published in 1881, he took the bracketing of the last twelve verses (denoting uncertainty about their authenticity) as a rebuke to his scholarship, and unleashed a torrent of criticism of the Revised Version. He wrote a series of polemical articles for the *Quarterly Review*, and then reached a much larger public by collecting them in a book called *The Revision Revised* (1883). At the heart of his disparagement of the RV lay a disagreement about the Greek source text. Burgon was an advocate of the Textus Receptus of the New Testament and a principled opponent of the Westcott and Hort text, which in his view was over-dependent on readings in the Vatican and Sinai codices. This was not, however, merely an arid technical debate between scholars, because the Greek text was deemed to be inspired. The precise nature of this inspiration was disputed, and Dean Burgon was an advocate of verbal inspiration, according to which every word of the Greek (and Hebrew) text was given by the Spirit of God. That meant that the argument was not about which was the better text, but rather about which text the Spirit of God had given. Burgon felt passionately that God had inspired the Textus Receptus of the New Testament, and wrote two works in defence of this view; they were published posthumously, in 1896. Burgon's attack was immensely damaging, and the reputation of the RV never recovered from his strictures. Even now, proponents of the King James Only position (discussed in Chapter 13) gather together in the Dean Burgon Society, whose members regard the *The Revision Revised* as the founding text of the society named in Burgon's honour.

At the other end of the spectrum, the publication of the RV New Testament gave rise to the most famous joke about the KJV. In the version of the story reported by Philip Schaff, a deacon is said to have opposed the revision on the grounds that, 'if St James's Version was good enough for St Paul, it is good enough for me'.

The Old Testament

The revisers of the Old Testament were still at work on their text when the obloquy of textual conservatives was unleashed on the New Testament, and there is some evidence that the criticism affected their deliberations. That said, the Old Testament lacked the theological importance of the New Testament for Christian readers, and the underlying Hebrew text had not changed radically (that lay ahead with the discovery of the Dead Sea Scrolls between 1947 and 1956 (see p. 270)), so there was less incentive to controversy. Nonetheless, an increased emphasis on the oral transmission of the Hebrew text led to some startling changes: 'Though he slay me, yet will I trust in him' (Job 13:15) in the KJV, for example, became its exact opposite in the Revised Version: 'Behold, he will slay me; I have no hope.'

The evidence of the notes of William Aldis Wright (secretary of the Old Testament Committee), which records proposed changes, gives no hint of the reasons for the proposals nor the methods by which the revisers worked. A section of the KJV marked up for revision, discovered by Diarmaid MacCulloch in the library of Wesley College (Westbury on Trym, Bristol), does, however, illuminate part of the process. The Wesley College manuscript is the section (1 and 2 Chronicles and part of Ezra) undertaken by the Hebraist Benjamin Harrison, and its existence may imply that the text was divided up and assigned to individual translators, as was the case with the Bishops' Bible of 1568. If so, this practice is consistent with the hypothesis that the heart of the matter was the perceived need to revise the New Testament at the fundamental level of its textual foundations, and that the Old Testament was simply given a sympathetic polishing to enable an entire Bible to be published. That said, the evidence of the Wesley College manuscript implies a more complex process. In the case of Harrison's revision of 2 Chronicles 4, for example, his recommendations for the revision of verse 6 (substituting 'belonged to' for 'they offered for') and verse 7 (substituting 'the ordinance concerning them' for 'their form') were clearly accepted, because that is how they appear in the RV. In the case of the first part of verse 5, however, there are clear indications that the verse was radically revised after it left Harrison's hands. The Blayney text from which he was working read:

> And the thickness of it *was* an handbreadth, and the brim of it
> like the work of the brim of a cup, with flowers of lilies...

In the revision that Harrison proposed, the text would have read:

> And the thickness of it *was* an handbreadth, and the brim thereof
> was wrought as the brim of a cup, like the flower of a lily...

The published text adopts the suggestion of 'wrought' (which was eventually changed to 'made') and concurs with Harrison's view, embodied in the KJV marginal note, that 'lily' should be singular, but it also reorders the opening phrase:

> And it was an handbreadth thick; and the brim thereof was wrought like the brim of a cup, like the flower of a lily...

This evidence seems to imply that the text was indeed divided and assigned to individuals, but that the company of which each reviser was a member did not accept revisions on trust, but rather considered every suggestion, either adopting it (as in the case of verses 6 and 7) or modifying it (as in verse 5).

A similar process may be observed in the two important books that describe the revision process. In 1897 Brooke Foss Westcott published *Some Lessons of the Revised Version of the New Testament*, which is a distinctly defensive account. By contrast, *A Companion to the Revised Old Testament* (1885) by Talbot Chambers, a Dutch Reformed member of the American Old Testament Committee, is a calm exposition of an altogether less contentious process whereby the committee sought to render the translation clearer and so more forceful. It is possible that on the British side of the Atlantic debate was more animated, but there is no evidence that this was so. The heart of the debate lay with the New Testament.

The Revised Version Revised

The principles that informed the Revised Version made further revision inevitable, in part because rival translations began to appear in the early twentieth century. The first revision of the looking toward the east: and the sea *was set* above upon them, and all their hinder parts *were* inward.

5 And the thickness of it *was* an handbreadth, and the brim ~~of it like~~ ~~the work of~~ the brim of a cup, ² ~~with~~ flowers of ~~lilies; and~~ it received and held ᵈ three thousand baths.

6 ¶ He made also ᵉ ten lavers, and put five on the right hand, and five on the left, to wash in them ⌊ ³ such things as ~~they offered for~~ the burnt offering they washed in them ⌊ but the sea *was* for the priests to wash in.

7 ᶠ And he made ten candlesticks of gold ᵍ according to their ~~form~~, and set *them* in the temple, five on the right hand, and five on the left.

8 ʰ He made also ten tables, and placed *them* in the temple, five on the right side, and five on the left. And he made an hundred ⁴ basons of gold.

9 ¶ Furthermore ⁱ he made the court of the priests, and the great court, and doors for the court, and overlaid the doors of them with brass.

10 And ᵏ he set the sea on the right side, ~~of the~~ east ~~end~~, over against the south.

11 And ˡ Huram made the pots, and the shovels, and the ⁵ basons. ~~And~~ Huram ⁶~~finished~~ the work that he ~~was to make~~ for king Solomon ~~for~~ the house of God;

12 ~~To wit~~, the two pillars, and ᵐ the ~~pommels,~~ and the ⌊chapiters *which were* on the top of the ⌊two⌉ pillars, and the two ~~wreaths~~ to cover the two ~~pommels~~ of the chapiters which *were* on the top of the pillars;

13 And ⁿ four hundred pomegranates ~~on~~ the two wreaths; two rows of pomegranates on each wreath, to cover the two pommels of the chapiters which *were* ⁷ upon the pillars.

14 He made also ⌊ bases, and ⁸ lavers made he upon the ⌊ bases;

15 One sea, and twelve oxen under it.

16 The pots also, and the shovels, and the fleshhooks, and all their ~~in-struments~~, did ✗Huram his father make ~~to~~ king Solomon for the house of the LORD of ⁹ bright brass.

17 ⁱIn the plain of Jordan did the king cast them, in the ²clay ground between Succoth and Zeredathah.

Revised Version was the Revised Standard Version (NT 1946, OT 1952, Apocrypha 1957). In 1937 the International Council of Religious Education, which held the copyright of the American Standard Version (ASV), assembled a committee of thirty-two members, chaired by Luther Weigle, charged with a revision of the ASV; there was a plan to create a corresponding British committee, but the Second World War made such collaboration impossible, so the committee remained entirely North American.

The translation panel used the seventeenth edition of the scholarly Nestle–Aland Greek text (which is now in its twenty-eighth edition) for the New Testament, and the established Hebrew Masoretic Text for the Old Testament. Translations of the Greek text were relatively uncontroversial, but the practice of incorporating occasional readings from the Dead Sea Scrolls was destined to attract criticism.

The RSV refined the scholarship of the RV and ASV, but there were points of difference. On language policy, the RV differed from the ASV on two points of principle. First, on the debate about the translation of the Tetragrammaton, it chose to use 'LORD' or 'GOD' instead of 'Jehovah'. Second, the RSV retained archaic pronouns (thou, thee, thy, thine) and verb forms (art, hadst, and so on) in references to God, but used modern pronouns and verb forms in references to humans.

The publication of the RSV New Testament in 1946 was greeted warmly, but the Old Testament published in 1952 met with a mixed response. There were accusations, perhaps tinged with anti-Semitism, that the presence of a Jewish scholar (the Canadian Harry Orlinsky) among the revisers had given undue prominence to Jewish understandings of the Bible, and so played down the Messianic prophecies in verses such as Genesis 22:18, in which God's promise to Abraham, which appears in the KJV as 'and in thy seed shall all the nations of the earth be blessed', is translated in the RSV as 'and by your descendants shall all the nations of the earth bless themselves'. The central point of contention, however, was the treatment of a word in Isaiah 7:14, for which the KJV and RV translate the Hebrew as 'behold, a virgin shall conceive', whereas the RSV reads 'Behold, a young woman shall conceive'. In Hebrew the word *almah* denotes a woman of marriageable age, and so, in a neutral context, might be translated 'young woman', 'maiden', 'virgin', or 'teenager'. In such situations the Greek text of the Old Testament is often a useful guide, and in this instance it uses *parthenos,* which means 'virgin'; similarly, Matthew's assertion that the birth of Jesus has fulfilled this prophecy (Matthew 1:23) also uses the word *parthenos.* Against this reading, however, is the availability of another Hebrew word, *betulah,* which means 'virgin'. Both words are problematical, and translators have to make choices. The decision of the RSV revisers to translate *almah* as 'young woman' left them open to the accusation of denying the virgin birth of Jesus. The decision alienated evangelical Protestants, who looked elsewhere for a Bible that was doctrinally sound.

In 1962 there was a minor revision of the RSV (sometimes known as the 'Modified Edition'), and it is clear that the revisers responded to doctrinal sensitivities. The Roman soldier who witnessed the death of Jesus, for example, had in the original RSV referred to Jesus as 'a son of God', but in 1962 the phrase became 'the Son of God'. The real significance of this edition did not lie in its minor revisions, but rather in the fact that this was the text used as the basis for what had previously been unthinkable: a

Roman Catholic edition of the RSV. In the early 1960s relations between Protestants and Catholics thawed, and from 1964 the Vatican designated Protestants as 'separated brethren' rather than schismatics. This ecumenical spirit led to the publishing, by the Catholic Biblical Association of Great Britain, of a Catholic Edition of the RSV, which is commonly known as the Ignatius edition or by its initials, RSV-CE. The New Testament appeared in 1965 and the Old Testament in 1966. The Catholic canon includes deutero-canonical books known to Protestants as Apocrypha, and, as the RSV did not contain these books, the English RV edition of 1895 was adapted for the purpose. In the same period, American scholars prepared the New American Standard Bible (NT 1963, OT 1971; revised edition 1995), a revision of the American Standard Version of 1901 that took into account recent scholarship on the Hebrew and Greek texts, and also aspired to a more literal style of translation. This full-scale scholarly edition should not be confused with the Sacred Scriptures Bethel Edition (1981), which is a revision of the ASV published by the Assemblies of Yahweh (a small Pennsylvania-based group) in which the most prominent change is the use of Yahweh (for Jehovah) and Yahshua (for Jesus).

The Ignatius edition made no changes in the text of the Old Testament, even retaining the Protestant system of numbering the Psalms (though the Catholic numbers were placed in parentheses). In the New Testament, however, changes were made to reflect Catholic liturgy (for example, Mary is 'full of grace' in Luke 1:28) or doctrine (for example, in Matthew 1:19 the RSV 'divorce her' is replaced by 'send her away'). There were also changes based on textual scholarship, notably the inclusion of the longer ending of Mark's gospel (Mark 16:9–20) and of the story of the woman taken in adultery (John 7:53–8:11).

The Ignatius Bible was a milestone, because it was the first time that a Protestant Bible had been adapted for Catholic purposes. The response of scholarly Protestants to this edition was similarly remarkable, because some of the textual changes in the Ignatius edition were adopted in the full revision of the RSV that was published in 1971, notably the restoration of the long ending of Mark and of the woman taken in adultery, both of which had been relegated to footnotes in the original RSV.

The 1971 RSV contained a major revision of the New Testament, and so was designated a second edition. The textual restorations included not only the two inaugurated by the Catholic edition, but the full text of the institution of the Last Supper in Luke 22:19–20 (which in the RSV had ended with 'This is my body'); on the other hand, the appearance of an angel to Jesus in Gethsemane (Luke 22:43–44) was relegated to a footnote because of doubts about its authenticity. In a gesture of internationalism, the notes explaining the value of money dropped the RSV's use of American currency in favour of equivalences based on how long it was deemed to take to earn each coin: in Revelation 6:6 a denarius ceased to be 20 cents and became a day's wage for a labourer.

The culmination of these converging Catholic and Protestant editions was the Ecumenical Edition of the RSV published 1973, which is popularly known from its cover and spine title as the 'Common Bible'. The challenge that such an enterprise posed was including the Apocrypha as variously defined. The solution was to divide the text into four sections: the Old Testament, the deutero-canonical books of the Catholic Church, the three books of the Protestant Apocrypha that are not included in the Roman Catholic canon, and the New Testament. The following year

Oxford University Press broadened the circle of inclusion to include the Orthodox Church by publishing *The New Oxford Annotated Bible with the Apocrypha: Revised Standard Version, Containing the Second Edition of the New Testament and an Expanded Edition of the Apocrypha*, which is known from its cover and spine title as the Ecumenical Study Bible. This edition included a fresh translation of Psalm 151 and 3 and 4 Maccabees, the canonicity of which is accepted only by the Orthodox Church.

In 1989 the National Council of Churches produced a major revision of the RSV entitled the New Revised Standard Version. Small adjustments were made to the Old Testament to reflect readings recently made available in the Dead Sea Scrolls, and recent textual scholarship was taken into account. The distinction drawn in the RSV between archaic forms (thou, thee, thy, thine) used with reference to God and modern forms in reference to humans was dropped in favour of entirely modern forms on the grounds that 'in the original languages neither the Old Testament nor the New makes any linguistic distinction between addressing a human being and addressing the Deity'. Most controversially of all, the editors of the NRSV decided to use gender-neutral language on the grounds (as explained in the preface) that 'many in the churches have become sensitive to the danger of linguistic sexism arising from the inherent bias of the English language towards the masculine gender, a bias that in the case of the Bible has often restricted or obscured the meaning of the original text'. 'Man' therefore became 'person' or 'adult', and 'brothers' was expanded to 'brothers and sisters'. Thus in 1 Corinthians 13:11, which in the RSV read 'when I became a man, I gave up childish ways', appears in the NRSV as 'when I became an adult, I put an end to childish ways'.

The NRSV has been adopted or approved by many Protestant denominations and by the Catholic Church. In addition to the Protestant edition, the NRSV appears in a Catholic edition, a Common Bible edition, and in editions with British spelling. It also appears in many study-Bible editions, including the *The New Oxford Annotated Bible with Apocrypha* (3rd edition, 2001), *The Oxford New Revised Standard Version Anglicized Cross-Reference Edition* (1995), and, most recently, *The Green Bible* (2008), an edition of the NRSV with an emphasis on environmental issues; this Bible is printed on recycled paper and uses soy-based ink, and biblical passages concerning the environment are highlighted in green.

Many evangelical churches, on the other hand, have little affection for the NRSV, in some cases because of its politically correct gender neutrality, but mostly because it fails the litmus test of Isaiah 7:14 and blots out prophetic understandings of Old Testament texts (e.g. Psalm 22:16 is translated 'my hands and feet have shriveled' rather than the KJV's 'they pierced my hands and my feet'). In 2001 evangelical scholars produced an alternative revision of the RSV called the English Standard Version (ESV), in which gendered language is restored and, in Isaiah 7:14, 'virgin' is restored. A study-Bible edition was published in 2008. In 2009 Oxford University Press, having noted the popularity of the ESV beyond evangelical circles, published what is in effect a 'common Bible' edition of the ESV with Apocrypha (including the deuterocanonical books of the Roman Catholic and Orthodox churches).

The Catholic Church also disliked the NSRV, in part because of its disapproval of the use of gender-neutral language in certain passages. Like the Protestant evangelicals, it decided on an alternative revision. In 2006 the Ignatius Press released what is in effect a second edition of the RSV-CE. Like the Protestant ESV, the RSV-SCE restores 'virgin' to Isaiah 7:14.

Revision or New Translation?

The Revised Version is, like Blayney's edition of 1769, a reworking of the text, but its incorporation of recent textual scholarship of the Bible took it a step further away from the Bible of 1611. Blayney had introduced some 16,000 changes, but the RV introduced another 36,000 changes. It is possible to view the RV as a modernization of the KJV, but it is also possible to view it as a new version of the Bible. The former was the view of the American revisers, whose edition was entitled *The Holy Bible, Containing the Old and New Testaments, Translated out of the Original Tongues, Being the Version Set Forth A.D. 1611, Compared with the Most Ancient Authorities and Revised A.D. 1881–1885, Newly Edited by the American Revision Committee A.D. 1901, Standard Edition*. The RV and its American cousin the American Standard Version were in turn revised as the Revised Standard Version and the New American Standard Bible, and the RSV has been revised in rival (or complementary) editions by liberal Protestants, evangelical Protestants, and Roman Catholics. This process evokes the old puzzle about the point at which a repeatedly darned sock ceases to be the original sock and becomes a new, reworked sock. It is possible to argue that the Revised Version inaugurated a series of revisions that gradually moved away from the KJV, but it is equally possible to argue that these new versions are simply means of keeping the power and spirit of the KJV alive for succeeding generations.

12

⌒⌒⌒

THE EARLY TWENTIETH
CENTURY

New Editions

In the first half of the twentieth century the rift between the King James Version (KJV) as a literary artefact and a sacred text widened. The Baskerville Bible of 1763 may be the most beautiful book that Cambridge University Press has ever produced, but it was intended to be used, not simply admired as an aesthetic object. In the early twentieth century, however, there was a further division. In addition to Bibles published for everyday use by Christians, scholarly editions were published to mark the tercentenary of the KJV in 1911, and two important Bibles were designed for aesthetic pleasure: the Doves Press Bible and the Oxford Lectern Bible.

There were three important tercentenary Bibles, all published by Oxford University Press in 1911. One was a facsimile in reduced size of the 1611 text, introduced by A. W. Pollard, the bibliographer and book historian who was the greatest living authority on the KJV. Pollard's book-length introduction (which was indeed soon to be published as a separate book) consisted of a scholarly narrative account of the origins and later life of the KJV, and an annotated edition of sixty-two documents relevant to an understanding of the KJV, ranging from a prohibition of 1408 (in Latin) against unauthorized translations of the Bible 'under pain of excommunication and the stigma of heresy' to the report of 1618 by Samuel Ward (again in Latin) on the background of the KJV to the Synod of Dort. For the historian of the 1611 Bible, this collection of documents is a treasure trove.

The second tercentenary Bible, again edited by Pollard, was a mechanical reproduction of the Oxford text in roman type published in 1833, to which was prefixed Pollard's historical introduction (but not his edition of the documents). The third tercentenary Bible originated in America (though it was published by Oxford University Press in England as well as in the USA) and was actually called *The 1911 Tercentenary Commemoration Bible: The Holy Bible Containing the Old and New Testaments Translated out of the Original Tongues and with the Former Translations Diligently Compared and Revised by King James's Special Command 1611: The Text Carefully Corrected and Amended 1911*. This careful correcting and amending of the text are said to have been undertaken by 'a committee of 34 eminent Hebrew and Greek scholars' in the USA and Canada, 'representing all the great evangelical bodies', and the edition featured 'a new system of references prepared by C. I. Scofield'. This is the Scofield of the Scofield Reference Bible, which is discussed below. The text of this Bible is an outlier in the textual history of the KJV, because it had no progeny, even in the Scofield Bible. The text is a bold reworking of the standard American text. Sometimes it introduces the marginal note into the text, so 'Thou hast multiplied the nation, and not increased the joy' (Isaiah 9:3) appears as 'Thou hast multiplied the nation, and increased the joy'. On many occasions it simply rewrites the text.

These three editions are indicative of the impact of the tercentenary on public consciousness on both sides of the Atlantic. There were many exhibitions (notably at the British Museum and at Yale) and many commemorative events. In England 26 March was declared to be Tercentenary Sunday, and on 29 March a public celebration was held at the Royal Albert Hall. There was a similar event in New York, where the *New York Times* reported that a gathering that filled the topmost balconies of Carnegie Hall heard letters from King George and President Taft. The vast audience stood while a former Secretary of State (John Foster) read President Taft's letter:

> The publication of this version of the Holy Scriptures in 1611 associates it with the early colonies of the English people upon this continent. It became at once the Bible of our American forefathers. Its classic English has given shape to American literature. Its spirit has influenced American ideals in life and laws and government.

These are strong claims, but they are broadly speaking true. It was indeed the KJV rather than the Geneva Bible that was read in the colonial period. The Bible pervades the classics of nineteenth-century American literature; readers seeing the opening line of *Moby Dick* ('Call me Ishmael'), for example, did not need a footnote to know that Ishmael was the illegitimate child of Abraham and his servant Hagar, and that he was cast out after the birth of Isaac. It is hard to be certain what President Taft meant by the 'spirit' of the KJV, but it is certainly the case that this translation has had a profound effect on American thinking about 'life and laws and government'.

The commemorative editions and celebrations are indicative of popular sentiment, but there were also editions produced for cultural elites. The Doves Press, for example, was the private press of the bookbinder and printer T. J. Cobden Sanderson, who was one of the presiding figures of the Arts and Crafts movement. The Doves Press Bible (5 volumes, 1902–5), which used Scrivener's text, was largely the work of Emery (later Sir Emery) Walker, who was the most influential typographer of the early twentieth century. Walker's Bible, like his editions of Shakespeare and Milton, eschewed illustration and ornament in favour of text in the Doves type (based on a Renaissance Venetian type) enhanced only by some initials drawn by the calligrapher and letter designer Edward Johnston and Johnston's pupil Graily Hewitt. The page design, like the typeface, was intended to recall the Renaissance, and Johnston's magnificent initials gesture at the work of the medieval rubricator, the specialist scribes who drew the headings in red ink in manuscripts (hence the notion of a 'red-letter day'). This is a Bible rather like a chair designed by Charles Rennie Mackintosh: both are meant to be admired rather than used, so, just as a Mackintosh chair would be uncomfortable to sit on (and might indeed collapse), so the Doves Bible is difficult to read.

The Oxford Lectern Bible, which was the work of the American book designer Bruce Rogers, was published by Oxford University Press in 1935. Rogers had formidable expertise in typography (in 1917 he had published an important 'Report on the Typography at the Cambridge University Press' during one of his sojourns in England) and was arguably the greatest book designer in American history. His expertise also extended to paper and equipment, and he was insistent that modern production methods were not inconsistent with fine design. His massive Oxford Lectern Bible (the pages are 12 inches × 16 inches) was not handset, but was produced on a monotype typecasting machine; the typeface was Centaur,

IN THE BEGINNING

GOD CREATED THE HEAVEN AND THE EARTH. ⟨AND THE EARTH WAS WITHOUT FORM, AND VOID; AND DARKNESS WAS UPON THE FACE OF THE DEEP, & THE SPIRIT OF GOD MOVED UPON THE FACE OF THE WATERS. ⟨And God said, Let there be light: & there was light. And God saw the light, that it was good: & God divided the light from the darkness. And God called the light Day, and the darkness he called Night. And the evening and the morning were the first day. ⟨And God said, Let there be a firmament in the midst of the waters, & let it divide the waters from the waters. And God made the firmament, and divided the waters which were under the firmament from the waters which were above the firmament: & it was so. And God called the firmament Heaven. And the evening & the morning were the second day. ⟨And God said, Let the waters under the heaven be gathered together unto one place, and let the dry land appear: and it was so. And God called the dry land Earth; and the gathering together of the waters called he Seas: and God saw that it was good. And God said, Let the earth bring forth grass, the herb yielding seed, and the fruit tree yielding fruit after his kind, whose seed is in itself, upon the earth: & it was so. And the earth brought forth grass, & herb yielding seed after his kind, & the tree yielding fruit, whose seed was in itself, after his kind: and God saw that it was good. And the evening & the morning were the third day. ⟨And God said, Let there be lights in the firmament of the heaven to divide the day from the night; and let them be for signs, and for seasons, and for days, & years: and let them be for lights in the firmament of the heaven to give light upon the earth: & it was so. And God made two great lights; the greater light to rule the day, and the lesser light to rule the night: he made the stars also. And God set them in the firmament of the heaven to give light upon the earth, and to rule over the day and over the night, & to divide the light from the darkness: and God saw that it was good. And the evening and the morning were the fourth day. ⟨And God said, Let the waters bring forth abundantly the moving creature that hath life, and fowl that may fly above the earth in the open firmament of heaven. And God created great whales, & every living creature that moveth, which the waters brought forth abundantly, after their kind, & every winged fowl after his kind: & God saw that it was good. And God blessed them, saying, Be fruitful, & multiply, and fill the waters in the seas, and let fowl multiply in the earth. And the evening & the morning were the fifth day. ⟨And God said, Let the earth bring forth the living creature after his kind, cattle, and creeping thing, and beast of the earth after his kind: and it was so. And God made the beast of the earth after his kind, and cattle after their kind, and every thing that creepeth upon the

27

FIGURE 36. Opening of Genesis, Doves Press Bible, 1903–5.

which had been designed by Rogers in 1914 for the Metropolitan Museum of Art in New York. This Bible is widely regarded as the mostly beautiful book of the twentieth century. Like the Doves Press Bible, it looks back to the Renaissance: the Centaur type used for the text was modelled on the pioneering roman type of Nicolas Jenson, a French typographer working in Renaissance Venice; the larger type used for book titles and running heads derived from one by Robert Estienne, the French Renaissance printer whose English Bibles had introduced division of chapters into verses. His predecessor, who had been the first to number verses in any language, was the Italian Sante Pagnini, whose translation of the Bible into Latin (published in France in 1527) introduced the paraph marks (of which the modern form is ¶) that are imitated in the verse numbering of the Oxford Lectern Bible; in Pagnini's Bible the paraphs, which are aggressively ugly, are used to signal the verse numbers in the margin, but in Rogers's design a subdued form of the paraph elegantly shelters each verse number. The pages contain neither chapter summaries nor marginal cross-references, and so are wonderfully uncluttered; the only exception is 'The Translators to the Reader', where marginal notes have been retained, possibly to allow Rogers to deploy his elegant Greek font. The result of the immense talent that Rogers brought to the project and of the care that was lavished on every detail is one of the finest triumphs of the art of the book-designer.

The Scofield Bible

The Oxford Lectern Bible was the work of an American designer in England. In America, the most influential product of early twentieth-century evangelical scholarship was the Scofield

The Gospel according to
St. JOHN

CHAPTER I

IN the beginning was the Word, and the Word was with God, and the Word was God. ⟨2 The same was in the beginning with God. ⟨3 All things were made by him; and without him was not any thing made that was made. ⟨4 In him was life; and the life was the light of men. ⟨5 And the light shineth in darkness; and the darkness comprehended it not.

⟨6 There was a man sent from God, whose name was John. ⟨7 The same came for a witness, to bear witness of the Light, that all men through him might believe. ⟨8 He was not that Light, but was sent to bear witness of that Light. ⟨9 That was the true Light, which lighteth every man that cometh into the world. ⟨10 He was in the world, and the world was made by him, and said they unto him, Who art thou? that we may give an answer to them that sent us. What sayest thou of thyself? ⟨23 He said, I am the voice of one crying in the wilderness, Make straight the way of the Lord, as said the prophet Esaias. ⟨24 And they which were sent were of the Pharisees. ⟨25 And they asked him, and said unto him, Why baptizest thou then, if thou be not that Christ, nor Elias, neither that prophet? ⟨26 John answered them, saying, I baptize with water: but there standeth one among you, whom ye know not; ⟨27 He it is, who coming after me is preferred before me, whose shoe's latchet I am not worthy to unloose. ⟨28 These things were done in Bethabara beyond Jordan, where John was baptizing.

FIGURE 37. Opening of John's Gospel, Oxford Lectern Bible, 1935.

Reference Bible, which was first published in 1909. Cyrus I. Scofield was largely self-educated. Little is known about his youth, and, as the *American National Biography* explains, 'he was secretive about his past and not above distorting the facts of his shadowy years'. He married well in St Louis, and then moved to Kansas, where he embarked on a promising career as a lawyer and Republican politician. His progress was hampered by debt, alcohol abuse, and criminal charges, and in 1879 Scofield deserted his wife and children to return to St Louis, where he experienced an evangelical conversion. In 1883 he divorced and remarried, and became a Congregationalist minister in Dallas, which in the twentieth century was to become the seat of Dallas Theological Seminary, which continues to represent the dispensational premillennialism that was the most distinctive feature of Scofield's teaching.

Scofield was a Congregationalist who later became a Presbyterian, but his significance does not lie in these confessional allegiances. On the contrary, he represents the tradition of trans-denominational (now known as non-denominational) evangelical Christianity, to which his central contribution was the edition of the KJV that bears his name. Scofield felt that the KJV needed to be supplemented with notes of guidance that would embody the doctrine that had emerged in the evangelical revival of the late nineteenth century, and so in 1903 resigned his pastoral ministry in order to devote himself to the preparation of an evangelical edition of the Bible, one in which the text would be supplemented by notes, chain references, and other aids to study. Theological annotation had been eschewed by publishers of the KJV from the outset, because King James had taken exception to the annotations in the Geneva Bible. In the nineteenth century commentaries had been added to Bibles, usually at the bottom of the page. Scofield's edition marked a new phrase in the history of the KJV, because his pages are often dominated by commentary, some of which intrudes into the text as headings. In the first chapter of John's Gospel, for example, the KJV has the simple chapter heading 'the divinity, humanity, and office of Christ'. The Scofield Bible scraps these words, instead summarizing the first fourteen verses as 'The Prologue: the Eternal Word Incarnate in the Son of God'. He then subdivides the fourteen verses into five sections, each with a heading ('The Deity of Jesus Christ', 'The preincarnate work of the Son of God', 'Witness of John the Baptist', 'Jesus Christ, the true Light: rejected and received', and 'The Word made flesh'); each of these headings is supplemented with a list of cross-references. In effect, Scofield acts as a guiding hand, at every point helping the reader to understand what the passage means. His detractors have never tired of pointing out that such heavy-handed guidance is at odds with the Protestant notion that every believer should read the Bible under the individual guidance of the Spirit. Indeed, there are analogies with the view of the Roman Catholic Church, as articulated at Vatican II, that the faithful should read the Bible under the guidance of the Church.

The teaching of the Scofield Bible shares with other evangelical enterprises an emphasis on the literal truth of the Bible, on the future fulfilment of biblical prophecies, on covenant theology, and on eschatological premillennialism, which is the belief that the return of Christ will inaugurate a literal 1,000-year reign over a restored Jewish nation. Within this framework, the most distinctive feature of the Scofield Bible is its advocacy of dispensationalism, which is the belief, initially formulated by John Nelson Darby (a member of the Plymouth Brethren in England), that God's dealings with humankind are characterized by a series of progressive changes in the course of the 'dispensations' or eras of biblical history. In this tool for understanding biblical history as an organic whole, the grand narrative of the Bible is divided into seven dispensations: Innocence (before the fall), Conscience (Adam to Noah), Government (Noah to Abraham), Promise (Abraham to Moses), Law (Moses to Jesus), Church (the current age), and Kingdom (the millennial kingdom), each of which is signalled whenever it becomes prominent in the text. To these seven dispensations the Scofield scheme adds seven covenants between God and humankind: Edenic (Genesis 2:16), Adamic (Genesis 3:15), Noahic (Genesis 9:16),

Abrahamic (Genesis 12:2), Mosaic (Exodus 19:5), Palestinian (Deuteronomy 30:3), Davidic (2 Samuel 7:16) and the New Covenant (Hebrews 8:8).

In 1917 Scofield published a second edition (out of copyright, and now available online). In this edition Ussher's dates were added to the notes, so the creation is dated 4004 BC, and the events recorded in Genesis are said to cover a period of 2,315 years. For most Americans this was the first time that they had encountered Ussher's chronology, which soon became embedded in the popular evangelical imagination. Whereas in the seventeenth century Ussher's dates were the result of serious scientific and historical study, and so were treated with the respect appropriate to recent scientific discoveries, in the early twentieth century they became a focus of the debate about the history of the earth, which ran alongside the struggle between creationists and evolutionists, in which the protagonists are still embattled.

Scofield's Bible became immensely popular, and in its first two editions sold more than a million copies by 1930 and two million by 1945. Its influence on American evangelical thought has been huge. Its systematic approach to Bible study rendered a complex narrative more accessible, and so facilitated a habit of Bible study that extended beyond ministers to the laity. More controversially, the eschatological emphasis of Scofield's approach focused attention on the last days, when Jews will return to Israel; this led in the second half of the twentieth century to widespread support among American evangelicals for Israel, and for the movement known as Christian Zionism, which became a significant strand in the thinking of the Republican Party in America. The identification of the Whore of Babylon (in Revelation) with the Church of Rome may have done little to enhance

Protestant–Catholic relations, but in the early twentieth century Scofield's Bible was an importantly unifying force within the fundamentalist movement.

By the 1930s, however, the fissiparous nature of evangelical Protestantism, which encourages individual believers to make individual judgements as they read their Bibles under the guidance of the Holy Spirit, led to a split in which Scofield's Bible became representative of one side. The dispute was not confessional (the principal protagonists on both sides were conservative Presbyterians), but in the event led to schism and the founding of the Orthodox Presbyterian and Bible Presbyterian churches. The rift was theological—dispensationalism versus covenant theology—and centred on soteriology and eschatology. The Scofield Bible stood at the heart of the debate, and the principal proponent of Scofield's dispensationalism was his pupil Lewis Sperry Chafer, the Presbyterian founder of Dallas Theological Seminary. The soterial issue centred on the accusation by covenant theologians that the Scofield Bible, in distinguishing the Mosaic age from the Christian age, promoted 'two ways of salvation'; the eschatological issue concerned the ordering of the events surrounding the return of Christ in Scofield's system.

The 'two ways of salvation' debate focused on Scofield's note on John 1:17, 'For the law was given by Moses, but grace and truth came by Jesus Christ'. Scofield observed that

> Law is connected with Moses and works; grace with Christ and faith.... Law blesses the good; grace saves the bad.... As a dispensation, grace begins with the death and resurrection of Christ.... The point of testing is no longer legal obedience as the condition of salvation, but acceptance or rejection of Christ, with good works as a fruit of salvation.

On eschatatology, Scofield (and Chafer) championed a position that was premillennial (that is, Christ will return before the 1,000 years mentioned in Revelation 20), dispensational (we are now living in the last days of the sixth age, the final period before Christ's return), and pretribulational (that Christians will be 'raptured'—that is, taken up through the sky to be united with Christ before the tribulation described in 1 Thessalonians 4). Opponents of these views, who therefore became opponents of the Scofield Bible, argued that there was only one way to salvation, and that Bible allowed for alternatives to the rigid eschatology of the Scofield Bible.

By the 1950s the debate seemed to some conservatives to have run its course, and it was decided to published a revised edition of Scofield; the task was entrusted to a team led by E. Schuyler English, and the edition was published as The New Scofield Reference Bible in 1967. The note on John 1:17 was rewritten, and now seemed to say the opposite of Scofield's original note, and the same was true of extensive notes on Genesis 15:18, Exodus 19 (1, 5, 6, 19) and Galatians 3:19. Other new notes caused considerable irritation, such as the use of the word 'sacrament' to describe baptism in Acts 8; this is not a term that Scofield would have used. What was most controversial, however, was the decision to insert into the KJV text modern equivalents of obsolete and archaic terms, because many readers felt that tampering with the King James text was inappropriate. In Daniel 3:25 'a son of the gods' was substituted for 'the Son of God', which was deemed to tamper with a messianic prophecy. In Numbers 33:52 'pictures' was changed to 'stone idols', which was deemed to destroy the prophetic reference to television. In many such cases, the nefarious influence of the American Standard Version was detected.

The solution eventually devised by Oxford University Press was to offer readers a choice of translations, and so in the early twenty-first century a third edition is available in six versions: New King James Version (2002), King James Version (2003), New International Version (2005), New American Standard Bible (2005), English Standard Version (2006), and Holman Christian Standard Bible (2007). Scofield's Bible remains a powerful force in the American evangelical movement.

The King James Version as Literature

The early twentieth century saw the high-water mark of adulation of the KJV as a great work of literature. Before the Second World War there were at least three books and a published lecture with the title *The Bible as Literature*: I. F. Wood and E. Grant's introduction to the subject (1914), Samuel Daiches's lecture (1929), Kathleen Innes's popular book (1930), and Arthur Sewell's more academic book (1939). There were also several editions of selections from the KJV arranged to facilitate the reading of the Bible as a work of literature, as this was the period in which 'The Bible as Literature' courses began to appear in American colleges.

The book that set the pace for such studies was John Hays Gardiner's *The Bible as English Literature* (1906), the printed version of a course of lectures that Gardiner had delivered at Harvard University. He advances the proposition that the King James Version is literature, whereas the Revised Version is not:

> Since this is a study in English literature I have confined myself wholly to the Authorized Version. If another generation should return to the general reading of the Bible the Revised Version may become English literature; but that is a

matter for the future to determine. For this reason all my
quotations come from the Authorised Version, even where the
translation is imperfect or incorrect. It is well understood that
the Revised Version is a better basis for the study of Hebrew
literature or of New Testament literature.

This passage seems to drives a wedge between a text suitable for
religious study (the RV) and one suited for literary study (the
KJV), but it immediately comes apparent that the religious and
literary approaches to the text overlap. Gardiner explains that he
has 'assumed the fact of inspiration, but without attempting to
define it or to distinguish between religious and literary inspiration'. The consequence of this conflation is that literary study of
the Bible should be 'reverent in tone'. This reverence means that
Gardiner's account is often gushy or declamatory where it might
have been analytical. That said, there is an agenda informing
what may seem the banal assertion that the KJV is 'the crowning
monument of English literature', because he uses the literary
supremacy of the KJV as a weapon to denigrate the literature of
his own age. As a student of English literature he was alert to the
Romantic notion that the true subject of art is the artist, and he
thoroughly disliked it. 'In our modern literature', he complained,
'it is hardly possible to find an author who has not some touch of
the restless egotism that is the curse of the artistic temperament:
in the Bible there is no author who was not free from it'.

The KJV therefore stands as a rebuke to the self-importance of
modern literature. The accusation of egotism is not a casual or
ill-informed judgement. As the literary critic John Carey has
observed in a shrewd book subtitled *Pride and Prejudice among the
Literary Intelligentsia, 1880–1939*, the self-centredness and obscur-
antism of much late-nineteenth and early twentieth-century

modernist literature was born of snobbish revulsion towards mass literacy. Writers such as Eliot, Joyce, and Virginia Woolf wrote solipsistic works designed to exclude the masses. The translators of the KJV, in marked contrast, made themselves anonymous (no verse can be attributed to an individual translator), and their intent was to create a text that could be read and understood by everyone.

In 1931 Charles Allen Dinsmore, who had written a study guide to Dante, declared in *The English Bible as Literature* that the KJV 'was made in the most vital period of our language' and so 'is a finer and nobler literature than the Scriptures in their original tongues'. A few years later, Wilbur Owen Sypherd, author of a book on English for engineers, declared that the KJV had 'given to the world a literature greater than that of the original tongues'. It might be objected that neither Dinsmore nor Sypherd could read the Bible in Hebrew and Greek, and so were not in a good position to make such a judgement, but that is not the point. The opinion became a commonplace. As the Bellman says in Lewis Carroll's 'Hunting of the Snark', 'what I tell you three times is true'.

The most important literary figure to take up the cause of the KJV was John Livingston Lowes. He was the son of a Presbyterian minister in Indiana, and his father encouraged him to learn Hebrew, Greek, and Latin. He was a self-taught student of English literature, and in 1927 he published a book on Coleridge (*The Road to Xanadu*) which rightly became the best-known work of literary scholarship of the early twentieth century. In 1935, at the height of his fame, he published a collection of *Essays in Appreciation*, which included an essay on the KJV entitled 'The Noblest Monument of English Prose'. The essay has never been out of print (it is often anthologized) and has been enormously influential, in part because of the elegance and lucidity of Lowes's own prose. Citing passages such as 'O God, thou art my God…my soul thirsteth for thee, my flesh longeth for thee, in a dry and thirsty land where no water is' (Psalm 63:1) and 'a little sleep, a little slumber, a little folding of the hands to sleep' (Proverbs 24:33), Lowes argues that, rather than merely naming an emotion, the words 'reproduce the physical sensation that attends it—the surging of blood to the face, the tingling of the nerves, the rising of the hair, the palsy of the tongue, the quickening of the breath'. Lowes readily acknowledges that earlier translations (notably Tyndale's) account for many of the finest passages in the KJV, but skilfully selects passages in which there is a palpable (or audible) difference. He adduces, for example, Isaiah 53:5, which in the Bishops' Bible reads 'he is such a man as hath good experience of sorrows and infirmities' and the Geneva Bible modulated to 'a man full of sorrows and hath experience of infirmities'. The KJV reads 'a man of sorrows and acquainted with grief', and Lowes celebrates 'the grave beauty of the perfect wording that we know'. For many modern readers the familiarity is enhanced by recollections of the alto (or counter-tenor) solo in Handel's *Messiah*, but that does not subvert Lowes's point: Handel's librettist chose the words precisely because of the qualities that Lowes adduced.

Lowes brings formidable learning to the task, asking his readers to compare the cadences of Latin with those of the KJV. At times his approach is celebratory rather than analytical, because he holds the beauty of the KJV to be a self-evident truth. He cites, for example, a medley of three passages: Ruth's plea to Naomi (Ruth 1:16–17), a passage from the Song of Solomon (8:6–7), and a vision of heaven from Revelation (21:4):

Intreat me not to leave thee, or to return from following after thee: for whither thou goest, I will go; and where thou lodgest, I will lodge: thy people shall be my people, and thy God my God: where thou diest, will I die, and there will I be buried: the Lord do so to me, and more also, if ought but death part thee and me.

Set me a seal upon thine heart, as a seal upon thine arm: for love is as strong as death.... Many waters cannot drench love, neither can the floods drown it: if a man would give all the substance of his house for love, it would utterly be contemned.

And God shall wipe away all tears from their eyes; and there shall be no more death, neither sorrow, nor crying, neither shall there be any more pain.

Lowes comments simply that 'there are no nobler passages in English prose', and the reader nods in assent. Lowes's only analytical observation is that of the 144 words that he has quoted, 'only ten are not of native origin'. The gist of his argument is that the Saxon strain that dominates English has 'a homely vigour, a forthrightness and vividness and concreteness', characteristics that he also sees in Hebrew. The foreign element, in Lowes's view, is Latinate syntax, a resource that gives the KJV 'a sonorousness, a stateliness, a richness of music, a capacity for delicate discrimination'. The blend of Latin syntax and English vocabulary leads Lowes to his most enduring metaphor, that of the KJV as organ music. English is 'an instrument of almost endlessly varied stops', and the KJV, along with the poetry of John Milton, has become 'the organ-voice of England'. Lowes elevates aural effect above meaning, so the fact that the phrase 'do so to me' in the passage from Ruth is incomprehensible to the modern reader (it means 'deal severely with me') is not a consideration deemed worthy of mention. Lowes sees the KJV as a noble conduit of emotion, not of meaning. In the passages that he cites, the ordering of simple words, mostly of one syllable, is both faithful to the original languages and dazzlingly accomplished as a work of English prose. None of this is to be dismissed lightly, but it should be recognized as a secular reading; Lowes is concerned not with the truth of the words, but rather with their fidelity and their aesthetic qualities. The secularism of the essay is part of the reason for its influence beyond the churches, notably in the colleges and universities in which it is a staple part of courses on the Bible as literature.

In Britain the only student of the KJV who could hold a flickering candle to the eloquence of Lowes was George Saintsbury, the English literary scholar who in 1895 abandoned a career in journalism to become the regius professor of rhetoric and English literature at the University of Edinburgh. Saintsbury was a thoroughgoing reactionary who delighted in his opposition to every reform since 1832. He was untroubled by any obligation to teach students, which left him free to write a long succession of lofty books. The judgement and analytical skills that he brought to wine (*Notes on a Cellar-Book* (1920)) are only intermittently in evidence in Saintsbury's literary works, of which the most important for readers of the KJV is *A History of English Prose Rhythm* (1912).

In this book Saintsbury pronounces the 'utterly magnificent' KJV rendering of Isaiah 60 to be 'one of the highest points of English prose'. Surveying the different versions, he calmly asserts his 'critical competence in Greek and in Latin, in French and in German' and his more modest competence in Italian and Spanish, and insists that the English of the KJV is superior to all of these. He then embarks on a dazzling comparative metrical analysis of the Greek (Septuagint) and Latin (Vulgate) versions, and concludes that, although they are glorious, 'we can meet and beat them both'. In this imagined sporting contest between the versions, he assures the reader that 'it is in the total rhythm and harmonic ordonnance that the game is most surely ours'. The notion of Bible translation as a competitive sport may seem bizarre, but most readers would acknowledge the rhythmical pulse of the verse. Indeed, the first verse of Isaiah 60 ('Arise, shine, for thy light is come, and the glory of the Lord is risen upon thee') was incorporated unaltered into Handel's *Messiah*.

And who was responsible for this prose? Saintsbury points to the secular literature of the time, and notes that Shakespeare and Bacon were active at the same time as the translators, adding in a footnote that the Baconians had made Bacon into a secret reviser of the draft translation of the KJV. Indeed they had, and, in the Baconian fantasy (in which Shakespeare's works were written by Bacon), the translators were deemed to have passed their draft to Bacon, who 'hammered the various styles of the translators into the unity, rhythm, and music of Shakespearean prose, wrote the Prefaces and created the whole scheme of the Authorized Version'. The absurd notion that Shakespeare (or a Baconian 'Shakespeare') was responsible for the revision was deemed to have been proved in the translation of Psalm 46, in which the 46th word from the beginning is 'shake' and the 46th word from the end is 'spear', an encoding meant to signal the work of Shakespeare, who was 46 in 1610, when the work of revision was undertaken. If the Bible is the noblest monument of English prose and Britain's greatest writer is Shakespeare, it seems inevitable that they would be brought together, and so they were. John Buchan wondered whether the KJV translators had consulted literary figures such as Shakespeare and Jonson, and

Rudyard Kipling picked up the idea in a short story called 'Proofs of Holy Writ', in which Shakespeare and Ben Jonson discuss the proofs of Isaiah, which had been brought to them by Miles Smith; the poets proceed to create the version of Isaiah 60 that Saintsbury had proclaimed as the apogee of English prose. This harmless lunacy has continued to our own time. An Internet search of 'Shakespeare' and 'Psalm 46' shows active debate about the issue, including the Baconian dimension. Common sense is no impediment to such debate.

The secularism of the literary adulation of the KJV invariably aroused the opposition of believers who valued the Bible as a sacred text rather than a literary masterpiece. The principal exponents of the believers' view were both important figures in the world of literature: T. S. Eliot and C. S. Lewis. Eliot was an American poet, critic, and playwright living in England, and Lewis was an English academic and writer whose posthumous reputation is highest in America, where admiration for his religious writings continues to the present day. Eliot, who memorably described himself as 'an Anglo-Catholic in religion, a classicist in literature and a royalist in politics', articulated his indignation with respect to secular approaches in an essay on 'Religion and Literature' first published in 1935:

> I could fulminate against the men of letters who have gone into ecstasies over 'the Bible as literature', the Bible as 'the noblest monument of English prose'. Those who talk about the Bible as a 'monument of English prose' are merely admiring it as a monument over the grave of Christianity.... The Bible has had a *literary* influence upon English literature *not* because it has been considered as literature, but because it has been considered as the report of the Word of God.

Echoes of the KJV can be heard in Eliot's writing (notably in *Murder in the Cathedral*), but in this essay he makes clear that he values it as a book given by God rather than as a work of literature.

C. S. Lewis took up the theme in a lecture delivered in 1950 at the University of London. His theme was 'The Literary Impact of the Authorized Version', and his intention was to subvert the notion that the Authorized Version (as opposed to the Bible in general) is an important influence on English literature. Here, for example, is his comment on rhythm:

> The influence of the rhythms of the Authorized Version seems to me to be very hard to detect. Its rhythms are in fact extremely various, and some of them are unavoidable in the English language. I am not at all sure that a resemblance in rhythm, unless supported by some other resemblance, is usually recognizable. If I say 'At the regatta Madge avoided the river and the crowd' would this, without warning, remind you of 'In the beginning God created the heaven and the earth'? Even if it did, is the common rhythm, thus separated from community of thought and temper, a matter of any importance? I believe that wherever an English writer seems to us to recall the scriptural rhythms, he is always recalling other associations as well.

At the end of the lecture Lewis turns his guns on 'the Bible as literature':

> Our age has, indeed, coined the expression 'the Bible as literature'. It is very generally implied that those who have rejected its theological pretensions nevertheless continue to enjoy it as a treasure house of English prose. It may be so. There may be people who, not having been forced upon familiarity with it by believing parents, have yet been drawn to it by its literary charms and remained as constant readers. But I never happen

to meet them. Perhaps it is because I live in the provinces. But I cannot help suspecting, if I may make an Irish bull, that those who read the Bible as literature do not read the Bible. It would be strange if they did.

He concludes with an impassioned assertion of the Bible as a sacred book. Indeed, he argues that it is

> not merely a sacred book but a book so remorselessly and continuously sacred that it does not invite, it excludes or repels, the merely aesthetic approach. You can read it as literature only by a tour de force. You are cutting the wood against the grain, using the tool for a purpose it was not intended to serve. It demands incessantly to be taken on its own terms: it will not continue to give literary delight very long except to those who go to it for something quite different. I predict that it will in the future be read, as it always has been read, almost exclusively by Christians.

Sixty years later, the debate seems to have died away. Books on the Bible as literature no longer appear on the lists of academic publishers. Perhaps the last important example of the genre was *The Bible as Literature* (1970), the final book of the Cambridge scholar T. R. Henn. It is a good book by a fine student of literature, but in its examination of the epic, lyric, and dramatic qualities of the KJV and of its style, narrative, and imagery, it looks back to a debate that had for the most part been closed down by C. S. Lewis. Courses on 'The Bible and Literature' scarcely exist in Britain, in part because of reservations about teaching sacred texts. In the United States such courses live on from the pre-war era, but in many cases have moved away from the study of the KJV towards a broader consideration of the Bible, often in modern translations.

By the middle of the twentieth century, literary adulation of the KJV had faded, though its reputation as the supreme classic of English literature has lived on to the present day, even, or perhaps particularly, in the opinion of those who seldom read it. In the world of literary study, the KJV is more honoured than read.

13

∞∞∞

THE KING JAMES VERSION
IN THE MODERN WORLD

New Translations and Editions

After the Second World War, the trickle of translations and revisions inaugurated by the Revised Version turned into a flood. New translations included a fresh version of the Vulgate by Monsignor Ronald Knox (NT 1945, OT 1950). In 1966 another new Catholic translation of the Hebrew and Greek texts was published as the Jerusalem Bible; its best-known contributor was J. R. R. Tolkien, who translated the Book of Jonah. This edition was revised in 1985 as The New Jerusalem Bible. A parallel development was The New American Bible, a Catholic translation conceived in the liberal atmosphere of Vatican II and published in 1970. Other denominations embarked on similar enterprises. In 1961 Jehovah's Witnesses, who had previously used the King James Version (KJV) in their Anglophone ministry, published their own New World Translation of the Holy Scriptures. Evangelical groups produced the immensely successful New International Version (NT 1973, OT 1978), which has been revised as Today's New International Version (NT 2002, OT 2005). This is a

259

scrupulous translation that has rightly been widely welcomed, but the decision to prune some forty doubtful verses from the text has caused unhappiness in some quarters. In the New Testament, for example, excised verses include 'For the Son of man is come to save that which was lost' (Matthew 18:11), 'For an angel went down at a certain season into the pool, and troubled the water: whosoever then first after the troubling of the water stepped in was made whole of whatsoever disease he had' (John 5:4), and 'And Philip said, If thou believest with all thine heart, thou mayest. And he answered and said, I believe that Jesus Christ is the Son of God' (Acts 8:37). The suppression of such verses was done for good scholarly reasons, but some KJV purists are sufficiently outraged to denounce what they see as a maimed Bible.

There have been many other translations and paraphrases in the post-war period, but the only one to achieve the prominence of the NIV has been the New English Bible (NEB: NT 1961, OT and Apocrypha 1970), which is jointly published by the university presses of Oxford and Cambridge. This is, like the NIV, an immensely scholarly translation, but is more liberal in its range of reference within the manuscript tradition, taking into account a wide range of Old Testament texts (for example, the Dead Sea Scrolls, the Samaritan version of the Pentateuch, Aramaic targums, and Greek and Syriac versions), manuscripts and translations of the Apocrypha, and early Greek texts and translations of the New Testament. The impact of the New English Bible has been greater in the UK than in the USA, because its lexical choices are resolutely British: in 1 Corinthians 16:8, for example, Whitsuntide is used rather than Pentecost. The NEB was revised in 1989 as the Revised English Bible; this revision aspires to a language that can be readily understood on both sides of the Atlantic, but the decision to use gender-neutral language has alienated some readers.

Alongside these new translations, the Revised Version and the American Standard Version continued to be revised (see Chapter 11). These revisions have run parallel to two other movements: the revision of the KJV itself (as opposed to the RV and the ASV) and the championing of the KJV as the best (or only) translation. The principal revision of the KJV is the New King James Version (NKJV; NT 1979, Psalms 1980, OT 1982). This edition, which arose from consultation within the Baptist and Presbyterian communities in America, has a conservative textual base, in that the Greek text is the one used by the original translators (the Textus Receptus), though the Hebrew text, while firmly based on the Massoretic version, attends to a early manuscript now in St Petersburg that was unknown to the KJV translators. In its choice of language, however, the NKJV is in several respects quite radical: archaic forms, including the -eth endings of verbs and the second-person pronouns (thee, thou, thine, thy, and ye) are replaced by modern forms. In adjusting grammar (including word order) and vocabulary (including spelling), the revisers adopted a principle that they called 'complete equivalence', which they distinguish from the 'dynamic equivalence' that governs other modern translations; in other words, they sought to capture the literal meaning of each word as well as the idea that lay behind the word, which meant that the rendering of the original wording in Hebrew and Greek took precedence over a translation governed by the need to produce wholly idiomatic modern English. This edition is quite distinct from the 21st Century King James Version (1994, known as KJ21), which retains many seventeenth-century forms (including thee, thou, and so on) but modernizes words whose meanings are not now readily apparent: 'astonied' in Ezra 9:3, for example, becomes 'stunned'. This edition also distinguishes typographically between 'more familiar' passages, which are emboldened, and 'less familiar' passages, in an unemphasized typeface. A recent edition of KJ21 with Apocrypha, which dispenses with the odd typography, is variously known as the Third Millennium Bible and (by its subtitle) the New Authorised Version (2004).

The New Cambridge Paragraph Bible (2005) is a good popular edition of the KJV, but there is still no scholarly edition of the KJV that takes into account all the textual evidence and preserves all the elements in the 1611 edition. The principal scholarly obstacle to such an edition is the lack of a transcription and analysis of the annotations written by KJV revisers in the marked-up copy of the Bishops' Bible of 1602 (now in the Bodleian Library). Beyond this scholarly gap, there is also a commercial issue: the market is not calling for a scholarly edition of the KJV, and the prospect of a new text supplanting Blayney's version is not high: his text may be a fossil preserved in clay in 1769, but after more than 200 years the clay has hardened into stone, and there is little prospect that the standard text is set to change.

The text of the KJV might not change, but the packaging of the text constantly changes. Oxford University Press offers the KJV in more than 100 different versions, and in the USA the Bible publishing giants Zondervan and Nelson also sell scores of different versions of the KJV. The principal edition of the standard text for the literary market is the Oxford World's Classics edition. Individual books of the KJV are often published separately, notably in the Pocket Canon series, in which literary, artistic, and scientific figures introduce favourite books, including Louis de

Bernières (Job; UK edition), Bono (Psalms), Nick Cave (Mark; UK edition), E. L. Doctorow (Genesis; US edition), Doris Lessing (Ecclesiastes), Steven Rose (Genesis; UK edition), Will Self (Revelation; UK edition), and Fay Weldon (Corinthians). In these volumes reverence is reserved for the style of the KJV, but its contents are sometimes vilified. The millions of copies of the KJV published every year cater to very different markets—religious, academic, literary, popular, secular—and the volume of sales is sufficient to sustain large-scale production.

Commercial, religious, and academic publishers sell huge numbers of KJVs, and still more are given away by Bible societies. The Gideons, an evangelical Protestant organization for business and professional men, was founded in 1899 with a particular focus on the supply of Bibles to hotel rooms; it now gives away some seventy-five million Bibles a year. Most of these Bibles are KJVs, but the Gideons also distribute the Bible known as the Modern English Version, which is another name for the New King James Version. The key Bible verse for the conversionist theology of the Gideons is John 3:16 ('For God so loved the world that he gave his only begotten Son, that whosoever believeth in him should not perish, but have everlasting life'), which is printed in a range of languages in the prefatory material. The range of target audiences for these Bibles is indicated by the colours of the covers of their New Testaments (which often contain an appendix with Psalms and Proverbs). Those intended for high-school pupils are orange if distributed on the street or at outlets such as school cafeterias, and red if they are distributed within the school (the latter practice has been challenged in the courts). Target groups with colour-coded Bibles include college students (green), the armed forces (digital camouflage and desert camouflage), police, firefighters, and ambulance crews (dark blue), and doctors and nurses (white). Other colours represent the donors. Bibles used by individual Gideons for 'witnessing' (conversionist counselling) are brown, Bibles distributed by the Auxiliary (an organization of Gideons' wives) are light blue, and Bibles used by auxiliaries for witnessing are periwinkle (lavender blue).

The King James Only Movement

The new translations and the revision of old translations have not satisfied all readers. Millions of Bible readers prefer the KJV for literary or religious reasons. Of the latter group, the most prominent are part of the King James Only Movement. The term and the controversy around it first emerged in the late 1970s, which saw the publication of books with titles such as *The King James Version Debate* and *The King James Controversy*. The notion of a unified King James Only 'movement' is problematical. There are organizations, notably the Dean Burgon Society in the United States (see pp. 225–7) and the Trinitarian Bible Society in the United Kingdom (see p. 160), that provide scholarly materials on which advocates of the KJV can draw, but there is no central leadership, not indeed concurrence on the status accorded to the KJV. The two societies agree that the KJV is not divinely inspired, but they differ on its standing in relation to other translations: the Trinitarian Bible Society argues that the KJV is the most accurate translation, while the Dean Burgon Society contends that the KJV is the only accurate translation.

Beyond these mainstream groups there are others who believe that the KJV was inspired and is infallible. More than 1,000 churches listed in the online Bible Believers' Church Directory subscribe to an evangelical statement of faith, of which the first tenet is:

> We believe the King James 'Authorized Version' Bible to be the perfect and infallible word of God. We believe the Bible was inspired in its origination and then divinely preserved throughout its various generations and languages until it reached us in its final form. By this we mean that the Authorized Version preserves the very words of God in the form in which He wished them to be represented in the universal language of these last days: English.

In this view, the KJV preserves the very words of God in the divinely chosen world language. A few, such as the Independent Baptist Peter Ruckman, go even further, arguing that the KJV constitutes a third revelation alongside (or superseding) those of the Hebrew and Greek Scriptures. Still others contend that modern translations, which are deemed to be of New Age origin, are a Satanic attempt to draw Christians away from the translation that God intended to be authoritative.

The notion that English speakers hold a privileged position in the eyes of God is not new. In the seventeenth century, John Milton had explained that God reveals himself 'first to his Englishmen' (see p. 10). In the nineteenth century, the British Israelite movement, which asserted that the English people were the descendants of the ten lost tribes of Israel and that the British royal family descends from the royal line of King David, promoted a form of English exceptionalism that sat comfortably alongside Britain's status as an imperial power. The KJV was in due course annexed to this widespread belief in the providential history of England. The publication of the Revised Version of the New

Testament in 1881 led its detractors (notably Dean Burgon) to contrast it adversely with the KJV.

Attacks on the Revised Version and on the American Standard Version (the American equivalent, published in 1901) affected sales, as did popular nostalgia for the KJV, and these versions never became as popular as the publishers had hoped. The debate died down, but was revived with the publication of the Revised Standard Version of the Old Testament in 1952, because the virgin of Isaiah 7:14 became a 'young woman' (see Chapter 11), and this seemed to many conservatives to be a denial of the doctrine of the virgin birth. The net effect of the debate was to increase allegiance to the KJV amongst those who disapproved of the RSV. There was no single leader of evangelical dissent from the RSV, but the most prominent figure was David Otis Fuller, the Baptist founder-president of the 'Which Bible?' Society and a passionate advocate of the KJV.

The publication of the NKJV did little to quell the debate, nor has KJ21. The attempt to render the Jacobean English of the 1611 Bible in a version more accessible to the common reader, while nonetheless preserving many of the features of the original, has satisfied neither side. Advocates of modern translations dismiss its archaisms, and advocates of the King James Only position see it as a compromised Bible.

Champions of the King James Only position are a small but vociferous minority amongst evangelicals, distributed across a variety of denominations. Many are Independent Baptists, but proponents may also be found among Pentecostals, Free Presbyterians, Strict Baptists, Plymouth Brethren, and members of Reformed Churches. Other churches that remain loyal to the KJV include Seventh-Day Adventists and Christian Scientists;

Mormons also use the KJV, along with Joseph Smith's 'Inspired Bible', a rescension of the KJV. In the UK, the most eloquent advocacy of the KJV is Ian Paisley's *My Plea for the Old Sword: The English Authorised Version (KJV)*.

The debate about the standing of the KJV has a popular dimension, often played out in polemical literature and combative websites. The interlocking triangle (known as the triquetra or trinity knot) on the cover of the Nelson edition of the NKJV, for example, is alleged to be a stylized form of 666, the number of the beast of Revelation 13, and so indicative of the Satanic New Age origins of this version. There is also a parallel scholarly debate about the source text. The KJV relied on the eclectic Textus Receptus established by Erasmus, but the publication in 1881 of a new Greek text by Westcott and Hort, which included newly discovered manuscripts such as the Codex Sinaiticus, posed a real problem. If every word of the Greek text of the New Testament was inspired by God, then which version represented God's words? The Codex Sinaiticus, which is divided between St Catherine's Monastery (Egypt), the British Library, Leipzig University Library, and the National Library of Russia in St Petersburg (but is now being reassembled in digital form), includes many readings that differ from those of the Textus Receptus. The New Testament portion, which is part of the 694-page section at the British Library, is central to the debate. It is, together with the Codex Vaticanus (which has been in the Vatican Library since the fifteenth century), the earliest text of the New Testament, but it was unknown to Erasmus and the KJV translators. The differences are important. To adduce one prominent example, neither the Vatican nor Sinaitic codices contains the last twelve verses of Mark (Mark 16:9–20). Are these words inspired or not?

Similar issues are raised for the Hebrew text by the discovery of the Dead Sea Scrolls, which together with early translations (the Septuagint, the Samaritan Pentateuch, the Syriac texts) provide alternatives to the Masoretic text that underlies the KJV. The Dead Sea Scrolls have been slow to make an impact, because publication has been agonizingly protracted; the last of the ten Qumran caves (on the north-western shire of the Dead Sea) was excavated in 1956, but publication by Oxford University Press of the forty mighty volumes of *Discoveries in the Judaean Desert*, which began in 1951, was completed only in 2010. Many of the 800 Qumran manuscripts supply readings identical to the Masoretic text, but manuscripts of Exodus and Samuel found in Cave Four are the source of a large number of textual variants, including significant differences in content. Such variants cannot be casually brushed aside, because the Dead Sea Scrolls antedate the earliest surviving Hebrew manuscript of the Old Testament (the tenth-century Aleppo Codex) by a millennium.

Readers

Who reads or hears the KJV now? It is important to distinguish between owners and readers. Books such as Stephen Hawking's *Brief History of Time* are often bought but seldom read. Similarly, most households that contain books own a Bible. In England the KJV tends to be respected at a distance, more revered than read. In 1944 George Orwell observed that 'within the last generation the Bible reading which used to be traditional in England has lapsed. It is quite common to meet with young people who do not know the Bible stories even as stories.' In twenty-first-century England, which is largely secular, knowledge of the Bible is fading even amongst university students. When the name of Moses came up at a seminar that I was leading, no one had any idea whom he might have been, though a Muslim student eventually asked if he was the same person as Musa in the Qur'an (which he is). The picture is very different in the United States, where church attendance is still common, though many young Americans, like their British counterparts, have little interest in the past. This is not a new phenomenon: on discovering that Moses had been dead 'a considerable long time', Huck Finn famously declared that he 'don't take no stock in dead people'.

Reading patterns are changing. Just as academics read research papers online rather than on paper, so young people in affluent parts of the English-speaking world increasingly read online or listen to audio books. There is a KJV in Microsoft Reader format, which, surprisingly, includes the Apocrypha and the translators' preface to the reader. Similarly, there is a Kindle edition of the KJV, and an MP3 version for those who prefer to listen. There is a free audio version read by volunteers, and, for those who prefer celebrity voices, an audio recording of the late Johnny Cash reading the entire New Testament in the NKJV. There are computer games that use the KJV, such as Scripture Solitaire, and there is a KJV available for Nintendo DS. A King James Games website offers 'study puzzles crafted for the learning and memorization of God's Word'.

The printed book is not yet dead, and most readers of the KJV prefer paper. Readers who are motivated primarily by religious reasons tend to fall into two disparate groups. On the one hand, the KJV is read aloud in some Anglo-Catholic Anglican churches in the UK and in their Episcopalian counterparts in other parts of the Anglican communion, notably in America.

In these contexts it is often coupled with the use of the 1662 Book of Common Prayer. At the other end of the ecclesiastical spectrum, at the greatest possible distance from the Prayer Book, the KJV remains the Bible of choice for King James Only churches, many of which are Baptist. Indeed, it remains the most widely owned and used translation in the United States, and the same may be true in Britain.

Annual sales of the KJV and its various revisions run into millions. Every year Oxford University Press alone sells more than 250,000 copies of the KJV in various versions, and publishers such as Zondervan (now an imprint of HarperCollins) and Nelson sell comparable numbers. Bibles are also donated in huge numbers, and KJV Bibles are a prominent part of the donations. In addition to the 75 million Bibles donated every year by the Gideons, many of the 145 national Bible societies working in more than 200 countries and territories mostly involved in local languages sell or donate KJVs, even though their principal mission is to supply Bibles in local languages. The lists of the British and Foreign Bible Society (now known as the Bible Society), the Scottish Bible Society, and the American Bible Society all include editions of the KJV sold at low prices. The Trinitarian Bible Society has remained true to its constitutional stipulation that all Bibles that it distributes in the English language will be KJVs.

The KJV and the English Language

The Bible, and especially the KJV, is sometimes said to have exercised a huge influence on the development of the English language. Alas, this is not so. As David Crystal has pointed out in a fine recent book (*Begat: The King James Bible and the English Language*), this contention is true only in a limited sense, which is that certain phrases in the KJV have passed into the English language. Many of these phrases exist in earlier versions, so it is more accurate to say that the KJV has been the conduit through which many phrases in sixteenth- and seventeenth-century English have survived up to the present. Sometimes the biblical origins of such phrases are unknown to the speaker. When people are said to be 'at their wits' end', for example, there is no awareness of the source of the phrase in Psalm 107:27; similarly, an escape by 'the skin of my teeth' no longer evokes Psalm 19:20, the 'salt of the earth' no longer recalls the words of Jesus at Matthew 5-:13, 'riotous living' is no longer associated with the prodigal son, and the Pauline origins of 'thorn in the flesh' (1 Corinthians 12:7) are no longer recognized.

Phrases that in the past were allusions have in many cases become free-standing, so the 'writing on the wall' has lost its association with Belshazzar (Daniel 5:5, 24-9), and the origins of the assertion that the leopard cannot change its spots (Jeremiah 13:23) and the problematical fly in the ointment (Ecclesiastes 10:1) have been largely forgotten. In many proverbs the language of the KJV has been forsaken, but the idea lives on, so 'go the second mile' originates in 'whosoever shall compel thee to go a mile, go with him twain' (Matthew 5:41) and 'you can't take it with you' comes from 'and shall take nothing of his labour, which he may carry away in his hand' (Ecclesiastes 5:15).

The one instance in which the language of the KJV may be deemed to have changed the meaning of a word occurs in the parable of the talents (Matthew 25:14–30). A talent, in the Greek of the New Testament, was a sum of money, typically a silver coin. In the parable of the talents, a man about to depart on a journey gathers his three servants together, 'and unto one he gave five talents, to another two, and to another one; to every man according to his several ability; and straightway took his journey'. The servants who were given five and two talents became traders, and managed to double their money; the servant who had been given one talent buried it in the ground for safekeeping. When the master returned, he heaped praise and rewards on the two traders, but denounced the servant who had buried his talent as 'wicked and slothful', insisting that 'thou oughtest therefore to have put my money with the exchangers, and then at my coming I should have received mine own with usury'. This is by some measure the most enigmatic of the parables, because as a story about money it seems to be a ringing endorsement of investment banking, a hymn to usury, and an attack on thrift. Readers had long sought to make sense of the parable, and the traditional solution, which had been articulated in English almost 200 years before the KJV appeared, was to take a lead from 'to every man according to his several ability' and to assume that the 'talent' in the sense of money was a symbol for ability. It is hard to judge whether that was indeed what Jesus meant, but it does facilitate a reading in which the parable makes sense, and so 'talent' came to mean 'ability'. In all Bibles before the KJV (Vulgate, Wyclif, Coverdale, and so on), the word 'talent' had been imported from the Greek text rather than translated as 'coin', and the KJV followed in this tradition. It was the KJV that disseminated the parable to subsequent generations, and so 'talent' has lost its monetary sense, and has become a word to denote ability.

The language of the KJV is deemed to be British English, and so it is in its origins. English is now, however, a world language, and in many ways the pace in the development of the language is set in America. The American Revolutionary War concluded with the Treaty of Paris (1783), in which Britain recognized the independence of the thirteen colonies that became the United States; more than 200 years later, hopes that America will return to Britain may be fading (though I remain an optimist), but the shared language of English has created many enduring cultural links, including overlapping religious traditions and intertwined biblical cultures. The KJV is an integral part of the religious cultures of both countries, and there is no serious sense in which Britain has a prior claim; indeed, in many ways the English spoken in America is closer to the language of the KJV than is British English. Consider Exodus 14:18: 'And the Egyptians shall know that I am the Lord, when I have gotten me honour upon Pharaoh.' In British English the word 'gotten' is not in use, though it survives as a fossil in the phrase 'ill-gotten gains'; in American English it is part of everyday speech. Similarly, the use of the objective pronoun 'me' as if it were a Latin dative of advantage still survives in colloquial American English (I'm going to buy me a car), but not in British English. In this linguistic sense, the KJV is as American as it is English.

The KJV in 2011

This book began with an assertion that the KJV is the most important book in the English language. That importance does not rest on the inception or execution of this particular translation, nor even in its excellence as a translation (some modern translations may be more accurate) or as a work of English prose. It lies rather in its long history at the centre of the religious culture of the English-speaking world. It is valued by everyone who is a

273

Christian by conviction or background, even by those who for one reason or another use another translation.

In a broader cultural context, the KJV has a popular life beyond its pages, because it has become a cultural institution. Visitors to the Shakespeare sites in Stratford or passengers on the Mark Twain Riverboats in the Disney theme parks in Anaheim, Paris, or Tokyo may never have read a word of Shakespeare or Mark Twain, but they nonetheless know that these are revered figures in literary culture, and are content to acknowledge their greatness because everyone does so. Similarly, many who never read the Bible stand ready to praise the solemn cadences of the KJV, and indeed choose it at moments such as funerals, when language of a higher register is deemed appropriate. The same is true at national ceremonies. At the funeral service for Princess Diana, for example, Prime Minister Tony Blair read 1 Corinthians 13 from the KJV, though he substituted 'love' for the KJV's 'charity'. Across the Atlantic, the almost entirely secular funeral service for Michael Jackson ended with a prayer in which Pastor Lucious Smith reminded mourners that 'even now the King of Pop must bow his knee to the King of Kings. And we pray that you would remind us Lord, that our lives are but dust.' The formality of the language acknowledges its origins in the KJV. The modern idiom would be 'bend his knee', but 'bow his knee' recalls the repeated use of this idiom in the KJV (for example, 'that at the name of Jesus every knee should bow' (Philippians 2:10)); similarly, 'our lives are but dust' recalls 'he remembereth that we are dust' (Psalm 103:14), but does so in an archaic construction in which a negative is suppressed (with the negative the phrase would read 'our lives are nothing but dust') and 'but' becomes adverbial, and means 'merely'. This construction is common in the KJV ('I count all things but loss…do count them but dung' (Philippians 3:8)) but is now obsolete, so Pastor Smith's deployment of it evokes the language of the KJV. This is an instance of resolute contemporaneity of popular culture incorporating the language of a 400-year-old translation of the Bible.

Indeed, no one is abashed by an enthusiasm for the KJV. Just as real men do not eat quiche, so, in a range of T-shirts sold on the Internet, 'real men use a King James Version Bible'. The defiance and self-assurance implicit in this claim are indicative of how important the KJV remains in 2011. Expression of the cultural standing of the KJV can take many forms. For secular readers, it is a repository of cultural values, a great work of literature, and a realization of the power and beauty of the English language. For believers, it is much more, because it renders into English content that is inspired: 'All scripture is given by inspiration of God, and is profitable for doctrine, for reproof, for correction, for instruction in righteousness: that the man of God may be perfect, thoroughly furnished unto all good works' (2 Timothy 3:16–17). The KJV has proved to be the most enduring embodiment of Scripture in the English language. It has been revised and re-revised, and the unintended consequence of that process has been new translations of the Bible, none of which is entirely independent of the best of all translations. Indeed, the KJV is the fountainhead of Bible translation into English, and, although the finest modern translations are models of good scholarly practice, they are admired rather than loved. It is the King James Version that has been loved by generations of those who have listened to it or read it to themselves or to others; other translations may engage the mind, but the King James Version is the Bible of the heart.

APPENDIX 1

―――― ⤬ ――――

THE COMPANIES AND
LATER REVISERS

Many of the translators and revisers of the King James Version (KJV) are the subject of entries in the *Oxford Dictionary of National Biography* (here abbreviated as *ODNB*), of which a print version was published in 2004; a regularly updated electronic version is available by subscription. Some of the translators are the subject of book-length biographies; at the other extreme, a few are virtually unknown, or their identities are uncertain. The surviving lists of translators identify some members by title rather than name, so I have reproduced the title (e.g. Mr Dean of Westminster) and then the name (e.g. Lancelot Andrewes); most but not all of the identifications are secure. In cases where members are named, I have initially printed the name in the predominant form in which it exists in early lists, and then used the spelling that is used in the *ODNB*. When the date of birth is unknown, I add the date of baptism or matriculation (i.e. university entrance). If Cambridge graduates are not in the *ODNB*, I cite Venn's *Alumni Cantabrigienses*, and, for Oxford graduates, Foster's *Alumni Oxonienses*.

1. First Westminster Company, Old Testament (Genesis to 2 Kings)

Mr Dean of Westminster (director) Lancelot Andrewes (1555–1626), was dean of Westminster from 1601 to 1605, and later bishop of Chichester (1605), Ely (1609), and Winchester (1619). Andrewes was the most learned of men in an age of learned men, and eventually came to be known as one of Europe's most able linguists, such was his command of Latin, Greek, Hebrew, Aramaic, Syriac, Arabic, and, as a contemporary phrased it, 'moderne *Tongues* to the number of *fifteene*'. At Pembroke College Cambridge, where he was a contemporary of the poet Edmund Spenser, he was a moderate Calvinist, but he was later to become England's leading ceremonialist; at the Hampton Court Conference, he defended the use of the sign of the cross in baptism. Throughout his career he enjoyed a reputation for elegant preaching, and, although little of his writing survives (he always refused to publish unless commanded to do so), it is clear that he was one of England's greatest prose stylists. His only leisure pursuit was walking, and as an undergraduate he used to walk to Cambridge from his parents' home in London. He chaired the First Westminster Company, but it is not clear how involved he was after he resigned his deanery a year later. (*ODNB*)

Mr Dean of Paul's John Overall (bap. 1561, d. 1619), formerly regius professor of divinity at Cambridge, dean of St Paul's Cathedral from 1602, and a theological ally of Lancelot Andrewes. He was said to have spent so many years lecturing in Latin (the language of all university lectures) that he found it troublesome to speak English in his sermons, which were known for their learning and dullness. At the Hampton Court Conference he spoke against double predestination, adducing the case of Christians who had committed adultery; as his wife was to have two very public affairs, he may have had occasion to recall his words. At the end of the conference Overall was instructed to add a substantial section on the sacraments to the catechism; this expanded catechism remained in use until the 1970s. (*ODNB*)

Mr Doctor Saravia Adrian Saravia (1532–1613), canon of Westminster, was born in French Flanders, the son of a Spanish father and a Walloon mother. He became a Franciscan friar and then dallied with Lutheranism before becoming a Calvinist. For many years he moved back and forth between England and the Netherlands, and in 1585 he became president (rector magnificus) of the University of Leiden. His alliance with the Earl of Leicester in the Netherlands led to a charge of treason and a death sentence, and he fled to England in 1586. In England he published a treatise in defence of episcopacy, which he thought divinely ordained, and attacked the Calvinism of Theodore Beza. His defence of episcopacy, and of the apostolic legitimacy of English church government, aligned him with Richard Bancroft and against the Presbyterians. (*ODNB*)

Mr Doctor Clark Richard Clerke (matriculated 1579, d. 1634), fellow of Christ's College, Cambridge, was as a young man an anti-Calvinist, and so clashed with the Calvinists of his College. His dislike of Calvinism gradually abated, but he remained on the conformist side of the ecclesiastical spectrum. It was his learned expertise in Hebrew that led to his being chosen as one of the translators of the KJV. (*ODNB*)

Mr Doctor Leifield John Layfield (1562/3–1617), a former fellow of Trinity College, Cambridge, who became rector of St Clement Danes, London. He had a good command of Greek as well as Hebrew, but was apparently recruited for his command of architecture: on one of the lists of translators someone wrote beside his name 'being skilled in architecture, his judgement was much relied on for the fabric of the Tabernacle and Temple'. (*ODNB*)

Mr Doctor Teigh Robert Tyghe or Tigue or Tighe (matriculated Cambridge, 1577; d. 1616), archdeacon of Middlesex (from 1601) and vicar of All Hallows Church in Barking. (Venn, s.n. Tyghe)

Mr Burleigh Francis Burley (matriculated Cambridge 1578/79, d. 1619), rector of St Benet Paul's Wharf, London (1604–12). He had been appointed in 1590 as vicar of Bishop's Stortford by Lancelot Andrews. (Venn)

Mr King Geoffrey King (matriculated 1583, d. 1630), fellow of King's College, Cambridge, regius professor of Hebrew at Cambridge 1607–8 (succeeding Robert Spalding), and royal chaplain. (Venn)

Mr Thompson Richard Thomson (d. 1613), fellow of Clare College, Cambridge, was known as 'Dutch Thomson' because he was born in the Netherlands, probably of an English father and a Brabantine mother. He was a prominent Arminian (and ally of Lancelot Andrewes), arguing that it was possible for someone who had been justified by faith to fall wholly from grace. His Calvinist opponents sought to discredit his Arminianism by pointing to his habitual drunkenness. He was reviled in England, but Thomson's learning had earned the admiration of prominent European intellectuals, and his expertise in philology led to his inclusion among the translators. (*ODNB*)

Mr Beadwell William Bedwell (bap. 1563, d. 1632), England's leading Arabist, was educated at Cambridge, where he fell under the influence of the circle of Lancelot Andrewes, who encouraged him to study Hebrew (both ancient and rabbinic), Aramaic, and Syriac, and, on recognizing his ability in these languages, encouraged him to embark on the study of Arabic, of which little was understood in England. Bedwell drafted a substantial Arabic–Latin dictionary, and planned an edition of the Arabic New Testament. He generously imparted his knowledge to friends and pupils, but few of his scholarly endeavours came to fruition. Lancelot Andrewes, acting as his patron, brought him on to the Westminster company. (ODNB)

2. First Cambridge Company, Old Testament
(1 Chronicles to Song of Solomon)

Mr Lively Edward Lively (*c.*1545–1605), former regius professor of Hebrew at Cambridge, died in May 1605 and so did not participate in the project. His expertise extended to rabbinical Hebrew, and so he would have been able to bring the insights of Jewish exegetes to the task of revision. (*ODNB*)

Mr Richardson John Richardson (matriculated 1678, d. 1625), fellow of Emmanuel College, Cambridge, and from 1607 to 1617 regius professor of divinity at Cambridge. He was a prominent Arminian in a university that was increasingly Calvinist, but nonetheless became master of Peterhouse, master of Trinity, and the university's vice-chancellor. His scholarly strength was in biblical Hebrew. (Venn)

Mr Chatterton Laurence Chaderton (1536?–1640) was one of the four puritan delegates at the Hampton Court Conference. He was raised as a Roman Catholic, but converted to evangelical Protestantism while an undergraduate at Christ's College, Cambridge. He was a committed presbyterian, and, according to a published sermon widely attributed to him, 'loathed...the calling of Archbishop, Bishop, Deans...and all such as be rather members and parts of the whore and strumpet of Rome'. He became the first master of Emmanuel College, which he shaped into a seminary for the godly. He opposed the surplice, the sign of the cross, and kneeling, but was sufficiently pragmatic to acknowledge that their use was not a sin. In his private life Chaderton was a keen gardener and herbalist, and his long life meant that he outlived trees that he had planted. He was said to have been able to read his Hebrew Bible without glasses when over the age of 100, and he was still scribbling vitriolic remarks in the margins of his books at the time of his death. (*ODNB*)

Mr Dillingham Francis Dillingham (matriculated 1583, d. 1625) was a prolific theologian who had been a fellow of Christ's College, Cambridge, until 1599, when he became a parish priest in Bedfordshire, where he seems chiefly to have devoted himself to writing. He was apparently well off financially, and was certainly powerfully connected with the aristocracy and the upper reaches of the Church, despite his enthusiasm for reform of the Church. These connections may account for his inclusion among the translators. (*ODNB*)

Mr Harrison Thomas Harrison (1555–1630) was a fellow of Trinity College, Cambridge, and a biblical scholar of formidable learning and remarkable expertise in Greek and Hebrew. He had been a contemporary of Lancelot Andrewes at Merchant Taylors' School and at Cambridge, and vied with Andrewes in learning. Harrison's sympathies, however, were with the puritan cause, and Archbishop Bancroft said that Harrison had participated in a meeting at St John's College in 1589 at which there was an attempt to promote the adoption in England of Knox's 'First Book of Discipline', article 8 of which advocated presbyterianism instead of episcopacy. (*ODNB*)

Mr Andrews Roger Andrewes (matriculated *c*.1590, d. 1635), brother of Lancelot Andrewes and fellow of Pembroke Hall, later master of Jesus College, Cambridge. He was widely disliked for his bad temper and lack of scruple, and was eventually forced by the king to resign his mastership. He was appointed to the committee because of his brother's influence. (Venn)

Mr Spalding Robert Spalding (matriculated 1585, d. 1626), fellow of St John's College, Cambridge; he succeeded Edward Lively as regius professor of Hebrew. (Venn)

Mr Binge Andrew Byng (1574–1652) was the son of Thomas Byng (regius professor of law and master of Clare College, Cambridge) and the godson of Archbishop John Whitgift, who became his patron. Byng became a fellow of Peterhouse, Cambridge, and later a prebendary of Southwell and subdean of York. Whitgift attended the Hampton Court Conference in the last month of his life, and the invitation to Byng may have been his final act of patronage, though Byng's standing as a Hebraist would also have justified his inclusion. (*ODNB*)

William Eyre or Eyres or Aiers (matriculated 1592, d. 1670), fellow of Emmanuel College, Cambridge (1599–1611), was appointed as an overseer for this company on the basis of his linguistic expertise. (Venn)

3. First Oxford Company, Old Testament
(Isaiah to Malachi)

Doctor Harding (director) John Harding (*c.*1562–1610), regius professor of Hebrew (1591–8 and 1604–10) and (from 1607), president of Magdalen College, Oxford. (Foster, s.n. Hardynge)

Dr Reynolds John Rainolds (1549–1607), president of Corpus Christi College, Oxford, had been the leader of the puritan delegation to the Hampton Court Conference, and was the person who had originally proposed the revision project to King James; although Harding was the director of the company, its meetings were held in Rainolds's lodgings at Corpus. At Oxford his resolute puritanism had impeded Rainolds's career for many years, because the Queen declined to approve appointments that would advance his university career. In the 1580s Rainolds had given a series of 250 lectures refuting the attempt of the Jesuit Robert Bellarmine to make the Apocrypha part of the Old Testament canon. He was, therefore, unhappy that the KJV was to include the Apocrypha, but achieved posthumous revenge when his lecture series was published in two vast volumes in 1611, the year in which the KJV was published. (*ODNB*)

Dr Holland Thomas Holland (d. 1612), regius professor of divinity in Oxford and rector of Exeter College, Oxford. He was a moderate puritan by conviction, and his formidable expertise in biblical languages included rabbinical as well as biblical Hebrew; he was also knowledgeable about law. (*ODNB*)

Dr Kilbye Richard Kilbye (1560/1–1620), rector of Lincoln College, Oxford, prebendary of Lincoln Cathedral and from 1610 regius professor of Hebrew at Oxford. His daunting command of Hebrew sources is illustrated by the survival in the Lincoln College Library of an unpublished manuscript commentary on Exodus that uses almost 100 Hebrew sources, many of which were unfamiliar to scholars. (*ODNB*)

Mr Smith Miles Smith (matriculated c. 1568, d. 1624) was a classical scholar with legendary expertise in oriental languages. After leaving Oxford, where he had studied at Corpus Christi and Brasenose colleges, he accepted a range of ecclesiastical appointments, including a prebendary at Hereford Cathedral. It was said of Smith that Hebrew, Aramaic, Syriac, and Arabic were as familiar to him as his own mother tongue. This exaggerates a formidable skill, of which evidence includes his annotations to works in those languages that he left to Hereford Cathedral Library at his death; his ability in rabbinical Hebrew enabled him to develop a detailed knowledge of the Jewish exegetes. Smith was one of a small number of translators with no current university connection, but his role was central, in that he also sat on the revision committee, conducted the final review of the translation with the bishop of Winchester, Thomas Bilson, and composed the magnificent preface to the reader. He was appointed bishop of Gloucester in 1612, but his episcopate was chiefly remarkable for his dispute with William Laud (the dean), of whose Arminianism and ceremonialism Smith was contemptuous. (*ODNB*)

Mr Brett Richard Brett (1567/8–1637) was a member of a Somerset gentry family who studied at Hart Hall (now Hertford

College), Oxford, and became a fellow of Lincoln College, Oxford. He was an outstanding oriental linguist with competence in Latin, Greek, Hebrew, Aramaic, Arabic, and Ethiopic. (Foster)

Mr Fairclough Probably Richard Fairclough (matriculated 1570, d. 1638), a former fellow of New College, Oxford; he left a Greek and Hebrew Bible to the College, and it is still there. It has also been suggested that Mr Fairclough may have been the controversialist Daniel Featley (1582–1645), whose father's surname was Fairclough (*ODNB*), but he seems too young to be a serious candidate. (Foster)

William Thorne (1568?–1630), dean of Chichester, does not appear on any of the lists of translators, but there is clear evidence that he was appointed to the First Oxford Company at an early stage, possibly as an overseer: a document signed by fifteen bishops in 1605 or 1606 recommends Thorne for promotion, referring to him as one of the Oxford translators. Thorne had served as regius professor of Hebrew until 1604, and his command of the language meant that he could compose poetry in Hebrew and read letters written to him in that language. He also knew Syriac and seems to have studied Arabic. (*ODNB*)

4. Second Cambridge Company, Apocrypha

Doctor Dewport (director) John Duport (d. 1617/18), master of Jesus College, Cambridge, from 1590; he also served as the university's vice-chancellor four times. He was a moderate puritan, and so a politically astute choice to chair the company responsible for the Apocrypha. (*ODNB*)

Dr Branthwait William Branthwaite (1563–1619), fellow of Emmanuel who in 1607 became master of Gonville and Caius College, Cambridge, by royal mandate. It may have been court connections that secured Branthwaite a place among the translators, but his command of Greek must also have been a factor. He served as vice-chancellor in 1618/19, and died in office. (Venn)

Dr Radclife Jeremiah Radcliffe (matriculated 1567, d. 1612), vice-master of Trinity College, Cambridge. (Venn)

Mr Warde, Eman Samuel Ward (1572–1643) was a fellow of Emmanuel College, Cambridge, who became master of Sidney Sussex College in 1610. Both were puritan colleges, and Ward was a firm member of the puritan party. At Cambridge he was aligned with Laurence Chaderton and William Perkins in his dislike of 'popish' ceremony in the Church, and he became a notable opponent of Arminianism; his college chapel remained unconsecrated, and communion was taken at an unrailed table rather than an altar. These Calvinist convictions and puritan practices were tempered, however, by Ward's advocacy of episcopacy and his practice of pluralism (he held a large number of ecclesiastical offices); he was also clearly willing to countenance the presence of the Apocryphal books in the new edition of the Bible. Ward's report to the Synod of Dort contains valuable information about the process of translation. Ward later contributed to the second Cambridge edition of the KJV, published in 1638. (*ODNB*)

Mr Downs Andrew Downes (*c.*1549–1628) was a fellow of St John's College, Cambridge, and regius professor of Greek at

Cambridge. Together with his pupil John Bois, Downes revived the study of Greek in their college. Both Downes and Bois served in the Apocrypha company, and both went on to serve on the Committee of Revisers, which met at the Stationers' Hall in London for nine months. Downes was apparently a reluctant participant in the London meetings, and 'would not go 'till he was either fetcht or threatened with a Pursuivant'. (*ODNB*)

Mr Boyes John Bois (1561–1644) was a fellow of St John's College, Cambridge. His prodigious learning was grounded in an enriched childhood education. Under the tuition of his father, he read the entire Bible by the age of 5, and by 6 he could write Hebrew and had some command of Greek. By the time he entered St John's College in Cambridge at the age of 14, his Greek was so good that his tutor Andrew Downes was able to induct him into the most demanding of Greek authors. Bois remained at St John's for more than twenty years, studying relentlessly and fretting about imagined ailments. In 1598 he left Cambridge for a career in the Church, and was working in a rural parish when he was invited to join the company responsible for the translation of the Apocrypha. Like Downes and Harmar, he also served as a member of the Committee of Revisers. His notebooks afford a glimpse into the process by which the work of the six companies was revised. Like Samuel Ward, Bois later contributed to the second Cambridge edition of the KJV, published in 1638. (*ODNB*)

Mr Warde, Reg. Robert Ward (matriculated 1588, d. 1629), fellow of King's College, Cambridge, and prebendary of Chichester Cathedral. (Venn)

5. Second Oxford Company, New Testament (Gospels, Acts, and Book of Revelation)

Mr Dean of Christchurch Thomas Ravis (b. in or before *1560*, d. 1609), dean of Christ Church College, Oxford, and later bishop of Gloucester and of London. In his capacity of dean of Christ Church he attended the Hampton Court Conference; the notes that he took were later used by Bishop Barlow to prepare the published account of the proceedings. He was a Calvinist by conviction, but nonetheless persecuted nonconforming clergy with zeal. (*ODNB*)

Mr Dean of Winchester George Abbot (1562–1633), later archbishop of Canterbury, was master of University College, Oxford, and also served as the university's vice-chancellor. He was an evangelical Calvinist and an advocate of the doctrine of double predestination, and his anti-Catholicism was forceful even by the virulent standards of the time. He nonetheless resisted pressure from the puritan party to make the Church less Catholic, instead defending the office of bishop as apostolic, supporting conformity in ceremony, and defending clerical privileges such as pluralism and non-residency. (*ODNB*)

Mr Dean of Worcester Probably Richard Edes (bap. 1554, d. 1604), a royal chaplain and court preacher under Queen Elizabeth and King James, but he died at Worcester on 19 November 1604, before he could embark on the project. (*ODNB*)

[John Aglionby] (1566/7–1610), a royal chaplain, former fellow of Queen's College, Oxford, and principal of St Edmund Hall,

Oxford, was appointed to replace Richard Edes after the lists had been drawn up. (Foster)

Mr Dean of Windsor Giles Thomson (1553–1612) was a royal chaplain to Queen Elizabeth and King James; he was dean of Windsor from 1603 and later bishop of Gloucester. He attended the Hampton Court Conference, but there is no record of what he said, if anything. (*ODNB*)

Mr Savile Sir Henry Savile (1549–1622), warden of Merton College, Oxford, and provost of Eton, was a mathematician and patristic scholar who became the most learned astronomer in sixteenth-century England. He was an intellectual of European standing, and a friend of both Roman Catholic and Protestant humanists. In 1604 Savile broke off his labours on his eight-volume edition of the works of Chrysostom to join the company of translators, which met in the warden's lodgings at Merton. (*ODNB*)

Dr Perne John Perrinne (matriculated 1575, d. 1615), prebendary of Christ Church College, Oxford, regius professor of Greek (1597–1615). (Foster)

Dr Ravens Probably Ralph Ravens (matriculated 1575), fellow of St John's College, Oxford. (Foster)

Dr Hutten In some versions of the list of translators Leonard Hutton (1556/7–1632), a student (i.e. fellow) of Christ Church, Oxford, appears instead of Dr Ravens. Hutton was a ceremonialist whose polemical work in defence of ceremony was dedicated to Archbishop Bancroft. (Foster)

Mr Harmer John Harmar (*c.*1555–1613), a former regius professor of Greek at Oxford who became successively headmaster and warden of Winchester College. He had particular expertise in patristic Greek, and in 1586 had edited six sermons of John Chrysostom, which was the first Greek book to be printed in Oxford. Like Downes and Bois, Harmar also served as a member of the Committee of Revisers. (*ODNB*)

6. Second Westminster Company, New Testament (Epistles)

Dean of Chester (director) William Barlow (d. 1613) had been educated at St John's College, Cambridge, and became a fellow of Trinity Hall, Cambridge. He was appointed dean of Chester and (from 1608) bishop of Lincoln. Barlow was a conspicuously loyal servant of the Crown, and, as the *ODNB* comments, 'his oleaginous pulpit manner was...much admired by Elizabeth, as by her successor, and it lubricated his passage to preferment'. He was present at the Hampton Court Conference, and wrote the official account of its proceedings. (*ODNB*)

Dr Hutchinson Ralph Hutchinson (1552?–1606), president of St John's College, Oxford. The reason for his inclusion among the translators is not clear, nor is it known how much he was able to contribute to the process of revision before his death on 16 January 1606. (*ODNB*)

Dr Spencer John Spenser (1558/9–1614), president of Corpus Christi College, Oxford, royal chaplain to King James and editor of Richard Hooker's *Laws of Ecclesiastical Polity*. His sympathy for Hooker's eirenic views is indicative of Spenser's combination of moderate puritanism and advocacy of episcopacy. (*ODNB*)

Mr Fenton Roger Fenton (1565–1616), rector of St Stephen Walbrook, London, and a friend of Lancelot Andrewes. Fenton campaigned for the abolition of usury, which he thought contrary to the laws of God. As a theologian he was interested in the role of the Holy Spirit in the life of the individual believer, and an advocate for an examined spiritual life. His sermons and publications were praised by a contemporary for 'the natural majesty of the style, like a master bee without a sting'. (*ODNB*)

Mr Rabbett Michael Rabbet (*c.*1552–1630), educated at Trinity College, Cambridge, from 1604 rector of St Vedast, Foster Lane, London. (Venn)

Mr Sanderson Thomas Sanderson (matriculated 1577, d. after 1614), a fellow of Balliol College, Oxford, and rector of All Hallows-the-Great, London. (Foster)

Mr Dakins William Dakins (1568/9–1607), fellow of Trinity College, Cambridge, and professor of divinity at Gresham College in London. (*ODNB*)

[**Arthur Lake**] (bap. 1567, d. 1626), a fellow of Winchester College who was later to become bishop of Bath and Wells, had been preparing for the academic exercises for the BD and DD at Oxford when he was invited to join the company; he was allowed to defer the exercises in order to become a translator. He was the younger brother of Sir Thomas Lake, secretary of state to James I, so his appointment may have been occasioned by royal patronage. (*ODNB*)

[**George Ryves**] (matriculated Oxford 1579, d. 1613), warden of New College, Oxford, was appointed as an overseer for this section. (Foster)

[**Nicholas Love**] (matriculated Oxford 1588, d. 1630), royal chaplain and headmaster of Winchester College (and father of the regicide of the same name), is named in the same document that mentions the involvement of George Ryves, but his duties in respect of the translation are nowhere specified. (Foster)

The Committee of Revisers (of which only these names are known)

John Bois (see p. 289)
Andrew Downes (see pp. 288–9)
John Harmar (see pp. 291–2)
'**Hutch**' (in Bois's notes) Possibly William Hutchinson (matriculated Cambridge 1568, d. 1616), fellow of Queens' College, Cambridge. Thereafter he held a series of livings in or near London, and became chaplain to the bishop of London, prebendary of St Paul's, and archdeacon of St Albans. (Venn)

The Committee of Two

Miles Smith (see p. 286)
Thomas Bilson (1546/7–1616), bishop of Winchester, was a scholarly theologian with a particular interest in church government: he rejected both papal supremacy and presbyterian democracy in favour of the episcopacy favoured by the Church of England, and secular governance presided over by a hereditary monarchy. Bilson opposed the convening of the Hampton Court Conference, but attended nonetheless and proved to be one of the most forceful and articulate delegates. He was by temperament a moderate, and, although a Calvinist, he was conciliatory towards ceremonialists.

He was regarded by Bodley's first librarian (a former pupil of Bilson) as 'one of the profoundest scholars' England had produced. (*ODNB*)

The Final Reviser

Richard Bancroft (bap. 1544, d. 1610), archbishop of Canterbury from 1604, was educated at Christ's College, Cambridge. He attended the Hampton Court Conference in his capacity of bishop of London, and, together with eight other bishops, represented the church hierarchy against the puritan reformers. A few weeks later John Whitgift died, and Bancroft became his successor as archbishop of Canterbury. As the text of the KJV was being finalized, he insisted on fourteen alterations, but it is not known what they were. (*ODNB*)

The Revisers of the Second Cambridge Edition, 1638

Samuel Ward (see p. 288)
John Bois (see p. 289)
Thomas Goade (1576–1638) was a product of Cambridge, where his father had been provost of King's College. He was a scholar, historian, controversialist, theologian, and poet with, as Thomas Fuller said, 'a *commanding* presence, an uncontrolable spirit, impatient to be opposed, and loving to steere the discourse...of all the Company he came in'. He attended the Synod of Dort, where the records show that Goade was a firm Calvinist. His puritan sympathies gradually faded, and he eventually became a Laudian with a distaste for puritanism. (*ODNB*)

Joseph Mede or Mead (1586–1638) was a senior figure at Christ's College with remarkably proficiency in Hebrew, Greek, Latin, and biblical studies, and his knowledge of patristics was incomparable; his biographer also described him as 'an acute logician, an accurate philosopher, a skilful mathematician, a great philologer, and an excellent anatomist', to which might be added that he had interests in astrology, botany, physics, and history. His biblical scholarship was focused on eschatology. Although he had some puritan sympathies, Mede enjoyed warm relations with the Laudian party. (*ODNB*)

The Revisers of the Revised Version

There were four committees, two British and two American. The names of members who died while the work was in progress are prefixed with †; those who resigned while the work was in progress are marked ®. I describe them as they are listed in the official documents.

The English Old Testament Company

The Right Rev. Edward Harold Browne, D.D., Bishop of Winchester (Chairman). (*ODNB*)

The Right Rev. Lord Arthur Charles Hervey, D.D., Bishop of Bath and Wells. (*ODNB*)

The Right Rev. Alfred Ollivant, D.D., Bishop of Llandaff. (*ODNB*)

The Very Rev. Robert Payne Smith, D.D., Dean of Canterbury. (*ODNB*)

The Ven. Benjamin Harrison, M.A., Archdeacon of Maidstone, Canon of Canterbury. (*ODNB*)

The Rev. William Lindsay Alexander, D.D., Professor of Theology, Congregational Church Hall, Edinburgh. (*ODNB*)

Robert Lubbock Bensly, Esq., Fellow and Hebrew Lecturer, Gonville and Caius College, Cambridge. (*ODNB*)

The Rev. John Birrell, Professor of Oriental Languages, St Andrews, Scotland. (*ODNB*)

Frank Chance, Esq., M.D., Burleigh House, Sydenham Hill, London.

Thomas Chenery, Esq., Reform Club, London [newspaper editor and orientalist]. (*ODNB*)

The Rev. Thomas Kelly Cheyne, Fellow and Hebrew Lecturer, Balliol College, Oxford. (*ODNB*)

The Rev. Andrew Bruce Davidson, D.D., Professor of Hebrew, Free Church College, Edinburgh. (*ODNB*)

The Rev. George Cunninghame Monteath Douglas, D.D., Professor of Hebrew and Principal of Free Church College, Glasgow. (*ODNB*)

Samuel Rolles Driver, Esq., Tutor of New College, Oxford. (*ODNB*)

The Rev. C. J. Elliott, Winkfield Vicarage, Windsor.

† The Rev. Dr Patrick Fairbairn, Principal of the Free Church College, Glasgow. (*ODNB*)

The Rev. Frederick Field, D.D. (*ODNB*)

The Rev. John Dury Geden, Professor of Hebrew, Wesleyan College, Didsbury, Manchester. (*ODNB*)

The Rev. Christian David Ginsburg, LL.D. (*ODNB*)

The Rev. Frederick William Gotch, D.D., Principal of the Baptist College, Bristol.

® The Rev. John Jebb, Canon of Hereford. (*ODNB*)

The Rev. William Kay, D.D., Great Leighs Rectory, Chelmsford. (*ODNB*)

The Rev. Stanley Leathes, D.D., Professor of Hebrew, King's College, London. (*ODNB*)

The Rev. Professor Joseph Rawson Lumby, D.D., Fellow of St Catharine's College, Cambridge. (*ODNB*)

† Professor Davies.

† Professor McGill.

The Very Rev. John James Stewart Perowne, D.D., Dean of Peterborough. (*ODNB*)

® The Rev. Edward Hayes Plumptre, D.D., Professor of New Testament Exegesis, King's College, London. (*ODNB*)

† The Ven. Henry John Rose, Archdeacon of Bedford. (*ODNB*)

The Rev. Archibald Henry Sayce, Fellow and Tutor of Queen's College, Oxford. (*ODNB*)

† The Rev. William Selwyn, D.D., Canon of Ely. (*ODNB*)

The Rev. William Robertson Smith, Professor of Hebrew, Free Church College, Aberdeen. (*ODNB*)

† The Right Rev. Dr Connop Thirlwall, Bishop of St Davids. (*ODNB*)

† Professor Weir.

® The Right Rev. Dr Christopher Wordsworth, Bishop of Lincoln. (*ODNB*)

William Wright, LL.D., Professor of Arabic, Cambridge. (*ODNB*)

William Aldis Wright Esq. (Secretary), Bursar of Trinity College, Cambridge. (*ODNB*)

The English New Testament Company

The Right Rev. Charles John Ellicott, D.D., Bishop of Gloucester and Bristol (Chairman). (*ODNB*)

The Right Rev. George Moberly, D.C.L., Bishop of Salisbury. (*ODNB*)

The Very Rev. Henry Alford, D.D., Dean of Canterbury. (*ODNB*)

The Very Rev. Edward Henry Bickersteth, D.D., Prolocutor, Dean of Lichfield. (*ODNB*)

The Very Rev. Arthur Penrhyn Stanley, D.D., Dean of Westminster. (*ODNB*)

The Very Rev. Robert Scott, D.D., Dean of Rochester. (*ODNB*)

The Very Rev. Joseph Williams Blakesley, B.D., Dean of Lincoln. (*ODNB*)

The Most Rev. Richard Chenevix Trench, D.D., Archbishop of Dublin. (*ODNB*)

The Right Rev. Joseph Lightfoot, D.D., LL.D., Bishop of Durham. (*ODNB*)

The Right Rev. Charles Wordsworth, D.C.L., Bishop of St Andrews. (*ODNB*)

The Rev. Joseph Angus, D.D., President of the Baptist College, Regent's Park, London. (*ODNB*)

The Rev. David Brown, D.D., Principal of the Free Church College, Aberdeen.

The Rev. Fenton John Anthony Hort, D.D., Fellow of Emmanual College, Cambridge. (*ODNB*)

The Rev. William Gilson Humphry, Vicarage, St Martin's-in-the-Fields, London. (*ODNB*)

The Rev. Benjamin Hall Kennedy, D.D., canon of Ely and regius professor of Greek, Cambridge. (*ODNB*)

The Ven. William Lee, D.D., Archdeacon of Dublin. (*ODNB*)

The Rev. William Milligan, DD., Professor of Divinity and Biblical Criticism, Aberdeen. (*ODNB*)

The Rev. William Fiddian Moulton, D.D., Master of the Leys School, Cambridge. (*ODNB*)

The Rev. Samuel Newth, D.D., Principal of New College, Hampstead, London. (*ODNB*)

The Ven. Edwin Palmer, D.D., Corpus professor of Latin, Oxford, and Archdeacon of Oxford.

The Rev. Alexander Roberts, D.D., Professor of Humanity, St Andrews. (*ODNB*)

The Rev. Frederick Henry Ambrose Scrivener, LL.D., Prebendary, Hendon Vicarage, London. (*ODNB*)

The Rev. George Vance Smith, D.D. (*ODNB*)

The Rev. Charles John Vaughan, D.D., Master of the Temple, The Temple, London. (*ODNB*)

The Rev. Brooke Foss Westcott, D.D., Canon of Peterborough, Fellow of Trinity College, Cambridge, and Regius Professor of Divinity, Cambridge. (*ODNB*)

The Rev. J. Troutbeck (Secretary), Dean's Yard, Westminster.

† The Right Rev. Dr Samuel Wilberforce, Bishop of Winchester. (*ODNB*)

† The Rev. Dr John Eadie, Professor of Biblical Literature in the United Presbyterian Church, Glasgow. (*ODNB*)

† Mr. Samuel Prideaux Tregelles, LL.D. (*ODNB*)

® The Rev. Dr Charles Merivale, Dean of Ely. (*ODNB*)

The American Revision Committee

Some members of the American Revision Committee are the subject of entries in the *American National Biography* (here abbreviated as *ANB*), of which a print version was published in

1999; a constantly updated electronic version is available by subscription.

Philip Schaff, D.D., LL.D., President of the General Committee. (*ANB*)

George E. Day, D.D., Secretary.

American Old Testament Company

Professor William Henry Green, D.D., LL.D. (Chairman), Theological Seminary, Princeton, NJ.

Professor George E. Day, D.D. (Secretary), Divinity School of Yale College, New Haven, Conn.

Professor Charles A. Aiken, D.D., Theological Seminary, Princeton, NJ.

The Rev. Talbot W. Chambers, D.D., Collegiate Reformed Dutch Church, NY.

Professor Thomas J. Conant, D.D., Brooklyn, NY.

Professor John De Witt, D.D., Theological Seminary, New Brunswick, NJ.

Professor George Emlen Hare, D.D., LL.D., Divinity School, Philadelphia. (*ANB*)

Professor Charles Portfield Krauth, D.D., LL.D., Vice-Provost of the University of Pennsylvania, Philadelphia. (*ANB*)

† Tayler Lewis, LL.D., Professor Emeritus of Greek and Hebrew, Union College, Schenectady, NY.

Professor Charles M. Mead, D.D., Theological Seminary, Andover, Mass.

Professor Howard Osgood, D.D., Theological Seminary, Rochester, NY.

Professor Joseph Packard, D.D., Theological Seminary, Alexandria, Va.

Professor Calvin E. Stowe, D.D., Hartford, Conn. (*ANB*)

Professor James Strong, S.T.D., Theological Seminary, Madison, NJ

Professor C. V. A. Van Dyck, LL.D., D.D., M.D., Beirut (Advisor on Arabic). (*ANB*)

American New Testament Company

Ex-President Theodore D. Woolsey, D.D., LL.D. (Chairman), New Haven, Conn. (*ANB*)

Professor J. Henry Thayer, D.D. (Secretary), Theological Seminary, Andover, Mass.

Professor Ezra Abbot, D.D., LL.D., Divinity School, Harvard University, Cambridge, Mass.

† Professor Henry Boynton Smith, D.D., LL.D., Union Theological Seminary, New York. (*ANB*)

The Rev. J. K. Burr, D.D., Trenton, NJ.

President Thomas Chase, LL.D., Haverford College, Pa.

® Rev. G. R. Crooks, D.D., New York.

Chancellor Howard Crosby, D.D., LL.D., New York University, New York.

Professor Timothy Dwight, D.D., Divinity School of Yale College, New Haven, Conn.

† Professor Horatio B. Hackett, D.D., LL.D., Theological Seminary, Rochester, NY.

† James Hadley, LL.D., Professor of Greek, Yale College, Conn.

† Professor Charles Hodge, D.D., LL.D., Theological Seminary, Princeton, NJ. (*ANB*)

Professor A. C. Kendrick, D.D., LL.D., University of Rochester, Rochester, NY.

The Right Rev. Alfred Lee, D.D., Bishop of the Diocese of Delaware.

Professor Matthew B. Riddle, D.D., Theological Seminary, Hartford, Conn. (*ANB*)

Professor Philip Schaff, D.D., LL.D., Union Theological Seminary, New York.

Professor Charles Short, LL.D. (Secretary), NY. (*ANB*)

® Rev. W. F. Warren, D.D., Boston. (*ANB*)

The Rev. Edward A. Washburn, D.D., Calvary P.E. Church, NY.

APPENDIX 2

∽∾∽

THE PRELIMINARIES
TO THE KJV

The first edition of the KJV contained seventy-four pages of preliminaries. Many modern Bibles do not preserve any of these documents apart from a version of the list of books in the Testaments. Some print the dedicatory epistle to King James and a few include the epistle from the translators to the reader, but the others have all disappeared. Here the twelve preliminaries are discussed in the order in which they usually (but not invariably) appear in copies of the first edition. They are printed in facsimile in the Quatercentenary Edition of the KJV published simultaneously with this book.

1. The Title Page

This elegant engraving (see p. 99) is the work of the Flemish artist Cornelis Boel. On the figures in the engraving, see pp. 98–102.

2. A Dedicatory Epistle to King James

The KJV is dedicated 'to the most high and mighty prince, James, by the grace of God king of Great Britain, France and Ireland'. The country of Great Britain existed only in the mind of King

James; he wanted England and Scotland to unite, but they were not to do so until 1707, almost a century later. The claim to the throne of France was the vestige of a claim first made in 1340 and not withdrawn until 1810, ten years after the throne of France had ceased to exist. In the dedication King James is said to be 'the principal mover and author of the work'; this is not meant to imply that he contributed to the process of revision, but rather that it was his commission that made it happen.

The author of the dedication is not known, but, as the style seems different from that of Miles Smith, who wrote the preface on behalf of the translators (see below), the obvious candidate would seem to be Thomas Bilson, bishop of Winchester.

3. The Translators to the Reader

The dauntingly learned address to the reader on behalf of the translators is the work of Miles Smith, who sat on the First Oxford Company (responsible for the Old Testament from Isaiah to Malachi) and on the Committee of Revisers. The language is sonorous and at times majestic; indeed, its Latinate cadences are cast in a much more formal idiom than that used by the translators of the Bible. The range of allusion to patristic sources is well beyond the educational thresholds of most twenty-first-century readers, and Smith quotes Greek and Latin, sometimes without translations. There is a helpful set of annotations to the epistle in the New Cambridge Paragraph Bible.

4. A Calendar

The information in the twelve pages of the liturgical calendar may be elucidated by reference to one month: March. The first horizontal column announces that March has thirty-one days. The second horizontal column asserts that the corresponding lunar month (one cycle of the moon) is thirty days long; this calculation (in which months with thirty-one solar days are assigned lunar months of thirty days, and the others twenty-nine days) is a traditional error, in that, if the solar and lunar calendars are to coincide every nineteen years, then one of the lunar months must be solar minus two.

The third horizontal column has four divisions: sunrise and sunset, Psalms, morning prayer, and evening prayer. The sun is said to rise (presumably on the first day of the month) at 0618 and to set at 1742. 'Psalms' is a heading for the column below. The Psalter is to be read through once every month, but on months with thirty-one days (such as March), the first and last day have the same reading (number 30); the thirty sets of readings are the subject of a later table. The final two columns are headings for lists of two 'lessons' (portions of Scripture to be read at services of worship) for morning prayer (matins) and two for evening prayer (evensong).

Of the ten vertical columns below, the five on the right set out readings from the Psalter (column 6), the Old Testament (columns 7 and 9), and the New Testament (columns 8 and 10). Of the five columns on the left, only column 2 is clear: it is a list of the days of the solar month. Column 4 is a list according to the Roman calendar, in which the day is identified by counting backwards from the three divisions of the month (*calends*, *nones*, and *ides*) rather than by counting forwards in ordinal numbers from the beginning of the month; the *ides* of March, of which Julius Caesar was famously told to beware, falls on the 15th.

Column 5 notes important dates in the church calendar: (1) Archbishop David, patron saint of Wales; (2) Bishop Chad of Mercia, d. 672; (7) Perpetua, martyr of Carthage, d. 203; (12)

Pope Gregory the Great, d. 604; (13) sun enters constellation of Aries (16); 'Aprilis', the beginning of the lunar month of April (lunar months were named after the solar months in which they ended); (18) Edward, King of West Saxons, d. 978; (21) Abbot Benedict of Nursia, d. c.550; (24) the anniversary of the accession of King James to the throne of England on 24 March 1603, and a day of fasting; (25) Annunciation of the Virgin Mary.

Column 1 consists of golden numbers, and column 3 consists of dominical (Sunday) letters. Both relate to the calculation of the paschal moon, and so of Easter. The golden number arises from the coincidence of the solar and lunar cycles every nineteen years. Each of these nineteen years is given a number; in the case of March, if the new moon falls on 1 (or 31) March, the golden number is 19, and if it falls on 2 March, the golden number is 8. Column 3, the dominical letter, relates the days of the week to the calendar of the year, and the letters A to G indicate the cycle of seven days beginning on 1 January; the dominical letter for the year is the one allocated to the first Sunday.

5. An Almanac for Thirty-Nine Years

This almanac implements the information in the Calendar by charting the seven principal moveable feasts in the ecclesiastical calendar for the years 1603 to 1641. The first four columns list the year, the golden number, the epact, and the dominical letter, and the next seven give dates for the seven events:

1. Septuagesima (the third Sunday before Lent, signalling the wearing of purple vestments until Holy Week, and the omission of the word 'Alleluia' from the liturgy until the end of Lent)

2. The first day of Lent (Ash Wednesday, six and a half weeks before Easter)
3. Easter Day
4. Rogation Week (Rogation Sunday, inaugurating the three Rogation Days of prayer and fasting)
5. Ascension Day (the 40th day, inclusively, after Easter)
6. Whitsunday (the 50th day after Easter)
7. Advent Sunday (the nearest Sunday to St Andrews Day, 30 November)

6. A Table for the Calculation of Easter

The calculation of the date of Easter had been a matter of contention since the paschal controversies of the early Church. In England the matter was settled at the Synod of Whitby in 664. This table is a tool that enables the reader to calculate the date of Easter for any given year.

7. A Table and Calendar Setting out the Order of Psalms and Lessons to be Said at Morning and Evening Prayers throughout the Year

These pages set out the principles for ensuring that all the required biblical passages are read at appropriate times, as set out in *The Book of Common Prayer*; the survival of this table in the KJV represented a defeat for the puritan party, who disliked orchestrated readings and prayers. The Psalter is to be read monthly, so the Psalms are grouped into thirty sections, and the lengthy Psalm 119 is subdivided into twenty-two portions.

8. A List of the Books of the Testaments and the Apocrypha

This list survives in modern texts of the KJV, save that the Apocrypha is not now normally printed, so its books are excluded from the list. Here the titles of two Apocryphal books seem to have been adjusted to acknowledge puritan sensitivities: the 'Historie of Susanna' appears here as the 'Story of Susanna', and the abbreviated title of 'Bel and the Dragon' is rendered emphatically as 'The idole Bel and the Dragon'. The catchword at the bottom is 'The', which refers to the title of Genesis ('The First Book of Moses') rather than to the licence that follows.

9. Royal Coat of Arms

A fine woodcut of the coat of arms of James I, underneath which is written *Cum privilegio Regiæ Maiestas* ('by authority of the king'). The royal coat of arms contains the motto of the royal family, *Dieu et mon droit* ('God and my right') and the motto of the Order of the Garter, *Honi soit qui mal y pense* ('shame upon him who thinks evil of it'). The shield is quartered. In heraldic terms, the first and fourth quarters depict the three passant guardant lions of England; the second quarter depicts the rampant lion and double tressure fleury-counter-fleury (i.e. floral border) of Scotland; the harp in the third quarter represents Ireland. The supporter on the left is a crowned lion of England; the supporter on the right is a Scottish unicorn. The rose of England and the thistle of Scotland are beneath the shield. A version of this shield is still in use, but the shamrock has been added to the rose and thistle.

10. Genealogies

The thirty-six pages of genealogies were compiled by the antiquarian John Speed, who collaborated with the Hebraist Hugh Broughton on the project. Speed's patent, which extended from 31 October 1610 for ten years (and was afterwards extended till 1638), gave him the right to print and insert his genealogies (and the gazetteer and map of Canaan) into every edition of the KJV; he therefore produced versions in large folio, small folio, quarto, and octavo. The genealogies begin with God's creation of Adam and Eve and extend as far as Christ.

11. A Table of Place Names in Canaan

This gazetteer is divided in half by the map, because it is a separate folio insert, with the map on one side and the gazetteer on the other.

12. A Map of Canaan

This map is a reduction of a fourteen-sheet wall map of biblical Canaan (with an inset map of Jerusalem) first published by John Speed in 1595; no copy of the original is known to survive. In one version of the map, Speed's engraver is identified as Renold Elstrack. A note on the map says that it was 'begun by Mr John More, continued and finished by John Speed'. John More, who came to be known as the Apostle of Norwich, was a learned clergyman who had spent many years researching the cartography of the Bible, but had been unable to publish his map before his death in 1592.

LIST OF ILLUSTRATIONS

The publisher would like to thanks the following individuals and institutions who have kindly given permission to reproduce the illustrations listed below.

Chapter 1

Chapter 2

Chapter 6

Chapter 7

Chapter 8

Chapter 9

Chapter 10

Chapter 11

Chapter 12

FURTHER READING

The *Oxford Dictionary of National Biography* has articles on many of the people mentioned in the text and in Appendix 1. Several figures connected with the translation (John Aglionby, Robert Barker, John Bill, William Branthwaite, Richard Brett, John Richardson) are described in a thematic *ODNB* article called 'Translators of the Authorized Version of the Bible.' The following are the subject of individual entries:

George Abbot
William Lindsay Alexander
Henry Alford
King Alfred
Lancelot Andrewes
Joseph Angus
John Bale
Richard Bancroft
Christopher Barker
William Barlow
John Baskerville
John Baskett
Bede
William Bedwell

Robert Lubbock Bensly
Edward Henry Bickersteth
Thomas Bilson
John Birrell
William Blake
Joseph Williams Blakesley
Charles James Blomfield
John Bois
Richard Bristow
Hugh Broughton
David Brown
Edward Harold Browne
John William Burgon
Andrew Byng

John Cassell
Laurence Chaderton
Thomas Chenery
Richard Clerke
Thomas James Cobden-
  Sanderson
William Cole
Miles Coverdale
Thomas Cranmer
Thomas Cromwell
William Dakins
William Daniel
John Nelson Darby
Andrew Bruce Davidson
John Nelson Darby
Francis Dillingham
George Cunninghame
Monteath Douglas
Andrew Downes
George D'Oyly
Samuel Rolles Driver
John Dryden
John Duport
John Eadie
Richard Edes
Queen Elizabeth
Charles John Ellicott
Renold Elstrack
Desiderius Erasmus
John Evelyn

Frederick William Faber
Patrick Fairbairn
John Fell
Roger Fenton
Frederick Field
Thomas Fuller
Stephen Gardiner
William Ged
John Dury Geden
Robert Gell
Anthony Gilby
Christian David Ginsburg
Thomas Goade
Christopher Goodman
Richard Grafton
James Granger
John Harmar
Benjamin Harrison
Thomas Harrison
Thomas Rice Henn
King Henry VIII
Lord Arthur Charles Hervey
Hans Holbein the younger
Thomas Holland
Richard Hooker
Fenton John Anthony Hort
William Howley
William Gilson Humphry
John Husbands
Ralph Hutchinson

Thomas Henry Huxley
John Jebb Edward Johnston
Benjamin Jowett
Franciscus Junius
William Kay
Benjamin Hall Kennedy
Richard Kilbye
John Kitto
Henry Knighton
John Knox
Vicesimus Knox
Arthur Lake
Sir Thomas Lake
William Laud
John Layfield
Stanley Leathes
William Lee
Clive Staples Lewis
John Lightfoot
Joseph Barber Lightfoot
Edward Lively
William Lloyd
Rowland Lockey
Joseph Rawson Lumby
Thomas Babington Macaulay
Richard Mant
Gregory Martin
Queen Mary
Joseph Mede
Sir John Baptiste de Medina

Charles Merivale
William Milligan
John Milton
George Moberly
John More
William Fiddian Moulton
James Murray
John Henry Newman
Samuel Newth
Bonham Norton
Alfred Ollivant
John Overall
Thomas Payne
Edward Hayes Plumptre
Alfred Pollard
Anthony Purver
Thomas Penson De Quincey
John Rainolds
Thomas Ravis
Alexander Roberts
John Rogers
Richard Rolle
Henry John Rose
Henry St John, Viscount
   Bolingbroke
George Saintsbury
Thomas Sampson
Adrian Saravia
Sir Henry Savile
Archibald Henry Sayce

James Scholefield
Robert Scott
Frederick Henry Ambrose
  Scrivener
Thomas Secker
John Selden
William Selwyn
William Shakespeare
George Vance Smith
Miles Smith
Robert Payne Smith
William Robertson Smith
John Speed
John Spenser
Arthur Penrhyn Stanley
Jonathan Swift
Connop Thirlwall
Giles Thomson
Richard Thomson
William Thorne
Laurence Tomson
Samuel Prideaux Tregelles
Richard Chenevix Trench

Cuthbert Tunstal
William Tyndale
Ambrose Ussher
James Ussher
Charles John Vaughan
George Villiers, duke of
  Buckingham
Sir Emery Walker
Samuel Ward
Brooke Foss Westcott
Edward Whitchurch
John Whitgift
William Whittingham
Samuel Wilberforce
Mary Wollstonecraft
Thomas Wood
Charles Wordsworth
Christopher Wordsworth
William Wright
William Aldis Wright
John Wyclif
Robert Young

The *American National Biography* has entries on the following:

Robert Aitken
Ethan Allen
John James Audubon
Lyman Beecher

John Gadsby Chapman
Charles Chauncy
Samuel Danforth
Samuel Davies

Timothy Dwight
Jonathan Edwards
Dwight David Eisenhower
John Watson Foster
Theodorus Jacobus
    Freylinghuysen
Warren Gamaliel Harding
George Emlen Hare
Charles Hodge
Henry Edwards Huntington
Andrew Jackson
Charles Portfield Krauth
Abraham Lincoln
Martin Luther King
John Livingston Lowes
John Pierpont Morgan
Thomas Paine
Matthew Brown Riddle
Thomas Secker

Edward Robinson
Bruce Rogers
Philip Schaff
Cyrus Ingerson Scofield
Charles Short
Henry Boynton Smith
Julia Evelina Smith
Miles Smith
Shubal Stearns
Calvin E. Stowe
William Howard Taft
Zachary Taylor
Gilbert Tennent
Cornelius Van Alen Van Dyck
William Fairfield Warren
George Washington
Benjamin West
George Whitefield
Theodore Dwight Woolsey

Bibles

[The title of the KJV remains constant, and so is not repeated in full in the list of later editions.]

The Holy Bible: Containing the Old Testament and the New. Authorised and Appointed to be Read in Churches (London, 1602) [The Bishops' Bible; a copy in the Bodleian Library in Oxford has annotations by the KJV translators].

The Holy Bible, Containing the Old Testament, and the New. Newly Translated out of the Original Tongues, and with the Former Translations Diligently Compared and Revised by His Majesty's Special Commandment. Appointed to be read in churches. Imprinted at London by Robert Barker, Printer to the King's Most Excellent Majesty. Anno Dom. 1611 [the 1st edn; 'He' Bible].

The Holy Bible... Commandment (London, 1611) [the 2nd edn; 'She' Bible].

The Holy Bible... Commandment (Cambridge, 1629) [the first Cambridge folio].

The Holy Bible... Commandment (London, 1631) [the Wicked Bible].

The Holy Bible... Commandment (Cambridge, 1638) [the second Cambridge folio].

The Holy Bible... Commandment (Oxford, 1675) [the first Oxford quarto].

The Holy Bible... Commandment (Oxford, 1679) [the second Oxford quarto].

The Holy Bible... Commandment (London, 1701) [includes Ussher's chronology].

The Holy Bible... Commandment (Oxford, 1717) [Thomas Baskett's 'Vinegar Bible'].

The Holy Bible... Commandment (Cambridge, 1743) [ed. F. S. Parris].

The Holy Bible... Commandment (Cambridge, 1763) [the Baskerville Bible].

Purver, Anthony, *A New and Literal Translation of the Books of the Old and New Testament* (2 vols, London, 1764).

The Holy Bible... Commandment (Oxford, 1769) [ed. Benjamin Blayney; a copy in the Cambridge University Library has extensive annotations by Gilbert Buchanan].

The Holy Bible According to the Authorised Version, with Notes Explanatory and Practical... together with Appropriate Introductions, Tables, Indexes, Maps, and Plans. Prepared and Arranged by George D'Oyly... and Richard Mant... under the Direction of the Society for Promoting Christian Knowledge (Oxford, 1817).

The Holy Bible: An Exact Reprint in Roman Type, Page for Page of the Authorised Version Published in the Year MDCXI (Oxford, 1833).

The Holy Bible: According to the Authorised Version, Containing the Old and New Testaments: With Original Notes, and Pictorial Illustrations (3 vols, London, 1836–8) [the Kitto Pictorial Bible].

The Illuminated Bible, Containing the Old and New Testaments... With Marginal Readings, References, and Chronological Dates. Also, the Apocrypha.... Embellished with Sixteen Hundred Historical Engravings by J. A. Adams, more than Fourteen Hundred of which are from Original Designs by J. G. Chapman (New York, 1846) [Harper's Illuminated Bible].

Scrivener, F. H. A. (ed.), *The Cambridge Paragraph Bible of the Authorised English Version, with the Text Revised by a Collation of its Early and Other Principal Editions, the Use of Italic Type Made Uniform, the Marginal References Remodelled* (Cambridge, 1873) [Zondervan uses this text for Bibles such as the *King James Life in the Spirit Study Bible: An International Study Bible for Spirit-Filled Christians* (2003)].

Palmer, Edwin, *ΚΑΙΝΗ ΔΙΑΘΗΚΗ. The Greek Testament with the Readings Adopted by the Revisers of the Authorised Version* (Oxford, 1881; republished London, 2007).

Schaff, Philip (ed.), *The Holy Bible, Containing the Old and New Testaments, Translated out of the Original Tongues, Being the Version Set Forth A.D. 1611, Compared with the Most Ancient Authorities and Revised A.D. 1881–1885, Newly Edited by the American Revision Committee A.D. 1901, Standard Edition* (New York, 1901) [American Standard Version; revised as New American Standard Bible (NT 1963, OT 1971; rev. edn, 1995)].

The English Bible containing the Old Testament and the New Translated out of the Original Tongues by Special Command of His Majesty King James the First and now Reprinted with the Text Revised by a Collation of its Early and Other Principal Editions and Edited by the Late F. H. Scrivener (5 vols, Hammersmith, 1902–5) [The Doves Press Bible].

The Scofield Reference Bible (1909; 2nd edn, 1917).

Pollard, A. W. (ed.), *The Holy Bible: A Facsimile in a Reduced Size of the Authorised Version Published in the Year 1611, with an Introduction by A. W. Pollard and Illustrative Documents* (Oxford, 1911).

Pollard, A. W. (ed.), *The Holy Bible: An Exact Reprint in Roman Type, Page for Page of the Authorised Version Published in the Year 1611, with an Introduction by A. W. Pollard* (Oxford, 1911).

The 1911 Tercentenary Commemoration Bible: The Holy Bible Containing the Old and New Testaments Translated out of the Original Tongues and with the Former Translations Diligently Compared and Revised by King James's Special Command 1611:

The Text Carefully Corrected and Amended (New York and London, 1911).

The Holy Bible Containing the Old and New Testaments: Translated out of the Original Tongues and with the Former Translations Diligently Compared and Revised by His Majesty's Special Command: Appointed to be Read in Churches (Oxford, 1935) [The Oxford Lectern Bible].

The Holy Bible, Revised Standard Version (London and New York, NT 1946, OT 1952, Apocrypha 1957; 'Modified Edition', 1962).

The Holy Bible: Revised Standard Edition: Catholic Edition (Oxford and San Francisco, NT 1965, OT, 1966; 2nd edn, 2006) [known as 'Ignatius Edition' or RSV-CE].

English, E. Schuyler (ed.), *The New Scofield Reference Bible* (New York and London, 1967).

The Holy Bible, Revised Standard Version. Containing the Old and New Testaments with the Apocrypha/Deuteroncanonical Books: An Ecumenical Edition (New York and London, 1973) [cover title: *Common Bible*].

May and Bruce M. Metzger (eds.), *The New Oxford Annotated Bible with the Apocrypha: Revised Standard Version, Containing the Second Edition of the New Testament and an Expanded Edition of the Apocrypha* (Oxford and New York 1977; 4th edn, 2010) [the 'Ecumenical Study Bible'].

The Holy Bible: New King James Version (London and Nashville, TN, NT 1979, OT 1982).

The Holy Bible: New Revised Standard Version (Oxford and New York, 1989) [this is the text used in *The New Oxford Annotated Bible with Apocrypha* (3rd edn, 2001), *The Oxford New Revised Standard Version Anglicized Cross-Reference Edition* (1995), and *The Green Bible* (2008).

The Holy Bible: English Standard Version (London, 2001) [evangelical revision of RSV].

21st-Century King James Version (Gary, SD, 1994, known as KJ21); later revision Third Millenium Bible, known by its subtitle as the New Authorized Version (2004).

The Scofield Study Bible III: King James Version (Oxford and New York, 2003) [3rd edn of the Scofield Reference Bible].

David Norton (ed.), *The New Cambridge Paragraph Bible with the Apocrypha: King James Version* (Cambridge, 2005) [this text has subsequently been published as *The Bible* in Penguin Classics (2006) and in a Folio Society edition (London, 2011)]

Robert Carroll and Stephen Prickett (eds.), *The Bible: Authorized King James Version* (Oxford and New York, 2008) [Oxford Classics edn].

Gordon Campbell (ed.), *The Holy Bible: Quatercentenary Edition* (Oxford and New York, 2010).

Books and Articles

Allen, Ward S., *Translating for King James* (Nashville, TN, 1969).

—— *Translating the New Testament Epistles, 1604–1611: A Manuscript from King James's Westminster Company* (Ann Arbor, MI, 1977).

—— and Jacobs, Edward C., *The Coming of the King James Gospels: A Collation of the Translators' Work-in-Progress* (Fayetteville, AR, 1995).

Barlow, William, *The Summe and Substance of the Conference . . . at Hampton Court* (London, 1604); facsimile ed. William T. Costello and Charles Keenan (Gainsville, FL, 1965).

Barnard, John, McKenzie, D. F., McKitterick, David, and Willison, I. R. (eds.), *The Cambridge History of the Book in Britain* (6 vols; 5 vols to date, Cambridge, 1999–2009).

Barnard, John, 'Politics, Profits and Idealism: John Norton, the Stationers' Company and Sir Thomas Bodley', *Bodleian Library Record*, 17 (2002), 385–408.

—— 'The Financing of the Authorized Version, 1610–1612: Robert Barker and "Combining" and "Sleeping" Stationers', *Publishing History*, 57 (2005), 5–52.

Bebbington, D. W., *Evangelicalism in Modern Britain: A History from the 1730s to the 1980s* (London, 1989).

Blagden, Cyprian, *The Stationers' Company: A History, 1403–1959* (London, 1960).

Bonomi, Patricia U., *Under the Cope of Heaven: Religion, Society, and Politics in Colonial America* (New York and Oxford, 1986; 2nd edn, 2003).

Boone, Kathleen C., *The Bible Tells Them So: The Discourse of Protestant Fundamentalism* (Albany, NY, 1989).

Boritt, Gabor, *The Gettysburg Gospel: The Lincoln Speech that Nobody Knows* (New York and London, 2006).

Brown, Callum, *The Death of Christian Britain: Understanding Secularization 1800–2000* (London, 2001).

Cadwallader, Alan, 'The Politics of Translation of the Revised Version: Evidence from the Newly Discovered Notebooks of Brooke Foss Westcott', *Journal of Theological Studies*, 58 (2007), 415–39.

Carey, John, *The Intellectuals and the Masses: Pride and Prejudice among the Literary Intelligentsia, 1880–1939* (London, 1992).

Carpenter, Joel A., *Revive Us Again: The Reawakening of American Fundamentalism* (New York and Oxford, 1997).

Carter, Harry, *A History of Oxford University Press: Volume 1, to the Year 1780* (Oxford, 1975).

Chambers, Talbot, *A Companion to the Revised Old Testament* (New York, 1885).

Corbett, Margery, and Lightbown, Ronald, *The Comely Frontispiece: The Emblematic Title-Page in England, 1550–1660* (London, 1979).

Cross, Whitney, *The Burned-Over District: The Social and Intellectual History of Enthusiastic Religion in Western New York, 1800–1850* (Ithaca, NY, and London, 1950).

Crystal, David, *Begat: The King James Bible and the English Language* (Oxford and New York, 2010).

Cummings, Brian, *The Literary Culture of the Reformation: Grammar and Grace* (Oxford and New York, 2002).

Curtis, Thomas, *The Existing Monopoly, an Inadequate Protection of the Authorised Version of Scripture* (London, 1833).

Daiches, Samuel, *The Bible as Literature: A Lecture* (London, 1929).

Daniell, David, *The Bible in English: Its History and Influence* (New Haven, 2003).

Dinsmore, Charles Allen, *The English Bible as Literature* (London, 1931).

Discoveries in the Judean Desert (40 vols, Oxford, 1956–2010) [Dead Sea Scrolls].

Eliot, T. S., 'Religion and Literature', in V. A. Demant (ed.), *The Faith that Illuminates* (London, 1935).

Faber, F.W., *An Essay on the Interest and Characteristics of the Lives of the Saints, with Illustrations from Mystical Theology* (London, 1853).

Ferrell, Lori Anne, *The Bible and the People* (New Haven, 2008).

——'Biblical Proportions: How the Art of Extra-Illustration Produced a Unique Version of the Bible', *Huntington Frontiers* (Fall/Winter 2006), 16–20.

Foster, Joseph, *Alumni Oxonienses: The Members of the University of Oxford, 1500–1714* (4 vols, Oxford, 1891).

Fry, Francis, *A Description of the Great Bible... [and] of Editions in Large Folio of the Authorised Version* (London, 1865).

Gadd, Ian, 'Covering God's Ass: New Light on the Wicked Bible of 1631', unpublished paper read at University of Reading and at Claremont College (conference of the Society for the History of Authorship, Reading, and Publishing), 2003.

Gaines, William H., Jr., 'The Continental Congress Considers the Publication of a Bible, 1777', *Studies in Bibliography*, 3 (1950), 274–81.

Gardiner, John Hays, *The Bible as English Literature* (London, 1906).

Gaustad, Edwin S., *The Great Awakening in New England* (New York, 1957).

Gell, Robert, *An Essay toward the Amendment of the Last English Translation of the Bible* (London, 1659).

Greenslade, S. L. (ed.), *The Cambridge History of the Bible: The West from the Reformation to the Present Day* (Cambridge, 1963).

Greg, W. W., *A Companion to Arber* (Oxford, 1967).

——and Boswell, E. (eds.), *Records of the Court of the Stationers' Company, 1576 to 1602, from Register B* (London, 1930).

Gubar, Susan, *Judas: A Biography* (New York, 2009).

Hammond, Gerald, *The Making of the English Bible* (Manchester, 1982).

Hatch, Nathan O., *The Democratization of American Christianity* (New Haven, 1989).

——and Noll, Mark A. (eds.), *The Bible in America* (New York and Oxford, 1982).

Herbert, A. S., *Historical Catalogue of Printed Editions of the English Bible, 1525–1961* (London and New York, 1968).

Howsam, Leslie, *Cheap Bibles: Nineteenth-Century Publishing and the British and Foreign Bible Society* (Cambridge, 1991).

Hunt, A., 'Book Trade Patents, 1603–1640', in A. Hunt, G. Mandelbrote, and A. Shell (eds.), *The Book Trade and its Customers, 1450–1900: Historical Essays for Robin Myers* (Winchester and New Castle, DE, 1997), 27–54.

Huxley, Thomas Henry, 'The School Boards: What they Can Do and what they May Do', *Contemporary Review*, 16 (1870), 1–15.

Innes, Kathleen, *The Bible as Literature* (London, 1930).

Jackson, W.A. (ed.), *Records of the Court of the Stationers' Company, 1602 to 1640* (London, 1957).

Jacobs, E. C., 'Old Testament Annotations in a Bishops' Bible, 1602', *Bodleian Library Record*, 9 (1974), 173.

——'An Old Testament Copytext for the 1611 Bible', *Papers of the Bibliographical Society of America*, 69/1 (1975), 1–15.

——'Two Stages of Old Testament Translation for the King James Bible', *Library*, 6th ser., 2/1 (Mar. 1980), 16–39.

——'King James's Translators: The Bishops' Bible New Testament Revised', *Library*, 6th ser., 14/2 (June 1992), 100–26.

Kilburne, William, *Dangerous Errors in Several Late Printed Bibles* (London, 1659 [i.e. 1660]).

Knott, David, 'James Gibbs's "Illustrations of Popular Literature"' (University of Reading Library Special Collections Service, 2008).

Lambert, C. S., 'The Printers and the Government, 1604–1637', in R. Myers and M. Harris, *Aspects of Printing from 1600* (Oxford, 1987), 1–29.

Larsen, Timothy, *Friends of Religious Equality: Nonconformist Politics in Mid-Victorian England* (Woodbridge, Suffolk and Rochester, NY, 1999).

——*Contested Christianity: The Political and Social Context of Victorian Theology* (Waco, TX, 2004).

Lewis, C. S., 'The Literary Impact of The Authorised Version'. The Ethel M. Wood Lecture delivered before the University of London on 20 March 1950 (London, 1950).

Lightfoot, J. B., Trench, Richard C., and. Ellicott, C. J., *The Revision of the English Version of the New Testament* (New York, 1873).

Lowes, John Livingston, *Essays in Appreciation* (Boston, 1931) [contains essay on 'The Noblest Monument of English Prose'].

McClure, Alexander Wilson, *The Translators Revived* (New York, 1853).

McGrath, A. *In the Beginning: The Story of the King James Bible and how it Changed a Nation, a Language and a Culture* (London and New York, 2001).

McKitterick, David, *A History of Cambridge University Press* (3 vols, Cambridge, 1992–2004).

McLoughlin, William G., *Revivals, Awakenings, and Reform: An Essay on Religion and Social Change in America, 1607–1977* (Chicago, 1978).

McMullin, J. B., 'The 1629 Cambridge Bible', *Transactions of the Cambridge Bibliographical Society*, 13 (1990), 381–97.

Mangum, R. Todd, *The Dispensational-Covenantal Rift: The Fissuring of American Evangelical Theology from 1936 to 1944* (Bletchley, 2007).

Marsden, George M., *Fundamentalism and American Culture: The Shaping of Twentieth-Century Evangelicalism, 1870–1925* (Oxford and New York, 1980; 2nd edn, 2006).

Martin, William, *With God on Our Side: The Rise of the Religious Right in America* (New York, 1996).

Morgan, Paul, 'A King's Printer at Work: Two Documents of Robert Barker', *Bodleian Library Record*, 13 (1990), 370–4.

Nicolson, Adam, *Power and Glory: Jacobean England and the Making of the King James Bible* (London, 2003); published in the USA as *God's Secretaries: The Making of the King James Bible* (New York, 2003).

Nord, David Paul, *Faith in Reading: Religious Publishing and the Birth of Mass Media in America* (Oxford and New York, 2004).

Norton, David, *A History of the Bible as Literature* (2 vols, Cambridge, 1993); revised and condensed into one volume as *A History of the English Bible as Literature* (Cambridge, 2000).

——'John Bois's Notes on the Revision of the King James Bible New Testament: A New Manuscript', *Library*, 6th ser., 18/4 (Dec. 1996), 328–46

——*A Textual History of the King James Bible* (Cambridge, 2005).

Paine, Gustavus S., *The Learned Men* (New York, 1959), republished as *The Men behind the King James Version* (Grand Rapids, MI, 1977).

Parkes, Malcolm, *Pause and Effect: An Introduction to the History of Punctuation in the West* (Aldershot and Berkeley, CA, 1992).

Plomer, Henry R., 'The King's Printing House under the Stuarts', *Library*, NS 2 (1901), 353–75.

Pollard, A. W., *Records of the English Bible* (Oxford, 1911; repr. Folkestone, 1974).

Rees, Graham, and Wakely, Maria, *Publishing, Politics, and Culture: The King's Printers in the Reign of James I and VI* (Oxford and New York, 2009).

Report on the History and Recent Collation of the English Version of the Bible, presented by the Committee on Versions to the Board of Managers of the American Bible Society (New York, 1851).

Roberts, Alexander, *Companion to the Revised Version of the New Testament, Explaining the Reasons for the Changes Made on the Authorised Version* (London, 1881).

Ryken, Leland, *The Word of God in English* (Wheaton, IL, 2002).

Saintsbury, George, *A History of English Prose Rhythm* (London, 1912; repr. Westport, CT, 1978).

Sandeen, Ernest, *The Roots of Fundamentalism: British and American Millenarianism, 1800–1930* (Chicago, 1970).

Sawyer, John, *The Blackwell Companion to the Bible and Culture* (Oxford, 2006).

Schaff, Philip, *The Revision of the English Version of the Holy Scripture* (New York, 1873).

Schaff, Philip (ed.), *Documentary History of the American Committee on Revision.* (New York, 1883; enlarged edn, 1885).

——*Historical Account of the Work of the American Committee of Revision of the Authorised English Version of the Bible* (New York, 1885).

Scholefield, James, *Hints for an Improved Translation of the New Testament* (London, 1832; 4th edn, Cambridge, 1857).

Sewell, Arthur, *The Bible as Literature* (Auckland, 1939).

Sheehan, Jonathan, *The Enlightenment Bible: Translation, Scholarship, Culture* (Princeton, 2005).

Shriver, F., 'Hampton Court Re-Visited: James I and the Puritans', *Journal of Ecclesiastical History*, 33 (1982), 48–71.

Scrivener, E. H. A., *The Authorised Edition of the English Bible (1611): Its Subsequent Reprints and Modern Representatives* (Cambridge, 1884; repr. Eugene, OR, 2004).

Shuger, Debora Kuller, *The Renaissance Bible: Scholarship, Sacrifice, and Subjectivity* (Berkeley, CA, 1994).

Smith, Walter E., *A Study of the Great 'She' Bible (1613 or 1611)* (London, 1890).

Sypherd, Wilbur Owen, *The Literature of the English Bible* (New York, 1938).

Thomas, John B. III, 'Tales from the Vault: Our Mayflower Bible', *Common-Place: The Interactive Journal of Early American Life*, 1/3 (Apr. 2001).

Venn, J., and Venn, J. A., *Alumni Cantabrigienses: A Biographical List of All Known Students, Graduates and Holders of Office at the University of Cambridge, from the Earliest Times to 1751* (4 vols, Cambridge, 1922–7).

Wakely, Maria, 'Printing and Double-Dealing in Jacobean England: Robert Barker, John Bill, and Bonham Norton', *Library*, 8/2 (June 2007), 119–53.

Walters, Kerry S., *The American Deists: Voices of Reason and Dissent in the Early Republic* (Lawrence, KS, 1992).

—— *Benjamin Franklin and his Gods* (Urbana, IL, 1999).

Watson, Justin, *The Christian Coalition: Dreams of Restoration, Demands for Recognition* (Basingstoke and New York, 1997).

Watt, David Harrington, *Bible-Carrying Christians: Conservative Protestants and Social Power* (New York and Oxford, 2002).

Westcott, Brooke Foss, *Some Lessons of the Revised Version of the New Testament* (London, 1897).

Westbrook, V., *Long Travail and Great Paynes: A Politics of Reformation Revision* (Dordrecht and Boston, 2001).

Wood, I. F., and Grant, E., *The Bible as Literature* (New York, 1914; repr. Folcroft, PA, 1979).

INDEX

Page numbers in *italics* refer to illustrations